A Student's Notes on Genesis

A Student's Notes on Genesis

The Bible for Public Schools

By Eleanor Grace Rupp

FOREWORD BY
Barbara K. Bellefeuille

WIPF & STOCK · Eugene, Oregon

A STUDENT'S NOTES ON GENESIS
The Bible for Public Schools

Copyright © 2016 Eleanor Grace Rupp. All rights reserved. Except for brief quotations in critical publications or reviews, no part of this book may be reproduced in any manner without prior written permission from the publisher. Write: Permissions, Wipf and Stock Publishers, 199 W. 8th Ave., Suite 3, Eugene, OR 97401.

Wipf & Stock
An Imprint of Wipf and Stock Publishers
199 W. 8th Ave., Suite 3
Eugene, OR 97401

www.wipfandstock.com

PAPERBACK ISBN: 978-1-61097-982-5
HARDCOVER ISBN: 978-1-4982-8793-7

Manufactured in the U.S.A.

King James Version (KJV) No permission needed

Maps used by permission of Oxford University Press

To the thousands of students, my friends,
who walked with me through that ancient forest
older than most ever enter,
that undying forest of living Hebrew narratives, poetry and prophecies

—the Bible—

the book whose words long ago turned this world upside down.

*A thorough understanding of the Bible is
better than a college education.*

Theodore Roosevelt,
twenty-sixth president of the
United States from 1901 to 1909

Contents

CONTENTS

Maps

The geography of the ancestral narratives

Foreword

Barbara K. Bellefeuille, Ed.D.

I APPROACHED MY FIRST public school teaching position with great antici-
pation. The year was 1977 and I would be teaching Bible as an elective to
middle school students. Eleanor Rupp was already a teacher in the same
school system. She did not know at that time that one day she would be
pouring her experience into writing for public schools nor did I know that
one day I would write my Virginia Tech doctoral dissertation on the same
subject, public school Bible teaching.

In our orientation at the beginning of each year, we reviewed in depth
the legal guidelines for teaching the Bible in public schools. Each week
throughout the year we also met with our supervisor to discuss our lesson
plans, to assure that we were keeping within those guidelines. *A Student's
Notes on Genesis* would have been a tremendous help during my years in
the public school, guiding me in my own teaching. This book represents
an investment of years in careful consideration of the best content and
delivery for public school classes. *A Student's Notes on Genesis* has been
scrutinized and refined over and over, continually evaluated in the light of
good teaching practices and the Supreme Court guidelines.

I am personally aware of the years of work this book represents. The
author's high standards automatically resisted "fast-tracking" a book of this
importance. Finally, Eleanor Rupp is an exceptional teacher! Her teaching
style, her devotion to her students, her depth of experience, and her never-
ending desire to learn, combine to make her a fine example of the art of
teaching. Rarely do those published have this unique package of talents.

Preface

A YEAR AFTER THE United States Supreme Court ruled on the place of teaching the Bible in the public schools, I was hired to teach the Bible to high school students in West Virginia. About a week after I began teaching, a kind lady in town politely told me that what I was doing was illegal, that the Court in 1963 had removed the Bible from our schools. Thankfully, she was wrong: the Court had not removed the Bible; rather, it wrote,

It certainly may be said that the Bible is worthy of study for its literary and historic qualities. Nothing we have said here indicates that such study of the Bible or of religion, when presented objectively as part of a secular program of education, may not be effected consistently with the First Amendment.[1]

In 1984 the Court clarified the ruling somewhat by saying that the schools may not convey a message either of *endorsement or disapproval.*[2] In other words, the teachers may show their students what the Bible says, but they may not press it upon them as beliefs to hold or as teachings to reject. Schools may expose students to religions and to the Bible, but they may not impose any of those beliefs upon them.

That meant students would study without fear of having their own religious views condemned in class and without fear that other views would be forced upon them.

These rulings meant that the classroom could be neither a church nor a synagogue nor a mosque nor a temple. If the schools stayed within the guidelines, they had perfect freedom to teach the Bible in the public schools.

1. *Abington v. Schempp*, (1963).
2. *Lynch v. Donnelly*, (1984).

A *Student's Notes on Genesis* guides students from Adam to Abraham (the first eleven chapters of Genesis) and then slows its rapid pace to spend the rest of Genesis (chapters 12 through 50) on Abraham's family extending to his great grandchildren. Bible readers stay with that family, not only throughout Genesis and the first five books of the Bible, but also to the Bible's very end. Hopefully, readers will see in that often frustrating, yet sometimes dazzling family, their own hopes, frustrations, and battles and will perhaps discover that they have found from Genesis new windows of wisdom.

Acknowledgments

Thanks to:

Dr. Charles Cauthen, former president of King College in Bristol Tennessee, and his wife, Hazel, who aided and encouraged me in the long and slow process of this project.

Dr. Barbara Bellefeuille, Vice President for Academic Services at Bethel College (IN) and former fellow Bible teacher, whose help opened up time for me to work and encouraged me with many insights.

Emma Stanley Cooper (Mrs. Donald), former fellow teacher, whose genius in Bible teaching helped me to see through periodic mental blocks.

Sarah Overstreet Midyett (Mrs. J. T.), teacher and writer of Bible study workbooks, for her instructions years ago, and her recent editing and suggestions.

Karen Schwind, author of *Her Life As She Knew It,* for her helpful thoughts about many of the chapters.

Mary Rupp McClure, a sister who refreshed me with her clear thinking.

Joy Gordon Beans, my niece, for her creative insights.

The Attorney General of West Virginia who in 1985 clarified the legality of teaching the Bible in our public schools.

ACKNOWLEDGMENTS

The thousands of dear students whose responses helped me see through their eyes, particularly Becky Taylor Goins, Emily Saunders Hooie, Kreston Tynes Lloyd, Alex Moore, and Loren Wells.

My family and my friends who have patiently (and sometimes despairingly) waited for the answer to when I would finish this volume.

Introduction for Students

*A heads-up on how to understand
this book's arrangement.*

- All Bible passages are printed in italics with the references at the end of the passage.

- Obsolete and rarely used words and phrases are followed by bracketed explanatory words printed in roman type rather than in italics.

- All spelling and punctuation follow the King James Version even when it horrifies modern grammar gurus. If you are not familiar with old versions of the Bible, it may take you a little while to get used to the old writing rules and the old vocabulary.

- Pronouns for *God* (he, him, his) follow the King James Version and are not capitalized. Names for God are, of course, capitalized just as your own are.

- In the Bible you sometimes see the word *Lord* written as LORD—a different font. The publishers do that to show you that each is a different word in the Hebrew language, the original language of the book of Genesis.

- You will learn the rules for writing Bible references (the *addresses* of Bible verses) in the fourth lesson.

LESSON 1

My Notes for the Genesis Bible Class

I AM A HIGH school student who loves movies, books, sports (especially basketball), and hiking with friends. Near the end of our summer break, about the time when I start to get bored, I realized I hadn't escaped into a single book this summer. That escape, I knew, was what I needed now. I wished I had a really good book waiting.

In that state of mind I bounced my basketball along the sidewalk, unaware that the ball was about to do me a favor. It bounced right out of my hand, rolled down the street, and wedged itself into the bottom step of a store. After freeing the ball, I noticed a sign on the window: *Jewish Books.* The sign jogged a thought. "Jewish books. Didn't the Jews have something to do with writing the Bible?"

I had often told myself I should read it. The Bible pops up everywhere I turn: English classes, history classes, discussions, debates, music, movies, and more. I have always had to drop out of those conversations. I know almost nothing about the Bible. Maybe it's time to get a copy and read one, so I entered the bookstore.

"Yes," the owner said, "we have Bibles, and yes, we Jews do have something to do with it. We wrote it. Do you want the Hebrew Bible or the Christian Bible?" I told him I couldn't read Hebrew and I was not a Christian; I just wanted an English Bible. He patiently explained that he didn't mean the Hebrew language. Realizing I was essentially ignorant of the book, he explained that what Christians call the Bible comes in two parts. Christians call the first and larger part the *Old Testament*, but Jewish people call the first part the *Hebrew Bible*. He said that Christians call the second part of the Bible the *New Testament* which is about a Jewish man named Jesus. The two parts together are what Christians mean by the *Bible*.

I knew that Jesus has something to do with Christmas, so wanting to learn all I could, I decided to get both parts. I was proud of my decision, but as I glanced through the pages, I realized it would take a lot of study. A short time later I heard that my school was offering a world literature elective that would include a unit on the book of Genesis—the first book in the Bible. I decided I would take the class.

The first day of the Genesis class

The first day of school the teacher took away any fears we might have. She explained that the Supreme Court's guidelines for studying the Bible in the public schools give protection to all beliefs and non beliefs—not endorsement, but protection. The guidelines free all students from fear of their beliefs being censored. She also made sure we knew that this would not be a comparative religions class and that our goal would be to know Genesis, a unit in itself and the gateway to the rest of the Bible.

To get some idea of how familiar we were with the Bible, the teacher asked us to write down as many Bible characters as we could remember in two minutes. Then she set the timer. I was sure (almost sure) of five people—Adam, Eve, Noah, Moses, and Jesus. A girl in front of me wrote and wrote and said she needed a lot more than two minutes. Fortunately, that's all the time the teacher gave.

She then asked us to give our ideas of what the Bible is about. Some said it was like an anthology, a collection of old miracle stories or maybe a mystical anthology. A few thought it was a book of old laws. Several said that every day they would read something in it. One girl said she usually opened her Bible up anywhere, put a finger on the page, and read a few sentences. She found it hard to understand, but thought it might do her good. It sounded like a rabbit's foot to me. All agreed that if they knew more about the Bible, it should help them in literature classes. I didn't say anything. I just knew the Bible had been too influential in the history of the world for me to be ignorant of it.

The teacher's next words surprised me: she said that since some interpret the Bible as myths and legend and some as true historical events, if in class she took a stand on one side or the other, she would be stepping outside of the Supreme Court's guidelines for public schools. The religion of both

Jews and Christians comes out of the Bible. Since the public school teacher may neither affirm nor deny any student's religious beliefs, the teacher said she would not take a stand on their differing religious viewpoints. Rather, she would teach its storyline—a storyline that lays a foundation for all that happens in the rest of the Bible.

As the class ended, the teacher explained that for several days we would study the formation of the Bible, the history of Bible translations, and the battles and bloodshed that brought it to us in our modern English. Although I was eager to start studying Genesis immediately, I could see by her introduction that those topics would answer some of my other questions—questions about where the Bible came from, who wrote it, when it was written, whether the original documents still exist, and how its story has survived to this day.

In order to make our study meaningful, at the end of each study, she will give us questions to discuss, checking our understanding and guiding us in analyzing those ancient characters and events. She said those characters were just like us, like every person—like all who sit around us in class.

I look forward to reading this book. I think I'll keep my notes as a journal—not just the information, but my expectations and reflections on each study. I don't want to forget my first impressions.

Overview of the Bible's Composition

My first thoughts

ON THE BOARD THE teacher had written the objective for the next few days: "Analysis of the Composition of the Bible." Realizing these lessons might be heavy, I took detailed notes. The following notes (brushed up some) were what I recorded from the teacher's lesson, as well as the comments from the class.

My notes on the teacher's lesson

This study is to cover the dates of the Bible writings, the different divisions of the Bible, and its languages, names, and writers.

The dates and age of the Bible writings

How years are dated

Before we can grasp the dates of the Bible writings, we must understand the changes in history's calendar. Thousands of years ago people dated their lives by important events such as a natural catastrophe, the rule of a great king, or the beginning of an important treaty. As the centuries passed, Christians who saw the work of Jesus (called Christ) as the great turning point in history began dating events according to his birth. From that estimated year, we have the dates we use today. The letters BC are the initials of *Before Christ*, meaning "before his birth." The letters AD are the initials, not of English words but of the Latin words, *Anno Domini*, meaning "in the year of our Lord." They refer to the years following his birth.

Events that happened one year *before* Jesus was born were dated as 1 BC. Events that happened one year *after* his birth were dated as AD 1. Notice that the letters BC *follow* the number of the year, and the letters AD *precede* the number of the year.

Making calendars with Christ as the center of history did not begin until over 500 years after his birth, gradually becoming a general world-standard. The best efforts of the calendar-makers in trying to line up his birth with the records of history, however, apparently missed the date by a number of years. The true date of Jesus' birth was probably about four or five years *before* the calendar date of 1 BC! Perhaps the only great problem created by that error was for those who were sure something cataclysmic would occur in AD 2,000. When the world celebrated the *calendar* year 2000 (at least four years too late), few knew that the *probable* two thousandth year had quietly come and gone about forty-eight months earlier with no cataclysm showing up for those parties.

The Bible's dates and age on a timeline

The teacher used a timeline to help us grasp the great age of the Bible. It surprised us all. The traditional view—the view held for hundreds of years—claims the writing, or the organizing of the writings, began about 1450 BC and was completed about AD 100. Some recent views place the beginning of the Bible writings about 1200 BC and the completion about AD 150.

Averaging the dates, Genesis was written over 3,300 years ago. Hearing that figure, a student interjected the words, "In fourteen hundred ninety-two, Columbus sailed the ocean blue." He then went on to say that Columbus's journey began a little over 500 years ago, a length of time that can seem endless to us; yet the writing of Genesis began over six times further back in history than Columbus, and the end of the Bible over three times further back. He remarked that compared to when the Bible writings began, Columbus's discovery of America was like last week! A student who is a history buff added that when Columbus discovered America, he had a copy of the Bible with him on the ship—and the Bible was already, at that time, very, very old.

According to traditional views, the length of time it took to write the complete Bible was about 1,550 years.

The two major divisions of the Bible

The Bible has two major divisions, the first division written before Jesus' life and the second division written afterwards. Jewish and Christian students in the class agreed that the first division of the Bible is *sacred scripture*—writings they see as holy and revered. The Jewish students call it the *Hebrew Bible*. The Christians call it the *Old Testament*.

The Hebrew Bible has twenty-four books. The Christian Old Testament has the same twenty-four books, though divided into thirty-nine rather than twenty-four. Some Christian Old Testaments have seven more books (and parts of books) called the Deuterocanonical books, or the Apocrypha.

The second major division of the Bible is the *New Testament* which Christians consider sacred scripture also. The New Testament has twenty-seven books.

The languages of the Bible

Except for a few passages, the writers of the Hebrew Bible, as would be expected, wrote in the Hebrew language.

Three centuries before the New Testament period, young Alexander (later called Alexander the Great) led his small armies in extraordinary victories from Greece to Egypt and eastward to India. No one could stop him. With his armies came the superb Greek language. No one could stop that language either. For hundreds of years and into New Testament times, even after the Greeks lost their military power, the Greek language dominated the Mediterranean world. The writers of the New Testament wrote in that Greek language making the New Testament readable and understandable over all the known world of their day.

The names of the Bible and its parts

Bible

We had to use our imaginations for part of this topic; it began with a time machine. Suppose by way of a time machine the men who wrote the Bible met to decide on a name for their sacred book. Suppose then that one of them said, "I think we should name our book after an ancient Phoenician city on the Mediterranean." That suggestion would have been insulting to them, for why would they write a book centered on their God and then place upon that sacred book the name of a pagan seaport! Yet that is exactly the origin of the word *Bible.*

Thirty-five hundred years ago the Mediterranean world did not have paper as we know it today. They wrote on sheets made from papyrus, a plant once growing abundantly in Egypt. The Egyptians shipped their papyrus to a city on the eastern shore of the Mediterranean Sea. The original name of that old city was *Gebal.* The Greeks called it *Byblos.*

Gradually, the Greeks began to call papyrus *biblos* from their name for the city Gebal. A papyrus book (think *scroll*) became a biblion, and more than one book became *biblia* from which we get the English name *Bible.* Our class easily understood the appropriateness of the name *Bible* (biblia) because that is exactly what the Bible is, a collection of books.

Tanakh

The name *Tanakh* (pronounced TAH nax) is another name for the Hebrew Bible. It is an acronym using the first letters of the three sections of the Hebrew Bible—*Torah* (Law or Teaching), *Nevi'im* (Prophets), and *Ketuvim* (Writings), forming the word *TaNaKh.*

Scripture

The word *scripture* comes from the Latin *scriptura,* meaning *writings.* Many use the name *Scripture* or *Scriptures* as another name for the Bible.

Testament

Testament is an important word in the Bible. It means *covenant* or *agreement* or sometimes *treaty*. Some covenants in the Bible are unilateral and some are bilateral. A unilateral covenant (think unicycle—a one wheeler) is a one-sided promise that one person makes and the other person is expected to gratefully receive as a gift.

If obligations are attached to a covenant, it is a bilateral covenant (think bicycle—two wheeler) made between two parties or people and with obligations for each. For example, when you agree to wash your neighbor's car if he will fix your computer, you have made a bilateral covenant.

The writers of the Bible

According to the traditional view, about forty people wrote the Bible. All of them (with the possible exception of Luke) were Jewish men. Most of the writers came from a small area of Asia not far from where the continents of Africa and Asia join. Since the writers lived in scattered time periods, few of them could have known each other, yet the teacher concluded our study with the comment that the writings of those men fit together like the instruments in an orchestra or like one of the movements in an inspiring, deeply moving symphony.

My reflections on the lesson

I can hardly believe that such an old book is still being published. It's hard to grasp—to think that people living thousands of years ago wrote the world's bestseller, the bestseller year after year; and I, with all my technology, am ignorant of what is in it. I know the Bible has had a huge influence on much of the world—that's why I took this class—but I didn't know it went back to a time when I thought writing didn't even exist. Some of the men who hang out at the barbershop tell me my generation has a little too much self-esteem—that we think we are wiser than we really are. Though we joke about it together, today I'm thinking maybe they are on to something.

Checking for understanding

1. What are two names Jewish people use for their scriptures—the section of the Bible that Christians call the Old Testament?

2. What do Christians call the second of the two major divisions of the Bible?

3. According to both traditional and recent views, approximately how many years have passed since the Bible writers finished their work?

4. What is the main language of the Hebrew Bible?

5. What language did the New Testament writers use?

6. Explain the difference between a unilateral covenant (or agreement) and a bilateral covenant.

7. From what you have learned in this study of the composition of the Bible and its age, tell at least one way the Bible stands alone as an impressive book.

LESSON 3

The "Original" Bible

My first thoughts

BEFORE TODAY'S CLASS STARTED, I asked, "Is the original Bible in existence today? Where can I go see it?" When our teacher wanted to know if anyone in the class had an answer to my question, many began making guesses. I thought maybe the Smithsonian, but no one was sure. The teacher also wanted to know if we knew what the *form* of that first Bible would have been. That question didn't make sense to me; no one else had an answer for that either. She then told us that since the Bible has been such an important book throughout history, today she would be discussing both these topics—the *form* of the original Bible, and the *location* of the original Bible.

My notes on the teacher's lesson

The form and location of the original Bible

Before the world had books with sheets of paper attached on one side as we have them today, they came as scrolls—long rolls of writing material. Some, as you remember, were made of papyrus sheets from the papyrus plant, and some were made of the more enduring parchment sheets made from the skins of animals. A scroll might have one long book on it, or it could have a number of shorter books. If it were a very long book, that one book would have to be written on two separate scrolls.

It was not until after the New Testament period that writers began making page-turning books as we have them today—a method that produced the whole Bible, every book, in one volume. None of the Bible writers, however, wrote on page-turning books; all wrote on scrolls. That leads to a slightly different question: "Are the original *scrolls* of the Bible in existence today?"

The answer disappointed us. Those scrolls either lie hidden away in unknown locations or because of time and decay have turned to dust, raising, we felt, a very serious problem. If no one has the original scrolls, how does anyone know what was in them? That is what we are to study today.

The studies of the ancient biblical scrolls fall into three main categories—the study of *manuscripts*, of *versions*, and of biblical *quotations*.

Manuscripts of the Bible

The word *manuscript* comes from the Latin words *manu* (meaning *hand*) and *script* (meaning *writing*). In its simplest form, manuscript means *handwritten*. When scholars speak of Bible manuscripts, they are not referring to the original writings, but only to ancient, handwritten *copies* of them.

For a copy of the Bible to be called a manuscript, it must be in the original language. A manuscript of the Hebrew Bible must be written in the Hebrew language (except for a few places in the Aramaic language), and a manuscript of the New Testament must be written in the Greek language.

The importance of manuscripts

If a fire burned down the National Archives and destroyed the Declaration of Independence written in 1776, would people then say, "O dear, no one will ever know for sure what was in that great document!"? Or if the original copy of the Constitution written in 1789 disappeared, would people fear that this country would never know its foundations? The answer to both is *No*. Those documents were reproduced on printing presses. The country has so many copies of both that we can easily find out exactly what was written in them from those earliest days of the nation. With early Bibles, however, it was different. Until that invention of the printing press about AD 1450, each Bible had to be copied by hand.

How the manuscript scrolls were produced

Jewish scribes (copyists) kept the Hebrew Bible in existence by their careful work of copying it. Later, other scribes copied the copies, and as time passed still other scribes copied copies of copies. Gradually the earliest copies of the manuscripts disappeared—some by the natural decay of time, some by intentional destruction, and some by formal burial! By the beginning of the twentieth century, the oldest known manuscripts of the Hebrew Bible (named the *Masoretic* manuscripts) were those made just before the 900s. That left a gap of thirteen hundred years between the end of the Hebrew Bible and the Masoretic copies.

Some argued that the Masoretic manuscripts surely must be filled with errors, believing that the scribes couldn't help but make mistakes. Then those mistakes would have been copied by later scribes who had accidentally added even more of their own. Critics were certain the ancient manuscripts would be quite different from the Masoretic copies. They believed no one knew what was written on those original manuscripts.

The Jewish scribes who made those Masoretic copies would not have agreed with the critics. They knew the many demanding requirements for copying the Bible:

1. The ink—black only—must be made from a special recipe.

2. The scribe could write only on the skins of clean animals.

3. The writer had to look at and speak aloud each word before he wrote it—it could not be written from memory.

4. Between letters there must be the space the width of a hair or thread.

5. Every line on a given page had to have the same number of words and letters as the original copy.

6. Every letter of the alphabet on every page had to be counted.

Someone said that it seemed they counted everything that could be counted.

The scribes also knew the words from Deuteronomy, the fifth book of Moses, *Ye shall not add unto the word which I command you, neither shall ye diminish ought* [anything] *from it . . . (4:2).* They were never to meddle with the words whether they liked them or not. When those men read a copy made by the Masoretes, they had confidence that they were reading what was in the manuscripts from ages past. That might sound bold except for a totally unexpected event that took place in 1947, an event sending shockwaves across the world.

The shocking discovery—the Dead Sea Scrolls

The discovery began with a shepherd boy looking for a lost goat. Suspecting the animal might be resting in one of the cool dark caves above the Dead Sea (the large inland sea at the lower end of the Jordan River), he threw a rock into a cave and listened. The sound he heard was not the bleating of a goat but the sound of something breaking—the first shockwave of what was to come.

When he and his friends explored the cave, they discovered large clay jars containing, to their disappointment, nothing but old scrolls written in a language they could not read. They decided to turn them over to a shopkeeper. Eventually, the scrolls came into the hands of Hebrew language experts who could hardly believe what they were reading! One of the first scrolls examined turned out to be a manuscript of the biblical book of Isaiah, far older than any other manuscript known to exist. The book had been copied many, many years before the New Testament period—centuries before the birth of Jesus and the births of Matthew, Mark, Luke, and John who wrote the accounts of Jesus' life!

After those finds, others began searching surrounding caves, finding more and more scrolls and fragments of scrolls. Except for the book of Esther, they found parts (sometimes only fragments) of every book in the Hebrew Bible plus many other religious writings. Those manuscripts, called the *Dead Sea Scrolls*, included scrolls that were about 1300 years older than the Masoretic copies.

The announcement of those finds stunned the world! At last, not only could they read what was copied one thousand years ago but also what was copied over two thousand years ago—almost as far back as the last events of the Hebrew Bible! Experts carefully examined the Isaiah scroll, comparing it to the Masoretic texts. The announcement of what they found was even more amazing than the "accidental" discovery of the scrolls. They were reading the same words. The Dead Sea Isaiah and the Masoretic Isaiah were ninety-five percent identical—the differences mainly being, not words, but only spelling changes, grammar changes or slips of the pen. Over all those hundreds and hundreds and hundreds of years the scribes had copied the book of Isaiah almost letter perfect!

The boys who found the scrolls probably had no idea that the land on which they led their goats had once been the site of an ancient Jewish sect. From what archeologists say of that sect, its members spent their time pursuing spiritual purity, making copies of the Hebrew Scriptures, and writing commentaries on them. Apparently they hid the scrolls in the remote caves to protect them from Roman armies, perhaps hoping when the wars ended to return for them. They could hardly have imagined that about two thousand years in the future, when doubts were arising over the reliability of their Hebrew writings, those old scrolls would be found, showing the great care and accuracy of the ancient scribes.

If scholars, after comparing all the known manuscripts of the same passage, were still not sure of the correct reading, what would they do? They would turn to versions.

Ancient versions and their importance

A *version* is a translation of the Bible into a language different from the original Hebrew or original Greek. The following illustration is only hypothetical:

What if scholars had only six manuscripts of a particular passage, three saying Noah had four sons and three saying Noah had three? If nothing else in the Bible referred to the number of his sons and the six manuscripts were divided on the number, they would have to turn to the ancient versions. If every one of the versions, even though written in different languages, said that Noah had three sons, they would assume that *three* was probably the correct number.

After comparing every known version of the same passage, what if the scholars were still not sure of the correct reading? They would next turn to quotations.

Quotations and their importance

By the word *quotations*, we mean written quotations of Bible verses and passages found in ancient books and sermons. Just as books and sermons today quote verses from the Bible, early writers also quoted them. The documents still in existence contain enough quotations from the Bible to reconstruct almost the entire New Testament several times, as well as much of the Old Testament—the Hebrew Bible.

Since quotations are not necessarily copied word for word, they are not as reliable as manuscripts and versions. However, they do show what readers long ago were reading: for example, in the illustration above about Noah's sons, if the manuscripts and the versions all were divided half and half—half saying Noah had three sons, and half saying he had four—the quotations might solve the problem. If all the quotations said Noah had only three sons, scholars would then assume that *three sons* was probably the correct reading.

The New Testament

The Masoretes who copied the Old Testament were not the people who copied the New. New Testament scholars did not follow the same rules for copying. Does that mean their manuscripts are full of errors? No. Did their copies contain errors? Yes, but they produced so many, many copies that by comparing them, scholars can still know the places where the copies are different. A reader who buys a study Bible should discover from that Bible's notes any place there are questions about the correct wording. The study notes will usually include alternate readings.

The teacher said she knew she had made a difficult study look simple, even too simple. Examining all the manuscripts, versions, and quotations is a complex work, greater than can be discussed fully in just a few days, but she felt it had at least given us an idea of how the process works.

One of my classmates commented on how much easier it is for us to make copies today and wished writers back then had had our technology, but the teacher was glad they didn't. She said that if the first documents had been written on computers, anyone could take them, cut and paste, and end up with something very different from the original writers's purposes. With scrolls you can easily see where changes have been made. Changes show up both on the front and on the back of the scrolls.

My reflections on the lesson

I now understand that my desire to know where the original Bible scrolls are located is an unanswerable question. I can see *copies* of the original scrolls, but at the present time, we do not have the originals. Who knows? Maybe someday we will.

Another student said he had seen a collection of Bible scrolls on display for a time in a seminary his brother attended. The scrolls were hundreds of years old and looked to him like the oilcloth his grandmother once had on her kitchen table. Although those scrolls at the seminary were very old, about as old as the travels of Columbus, they were new compared to the original writings of the Bible. I plan to search the Internet to find out where I can see them myself. (Maybe I'll find out what happened to the lost goat too.)

Checking for understanding

1. In your opinion, which would be easier: reading from a scroll or reading from a page-turning book. Explain your answer.

2. List the three types of documents scholars use in their search to determine what was written in the original Bible scrolls.

3. Describe the difference between a manuscript and a version.

4. Explain why the Dead Sea Scrolls are so important to Bible scholars in helping determine what was in the Hebrew Bible.

5. Using the Internet if you have access to it, do a search on *Ancient Jewish rules for copying the Hebrew Bible*. Then make a list of any of the rules we did not discuss in class.

Ancient and Recent Changes
that Assist Readers

My first thoughts

ON THE FIRST DAY in this class, our teacher had told us we would each have to write a research paper on a topic that we would later study. Not knowing anything about finding my way in the Bible, I chose to take that topic. I had no idea of what I was getting myself into. The teacher gave me unusual (and I thought fun) instructions for what I was to do. She gave me the first part of a story. My report was to complete it with the knowledge I had gained from my research.

My teacher's unusual instructions
for my report.

"I want you to imagine that you are a teenage genius—a super-mind. Like Clark Kent in Superman movies, you and your parents have hidden your intelligence from all but a few. You must be very careful; if evil people heard of your abilities, your life could be in danger. Not a single soul in your school has a clue of how brilliant you are.

"You can read and speak ten ancient languages. In fact, you have such outstanding abilities that universities around the world frequently call you to help examine old documents. Over the summer you received a call from a friend of your family, a rich executive in London, England. His workers had come upon a secret room in the foundation of an old tower and in that room had found treasures that included old Bibles. He begged you to come and examine them.

"You got permission from your parents, packed, and got on a plane headed to London. Your parents had one requirement: You had to keep a journal of all that happened so they would be able to hear all about that great opportunity.

"The following is my journal of how I helped my family's friend identify the ages of the Bibles and of how I helped him and his workers navigate the Bible for studying it on their own."

Identifying the ages of the Bibles

When I arrived in London, newspaper reporters were swarming everywhere, eager to get news on the books. Some, I learned, were already making claims that among the newly discovered documents was the very first Bible. They were confident the other books were likely to include at least the first few manuscripts of it (the first copies made from the original Bible).

When I saw the books, I knew in an instant the reporters were wrong. I turned the pages of the oldest looking Bible and came to the title *Genesis*. On that page I saw a chapter number and many verse numbers. The first words read, *In the beginning God created the heaven and the earth.* Every page I turned cried out that those Bibles were made sometime after AD 1550 and resembled modern Bibles, rather than ancient ones. A Bible produced 500 years ago would truly be old, but since the original writings were completed approximately 1900 years ago, the oldest Bible in the tower was relatively new. The reporters and my disappointed friend had no idea that their discoveries had little resemblance in either appearance or layout to the most ancient copies.

The differences between ancient Bibles and modern Bibles

The reporters asked how I knew at once that not even one of those Bibles in the tower's foundation was ancient, so I made a list of my reasons for their newspapers.

- The original Bible and the oldest manuscripts were written on scrolls, not in page-turning books.

- The words, *In the beginning God created the heaven and the earth* are in English. The Bible writers wrote in Hebrew and Greek.

- Even though the original Bible contained individual books, the books had no names. Names were added later. The books in these Bibles had names, such as *Genesis, Exodus, Leviticus*, all the way through to the end—names for every book.

- All early Bibles were handwritten. The Bibles in the tower had been produced on a printing press that was not invented until about AD 1450.

- Ancient Hebrew Bibles did not have vowels (a, e, i, o and u) within their words.

- Hebrew and Greek early manuscripts had no lowercase letters, no punctuation, and no spaces separating the words. If English Bibles today left out capitals, punctuation, spaces, and vowels as the Hebrew Bibles once did, the beginning of the first verse of Genesis (in the King James Version), which reads, *In the beginning God created the heaven and the earth*, would read, "NTHBGNNNGGDCRTDTHH-VNNDTHRTH" with no period at the end. (Additionally, the letters would have begun on the right and moved from right to left.)

- Ancient Bibles did not have chapter and verse divisions either. In the 1200s, long after the completion of the whole Bible, a scholar—Stephen Langton—divided the books of the English Bible into chapters, each chapter having a number. Although he was not the first to do this, his chapter divisions are the ones used in Bibles today.

- In 1448 a Jewish rabbi, Nathan, put verse numbers into the Hebrew Bible. One hundred years later, a printer took Nathan's numbers, gave verse numbers to the New Testament too, and in 1555 printed the entire Bible with both chapter and verse numbers. These are the same numbers we have today. The Bibles from the London tower had both chapter and verse numbers; therefore, they had to have been printed after 1555.

How to navigate modern English Bibles

Even though I answered the reporters's questions, the friend who asked me to go to London had more. He told me he was generally unfamiliar with the Bible. He did not know how to find his way in its pages, and he didn't understand the number system. No matter how many times he searched for familiar stories and quotes, he could never find them. He asked me to teach him those "mysteries." Since the workers who discovered the books had the same questions, they were glad when I offered to give them a class in how to navigate the Bible—how to find their way around in it. My instruction included how to read and write Bible references and how to find verses using a concordance.

Bible references

I began by explaining that just as houses have addresses, sentences in the Bible (and sometimes parts of long sentences) have addresses called *references*. It is important to understand how to read and write Bible references.

All books of the Bible are divided into chapters. Several short books have only one chapter, but the book of Psalms has one hundred and fifty. Each chapter is divided into numbered verses. Most verses are about one sentence in length. The spoken reference, *Genesis 23, one and two,* means *the book* of *Genesis, chapter 23, verses 1 and 2.*

A system of punctuation and abbreviations simplifies the writing of Bible references. The following are the basic punctuations:

1. *Colon* (:) The number before a colon is a chapter number, and the number after the colon is a verse number. The colon replaces the words, *chapter* and *verse,* shortening the reference *Genesis, chapter three, verse five,* to *Genesis 3:5.*

2. *Dash* (–) A dash means *through.* Genesis 3–5 means, *Genesis chapter 3 through chapter 5.*

3. *Comma* (,) A comma means *and.* Genesis 3:17, 20 means *Genesis chapter 3 verse 17 and verse 20.*

4. *Semicolon* (;) Semicolon also means *and* but is used between chapters, not between verses. Genesis chapter 3:5; 19 reads, *Genesis chapter 3 verse 5 and chapter 19* (not verse 19).

5. *Letters* (a, b, c) If only a small part of a long verse is used, a letter, *a*, *b*, or *c* might be added to the reference: *a* is the first section, *b* is the second section, *c* is the third section of the verse, and even *d* if the verse if very long Genesis 3:5b in this verse with three or four phrases

reads " . . . then your eyes shall be opened . . ." leaving out all the rest of the verse.

The concordance

Imagine a man who goes to a funeral and hears the words, *The LORD is my shepherd I shall not want.* He is almost certain the words come from the Bible, but though he has thumbed here and there through its pages, he cannot find them anywhere. If he had a concordance, he could find that verse in less than a minute.

Over eight hundred years ago (shortly after Stephen Langton added chapter numbers), Dominican friars, or monks, listed key Bible words in alphabetical order. With each word they included where that word is found in the Bible, both by the book and by the newly created chapter numbers. That made those key words and subjects much easier to find. Perhaps that was the first concordance. Today's concordances include far more. A complete concordance has every word in the Bible (not just some) in alphabetical order.

The person looking for the words *The LORD is my shepherd I shall not want* should first choose a key word in the verse, such as *shepherd,* and look it up in the alphabetical listing. (Better to take *shepherd* than LORD since there are thousands of entries of the word LORD and far fewer of *shepherd.*) In a complete concordance, every single time the word *shepherd* occurs in the Bible it is listed by reference, and with each reference the publisher has included a fragment of the verse.

So next to every word *shepherd* (which is shortened to the letter *s*) this man will see at least a fragment of the words surrounding each *shepherd.* As he works his way down the list, reading the fragments, finally he will come to "LORD is my *s* I shall not." The reference given with it is Psalm 23:1. He has easily found the correct passage.

Some publishers today include an abbreviated concordance at the back of their Bibles. (With the Internet a person can usually find the location of a Bible verse simply by typing a few of its words into a search engine.)

The teacher's wrap-up

The teacher read her directions as well as my report to the class, but didn't say who wrote it so that she wouldn't give away my identity yet. Everyone enjoyed it, and everyone claimed to be that genius. They all agreed that the report was a big help to them. When the teacher finally told them I was the one who wrote it, I got the short-lived nickname *Supermind*.

My reflections after the report

The "teenage genius" (which I enjoyed being for a day—well, maybe for an hour) has freed me from a false idea—the idea that the Bible is extremely complicated. Now that I understand the mechanics of using the Bible, I have taken a big step toward reading without confusion and toward exploring this remarkable book. I now feel prepared to work my way through its pages. (I do wish I really and truly *were* a teenage genius, but I'm thankful I can stand on the shoulders of many real-life smart people.)

Checking for understanding

1. Give four additions or changes that have made modern Bibles easier to use than ancient copies.

2. Leaving out the words in italics, punctuate the following references:

   a. Genesis *chapter 4 and chapter 7*

   b. Genesis *chapter 4 through chapter 7*

   c. Genesis *chapter 4 verse 7*

   d. Genesis *chapter 4 verse 7 through chapter 8 verse 3*

   e. Genesis *chapter 4 verse 7 and chapter 8 verse 3*

   f. Genesis *chapter 4 verses 7 through 9*

   g. Genesis *chapter 4 verses 7 and 9*

   h. Genesis *chapter 9 verse 12 and chapter 14*

3. What is the purpose of a concordance?

4. From the story written at the beginning of this lesson, list and explain three different reasons why none of the books found in the old tower could have been the original Bible.

History of English Bible versions, Part I

My first thoughts

Today and tomorrow we have a guest speaker who will take the class on a journey that covers over 2300 years. That journey, he said, will introduce us to a long line of Bible translators, many for whom the reward for their work was disgrace and death. I wondered why a person would suffer disgrace for translating the Bible into English. Our teacher wants us to make a timeline for this study—a timeline that will cover those 2300 years.

My notes on the guest speaker's lesson

The speaker's plan

The speaker will first tell us about two ancient, non-English translations. After that, he will take us from the Mediterranean area northward to England. There we will discover Bibles in an English that only scholars can read. That English is as foreign to us, he said, as Hindustani is to my little sister. From those translations he will take us on the trail to the most famous English Bible in the history of English translations: The King James Version, the one our class will use.

Early non-English versions, or translations

The Bible in Greek

Three hundred years before the New Testament period, Alexander the Great had spread his Greek language throughout the Mediterranean world. The Greeks, loving to learn, collected the scrolls of conquered lands, translated them into their superb language, and stored them in their famous library in Alexandria, Egypt. That included a Greek translation of the Hebrew Bible.

According to tradition, the librarian had asked the Jewish high priest in Jerusalem to send men who could translate the Hebrew Bible into Greek. The high priest sent seventy-two Hebrew scholars, each scholar working in a separate cell or room. As the story goes, at the end of seventy-two days, the seventy-two scholars had completed the Greek translation of the first five books of the Bible, all translations identical. The name *Septuagint,* from the Latin word *septuaginta* meaning seventy, became the name of the Greek translation of the first five books. The entire Hebrew Bible was translated into Greek before New Testament times. By then, the whole translation was called the *Septuagint.* Jesus and his disciples often quoted from that Greek Old Testament.

The Greeks ruled for 300 years, but their rule would not last forever. Shortly before New Testament times, disciplined Roman armies advanced across the Mediterranean world, conquering all in their paths. The new foreign rulers brought with them their Latin language. Although it was a slow process, Latin slowly displaced Greek, and fewer and fewer could read the Greek Bible. The time had come when their world needed a new translation.

The Bible in Latin

Many Christian began translating the Bible into Latin, the language of the Romans. Unfortunately, some less-skilled translators made errors that mislead and confused the churches. To end the problems, leaders asked the brilliant scholar Jerome to make a Latin translation that corrected the errors. When he completed his work in AD 405, he believed it was better than any of the others, but those who had grown accustomed to the old translations had no appreciation for what Jerome had done. They called it a work of the devil.

Though Jerome died without receiving recognition, scholars who came later, seeing the quality of his work, laid aside their older versions and replaced them with Jerome's. They called that translation by the name, *Jerome's Latin Vulgate,* Latin being the "vulgate" or *the common language* of the empire. For about a thousand years, it was the official Bible of the whole western world. Jerome, so humiliated and discredited by people who disliked his translation, had no idea that one day the Christian world would give him an honored name, *Saint Jerome.*

Old English, or Anglo-Saxon, translations and translators

Our study now moves from the Mediterranean world northward to England. The time is about 700 years after Christ, when the people of England spoke an English called *Anglo-Saxon*—but what an English it was! The teacher suggested that sometime we might use the Internet and find a sample of it. It is like a foreign language. Even many of the letters of their alphabet are different from our letters. From the Anglo-Saxon, also called *Old English,* modern English slowly and gradually developed.

Bede's translation of the Gospel of John

Although missionaries had spread Christianity into parts of England, few people there had ever seen a Bible, and even if they had seen one, without knowing Latin they could not have read it. The nonexistence of Bibles in English greatly troubled a monk named Bede [pronounced BEED]. As well as being a monk, he was a priest, a writer, and a brilliant historian. He realized he must begin translating the Bible into the English of England, the Anglo-Saxon language. Bede chose to start with the fourth book of the New Testament, *The Gospel According to John.* A young priest worked with him recording his words. That was unusual for Bede because he preferred to do his own writing, but this time it was impossible—he was too sick to write.

The young scribe copying Bede's words begged him to rest, but the priest responded, "I don't want my boys to read a lie." As he began the last chapter, the scribe again begged him to rest, but he went on. Finally, breathing with difficulty, Bede translated the last verse and then said, "It is finished." That same day he died. The year was 735; England finally had one book of the Bible in its own Anglo-Saxon language.

Gradually, in the next 300 years, others translated several books of the Bible into Anglo-Saxon, but there was not yet a complete English Bible.

The Anglo-Saxon Bible portions become unusable

Events occurred in 1066 that eventually, though unintentionally, turned the few Anglo-Saxon scriptures into a closed book. Northern France, called Normandy, moved its armies across the waters of the English Channel to battle against the Anglo-Saxons. In that war, called the *Battle of Hastings*, the French-Normans won, and William the Conqueror became England's new king. He gave all positions of leadership to the French-Normans— men who often did not speak the Anglo-Saxon language. Even the leaders of the churches could not speak the language of the people.

With the French-Norman language placed over the Anglo-Saxon, a change took place: the two languages merged and became Middle English, neither French nor Anglo-Saxon. In less than 300 years, the Anglo-Saxon language passed away, and England no longer had any part of the Bible in its own language.

My reflections on the study

It is amazing to me that so many people were intent on putting the Bible into new languages and making sure it could be read by those who were not scholars. I am wondering if any other book has that kind of history.

Checking for understanding

1. How did Greek become the language of the world?

2. Name the Greek translation of the Hebrew Scriptures used during the lifetime of Jesus.

3. Explain how it came about that a Latin Bible was needed.

4. How was the work of Jerome supposed to solve the problem of wrong teachings that were dividing the churches?

5. What was Bede's great worry that caused him to begin translating the Latin Bible into Old English (Anglo-Saxon)?

6. Explain what caused the Anglo-Saxon language to change into Middle English.

History of English Bible Versions, Part II

My first thoughts

THE GUEST SPEAKER IS back today to continue the stories of Bible versions (translations). As several of us chatted with him before class, he said we were lucky we didn't live in England in the Middle Ages, the period he would be teaching about today. He commented, "Back then if you had been caught with an English Bible, you would have been in serious trouble." I know that's true in some places today, but I had no idea it was once true in English-speaking countries.

My notes on the guest speaker's lesson

Middle English translators and translations

The guest's talk moved the study three hundred years past the French-Norman takeover in 1066 to an even more dangerous period in England's history—dangerous, that is, for any who had an English Bible.

John Wycliffe's Bible-related crime

John Wycliffe, a popular teacher at Oxford University in England, had powerful enemies who wanted him executed—burned alive. They thought burning him to death would be a mercy because the flames might cause him to repent of his sins and crimes before he died.

What were his sins and crimes? The authorities at that time believed it was dangerous for uneducated people to read the Bible in English. They might read, misunderstand, and fall into error. Wycliffe, though, believed that ignorance of what is clear is far worse than confusion over what is not clear. Therefore, with the help of others, he translated the Latin Vulgate Bible into the new language, Middle English, and made copies to distribute to others. Those were his sins and crimes.

As handwritten copies of the Bible spread throughout the country, searchers went from house to house to find and arrest anyone who had that forbidden book. Parents who taught their children the Lord's Prayer and the Ten Commandments in English were tied to beds of straw, and their children were forced to set the beds on fire.

Why was Wycliffe not burned at the stake as the law of the land demanded? He was too popular, but if he had lived four decades later, he would not have escaped. In 1428, forty-four years after his death, the authorities dug up Wycliffe's bones, burned them, and cast them into a nearby river, symbolizing the belief that he was even then suffering in eternal fire.

One hundred and fifty years passed before the English-speaking people could safely own an English Bible. During those years, even if their ancestors had secretly kept Wycliffe's English Bible, the many changes in the English language would have made it difficult to understand.

The inexpensive mass-production of books

Until about 1450 producing one Bible required ten months of careful, painstaking handwriting. That would make the cost of one Bible equal to what a person might make in ten months, which few could have afforded. Thankfully, Johann Gutenberg would change all that. His invention—the printing press—created around the year 1450, meant that hundreds of affordable Bibles could be mass-produced in a short time. Unfortunately, the invention did not help readers in England because possession of English Bibles was still a crime.

William Tyndale's fearless work

Two years after Columbus discovered America, a genius was born in England—William Tyndale—a genius who easily learned to speak eight different languages, speaking each language as if it were his own. When a friend gave him a Greek New Testament, Tyndale had nothing to fear because reading a Greek or Latin Bible was legal; it just could not be written in English. The words of the book kindled a determination in him that every person in the land should have an English Bible.

When the authorities refused his request to make such a translation, he left England for Germany where he could have greater freedom. Within a year he had completed a hasty English translation of the New Testament and found a man who would secretly print it.

On a night in 1525, Tyndale raced to the print shop, broke in, grabbed every sheet of his work, and fled from the town. What had happened? His printer, drinking heavily at the local saloon, began talking, and the secret of Tyndale's English translation was out. By the time the horrified authorities heard, it was too late; Tyndale and his papers were gone.

In the city of Worms, Tyndale found a sympathetic printer who promised to keep the work secret. Soon copies of English New Testaments began arriving in England hidden in sacks of corn, and flour, and inside bales of cloth. In spite of searches made at English ports and in spite of the many copies destroyed, thousands of New Testaments spread throughout England. The leaders, seeing they could not stop that flood of books, ordered Tyndale to return to England for trial.

Wisely, Tyndale refused, knowing he could not trust the promise of safety. Unfortunately for him, he was not as wise in choosing his friends. An Englishman named Phillips befriended him, pretending great sympathy for his work even as he carefully watched for a chance to betray him. Phillips succeeded; soldiers arrested Tyndale and took him to a dreadful prison in Brussels. Powerful friends of Tyndale wrote to King Henry VIII of England begging that Tyndale not be burned at the stake and that he be released from prison. The king refused to release him, but made one concession. Before the executioner started the fire, he was to kill Tyndale by strangling him.

It was 1536. The executioner tied him to the stake, placed both a chain and a noose around his neck, and piled wood at his feet—the chain to hold up his body, the noose to strangle him, and the wood for the fire. Excited crowds gathered to see the execution. Grim lawyers and officials also came. They came to give Tyndale one last chance to repent of his sin—the sin of translating the Bible into English. Tyndale's response was a fervent prayer, "Lord, open the King of England's eyes!"

The shocking change

Tyndale would not have guessed that within three years after his death every church in England would be required to have a copy of an English Bible. That copy, called the Great Bible because of its large size, was chained to a reading stand where anyone could read it, but no one could carry it away. King Henry even encouraged his people to go their churches and read from it. Though Tyndale's body had gone up in flames, his influence had not. He, himself, was the main translator of that Great Bible!

English versions between the Great Bible of 1539 and the version of 1611

Several more English Bible translations came out in the 1500s—translations that, like Tyndale's work, went back *beyond* the Latin Vulgate to the old Greek and Hebrew manuscripts—thus getting closer to the original writings. The most popular was the Geneva Bible (filled with many explanatory notes), the Bible the Puritans brought with them to America.

A new king, James I, came to England's throne in 1603. Once he saw the notes in the Geneva Bible, notes that challenged some of a king's rights, he decided England needed a new translation with no study notes at all—just the Bible! He authorized a committee of about fifty Bible scholars to make a new translation.

At the same time, English Roman Catholic scholars, exiles from England, worked on another translation. In 1610 they produced the Douai-Rheims Version, named for the two places in France where they did their work.

One year later in 1611, the version authorized by King James came off the presses. Little could the king have known that even 400 years later the *King James Version* would be the most popular, most read, and most quoted translation ever made, a translation that eventually became the bestseller over every version produced even to this day.

English translations of the Bible since the King James Version

Languages do not stay the same; new words come and old words take on different meanings. In the 400 years since the translation of the King James

Version, the English language has continued to change. For example, Numbers 16:30 (the fourth book of the Bible) describes a punishment about to come upon some rebels. The earth was going to open up and swallow the rebels *quick*, a word we use today for something that is fast. *Fast*, though, is not what the translators meant. The English word *quick* once meant *alive*. The earth was going to open up and swallow the rebels *alive*.

In the twentieth century and into the twenty-first, because of language changes as well as discoveries of even older Bible manuscripts, scholars continue to make new translations. Honest translators do not, as some have said, just take previous translations and tweak them. The goal of good translators is to take the oldest Hebrew and Greek manuscripts that we have and in the clearest English produce the most accurate, reliable, and understandable English Bible possible.

English readers in the days of Wycliffe and Tyndale could only dream of the day when all people could freely, and for such little cost, have their own understandable Bibles in their own homes for their own personal reading.

My reflection on the sufferings that once accompanied English Bibles

The speaker's words continue to surprise me. It's hard to imagine that at one time English speaking readers did not have the liberty to read what they wished and could be tortured and killed for having a Bible! It makes me even more curious to know what is in this book!

Checking for understanding

1. As time passed and people could no longer read the Anglo-Saxon language, who translated the Bible into Middle English?

2. What was the punishment that came to some parents who had taught their children the Bible?

3. Tell why the invention of AD 1450 was so significant in the history of the Bible.

4. In your estimation, if one Bible today cost what a skilled worker would make in ten months, how much would we have to pay to buy one?

5. As Tyndale was led out to the stake where he was to be burned, do you think there was anything he could have said that would have made the authorities let him go free? If so, what would it have been?

6. Tell which translation of the English Bible has had the greatest influence and popularity.

7. Why do scholars continue making new translations?

8. Give some illustrations, if you can, of how language has changed in your own lifetime. For example, think of new words that may not have existed when your grandparents were your age, such as technology words, or expressions that have arisen because of movies, expressions such as *bucket list*.

LESSON 7

———

Genesis Background

My first thoughts on what
seemed an easy question

THERE ON THE BOARD was a simple question. "Who wrote Genesis?" I felt I knew the answer. After I bought my own Bible and before I enrolled in this class, I began reading it. The title of the first book read *The First Book of Moses, called Genesis*. Evidently, whoever this Moses was, he wrote more than one book, so out of curiosity I had moved to the first page of the second book, and there it was again, *The Second Book of Moses, called Exodus*. How many did he write? I continued looking and found another, *The Third Book of Moses, called Leviticus*, and another, *The Fourth Book of Moses, called Numbers*. And finally, *The Fifth Book of Moses, called Deuteronomy*.

My search came to an end after Deuteronomy, for the next book simply said *The Book of Joshua*.

My notes on the teacher's lessons

Two views on who wrote Genesis

When the teacher asked the class if anyone knew who wrote Genesis, I thought it was a trick question—the answer was so obvious—but she said there were several views and gave our class an assignment to look up that question in an encyclopedia on the Internet or in the library, and to write a summary statement of two main views. This was my answer:

"For over two thousand years Jewish scholars agreed that a man named Moses wrote, or edited, the first five books of the Bible. Christian scholars agreed. The titles in many English language Bibles included his name—*The First Book of Moses called Genesis, The Second Book of Moses called Exodus*, right through the five books.

"A new theory arose about two hundred years ago proposing that long after Moses' time, a group of unnamed Hebrews, not Moses, had assembled and edited the Jews's sacred writings. That theory, called the Documentary Hypothesis, has given rise to at least two centuries of debate, discussion, books, and disagreements with no accord reached even to this day."

The classroom approach to studying Genesis

The teacher said that several reports, including mine, correctly showed the different sides. She made it clear that she would not try to prove one view over the other. Those questions could involve religious issues, and religious issues cannot be solved in a public high school course.

Instead, the class would be viewing Genesis as the writers and caretakers of the Hebrew Bible viewed it for thousands of years. We would see it as the writing of a man named Moses who grew up in the land of the Pharaohs about 1400 BC.

But who was Moses? What qualified him to write this book? To answer that question she said she would take us on a quick overview of the whole book of Genesis.

Moses life in relation to the whole book of Genesis

Genesis 1-11 is the Bible's record of the beginning or origin of everything; in fact, the name *Genesis* can be defined as *origins*. In those chapters Moses wrote of the beginning of everyone and everything in existence—the universe, life, family, death, languages, nations, troubles. Everything! He believed that the *genesis* of his own life and of all life is found in those early Genesis chapters.

In Genesis 12 - 50 Moses moved from looking at the whole world with its troubles to looking at one family, the family of a Hebrew named Abraham. Moses wrote in chapter 12 that God promised to bring great blessings to Abraham and through his family to bring great blessings to all the nations of the earth. By the end of Genesis, Abraham's family was living as honored guests in the most powerful country in the world Egypt, honored because of the great blessing one of Abraham's descendants had already brought to them. Moses would be born into that family, but not until hundreds of years later.

Moses' life in Exodus

In the years between Genesis and Exodus, the population of Abraham's family, still in Egypt, increased so greatly that a new king (called a *Pharaoh*) trembled. He feared they would turn against him and side with his enemies, so to hold down their numbers, he put them into brutal slavery. When that didn't stop their growth, he made a new law—all newborn Hebrew sons (Israelites) must be cast into the river (Exodus 1).

Pharaoh's order to drown the infant sons came just before a slave woman gave birth to a beautiful boy. The book of Exodus tells that through many extraordinary events, Pharaoh's own daughter saved that infant from death. She hired a Hebrew woman to nurse him, gave him the name *Moses,* and raised him as a prince of Egypt. (Exodus does not tell whether or not the princess knew that the woman she hired to nurse Moses was his own birth mother.) Both the book of Acts in the New Testament and Jewish tradition say that Moses was educated in all the wisdom of Egypt which would have included reading, writing, mathematics, astronomy, medicine, history, public speaking, and military training—the best education any Egyptian could have had. Perhaps the Pharaoh thought that this outstanding young son would someday be the next ruler of his country.

Neither Pharaoh nor his daughter had any idea in their forty years of raising and educating Moses that they were raising the very person who would one day free the slaves from Egypt. Though the king probably knew the adopted son was the child of slaves, only when the son became a man did he realize Moses was on the side, not of Egypt, but of the Hebrews. How did he know Moses was not on his side? A report came to him that Moses murdered an Egyptian slave master who was beating a Hebrew. Learning that Pharaoh planned to kill him, Moses escaped by fleeing to the desert east of Egypt.

Moses at eighty years of age

Forty years later, at the age of eighty and in full strength, Moses returned to the king of Egypt with a command from the LORD—*Let my people go.* It took a year for Pharaoh to bend, but at the end of that time he was ordering and rushing the slaves out of his land as fast as they could go. Moses then had the burdensome task of leading the people throughout the many years recorded in Exodus, Leviticus, Numbers, and Deuteronomy. According to those books, he also had the task of being sure his people forgot neither who they were, nor the purpose for their lives. That meant assembling their records and stories and writing an account of the family starting from the beginning. The first part of that account is the book of Genesis.

So what qualified Moses to write this book and the next four? Who else of all the Israelite men, working all their lives as slaves, could have undertaken those tasks? Who else had the training, education, and experience to face the Pharaoh, lead the Israelites out of Egypt, and form them into a nation. Who else could have taken records (perhaps carried by their ancestors into Egypt) and then recorded the family's history in the first five books of the Bible?

My reflections on the overview of Moses and his writings

What a story! Whoever recorded the ending of Moses' life wrote that he died at 120—his body as strong as ever. For forty years he had led, organized, taught, written, and kept the family (by then a nation) all together bringing them up to the edge of Canaan. I wish I could have a record like that. I'll really be happy if the last forty years of my life are so productive! That would mean that probably from the quite-old-age of forty to the really-old-age of eighty, I'd be a dynamo. It would be nice to do so much good throughout all those years!

Checking for understanding

1. Explain the two main views of who wrote Genesis.

2. You would think slave owners would be happy to have many slaves who could do a great deal of work and increase their owners riches. Why did Pharaoh want his slaves to decrease in number?

3. Tell the meaning of the word *Genesis.*

4. What is the difference between Genesis 1 to 11 and Genesis 12 to 50.

5. According to Moses' writings, how are you connected to Genesis?

6. Based on Moses' background, what made him especially suited to be the leader of the Hebrews?

LESSON 8

The Beginnings

Based on Genesis 1:1—2:3

My first thoughts

AT THE END OF our last class, the teacher gave us a heads up on Genesis 1. She wanted us to read it as if we had grown up as slaves in Egypt where the successful people worshipped many gods—even worshipped Pharaoh himself. Since many of the Israelites might have secretly worshipped those gods rather than the God of the Israelites, we were to see Genesis 1 as a challenge against Egyptian polytheism, the worship of many gods.

My notes on the teacher's lesson

Ancient Egyptian beliefs about the world

The Egyptians at the time of Moses were polytheists, believing that a multitude of gods created the world and everything in it. They believed those gods lived within creatures such as animals and birds, inanimate objects such as the sea and the earth, and even within their rulers, the Pharaohs. That meant if an Egyptian decided to go for a walk, he believed that the animals, birds, and insects that he might see along the way were superior to him, able to answer his prayers. The Egyptians also believed that when they looked upwards they saw more of their gods—the sun, the moon, and the stars—gods that perhaps, even then, were ordering and controlling their daily lives.

The Genesis account of the world

No doubt Moses' creation account in Genesis 1 would have disturbed many of the Hebrews who were accustomed to those Egyptian beliefs.

Introduction to the biblical creation days

The first verse in the Bible describes the world's condition. *In the beginning God created the heaven and the earth. And the earth was without form, and void* [or empty]; *and darkness was upon the face of the deep (1:1–2a).* No landforms rose above the waters and no sea creatures swam in the oceans. Neither life nor light yet existed on the earth. *And the Spirit of God moved upon the face of the waters (1:2b).*

The rest of the chapter is like listening to a recording of God as he *speaks*, commanding the world into existence. In the first three days, he commanded into existence *spaces and places* (the wording some use). On days four through six he commanded into existence the *occupants* that would live in those spaces and places.

Before starting the Genesis 1 creation days, our teacher had us draw a line down the middle of a paper to make a simple chart. She said it would give us a way to remember the order of the creation. We put the words *Spaces and Places* over the column on the left and under that listed the numbers from one to three. We put the words *Occupants* over the column on the right, and below that word listed numbers four through six opposite numbers one to three. She said we would understand why we are listing them that way after we study the days.

Days one through three: Spaces and places

Day one

And the Spirit of God moved upon the face of the waters. And God said, Let there be light: and there was light. And God saw the light, that it was good: and God divided the light from the darkness. And God called the light Day, and the darkness he called Night. And the evening and the morning were the first day (1:2b–5).

Day two

And God said, Let there be a firmament in the midst of the waters, and let it divide the waters from the waters (1:6). After reading this verse, our teacher asked us what we thought the *firmament* was. Since the firmament divided the waters, it sounded to all of us like land, but when she had us read verse seven, we changed our minds.

And God made the firmament, and divided the waters which were under the firmament from the waters which were above the firmament: and it was so. And God called the firmament heaven. And the evening and the morning were the second day (1:7–8). Clearly, the word *firmament* meant the heavens, the space above the earth. The teacher said we would see the occupants of the firmament and the occupants of the waters on days four and five.

Day three

And God said, Let the waters under the heaven be gathered together unto one place, and let the dry land appear: and it was so. And God called the dry land Earth; and the gathering together of the waters called he Seas: and God saw that it was good. And God said, Let the earth bring forth grass, the herb yielding seed, and the fruit tree yielding fruit after his kind, whose seed is in itself, upon the earth: and it was so. . . . And God saw that it was good. And the evening and the morning were the third day (1:9–13). We will see the occupants of the place (dry land) on day six.

Days four through six: Occupants, or inhabitants

Day four: Occupants of the light and of the firmament

On the fourth day *God said, Let there be lights in the firmament of the heaven to divide the day from the night; and let them be for signs, and for seasons, and for days, and years: and let them be for lights in the firmament of the heaven to give light upon the earth: and it was so (1:14–15).*

And God made two great lights; the greater light to rule the day, and the lesser light to rule the night: he made the stars also. And God set them in the firmament of the heaven to give light upon the earth, And to rule over the day and over the night, and to divide the light from the darkness: and God saw that it was good. And the evening and the morning were the fourth day (1:16–19).

This was saying that the occupants of the farthest spaces would give order to life far beneath them upon the earth. Those light bearers—the greater light, the lesser light, and the stars—would give order to the seasons, days, and years.

Moses' account of day four might have held a special surprise for any Egyptians who came out of Egypt with the slaves—a special surprise if they believed the Egyptian view of creation. Though Egypt's popular stories agreed that water once covered the earth as in day one of Genesis, the Egyptian priests taught that a hill rose up out of the water, an egg on the hill hatched, and out came the greatest of their gods, the sun god. In contrast, Moses taught that the Israelites's God had created the sun and had created it to do his own bidding. That was claiming that the God of the Hebrews was not only far greater than Egypt's sun god Ra, but that the God of the Hebrews had created the sun and that it belonged to him.

Readers have to wonder if Moses was showing his rejection of Egyptian beliefs by not even mentioning the names of the *greater and lesser lights*—the *sun* and the *moon*—since the Egyptians might think of those names as god-names.

Day five: Living occupants of the water and the firmament

Day five tells of the living creatures that would live in the firmament above the earth and within those waters beneath it.

And God said, Let the waters bring forth abundantly the moving creature that hath life, and fowl that may fly above the earth in the open firmament of heaven. And God created great whales [or great sea creatures] and every living creature that moveth, which the waters brought forth abundantly, after their kind, and every winged fowl after his kind: and God saw that it was good. And God blessed them, saying, Be fruitful, and multiply, and fill the waters in the seas, and let fowl multiply in the earth. And the evening and the morning were the fifth day (1:20–23).

Like the surprise of day four, Moses told the Israelites that their God made all the creatures of the air and the water—fish, fowl, and great sea creatures—more gods of Egypt's worship.

Day six: Living occupants of the dry land. Part I

Day three had described the dry land and its plant life; day six describes the occupants that would live on the dry land and would live by its plant life. *And God said, Let the earth bring forth the living creature after his kind, cattle, and creeping thing, and beast of the earth after his kind: and it was so. And God made the beast of the earth after his kind, and cattle after their kind, and every thing that creepeth upon the earth after his kind: and God saw that it was good (1:24–25).*

Day six: Living occupants of the dry land. Part II

The best, I thought, was saved for the last. *And God said, Let us make man in our image, after our likeness: and let them have dominion* [or rule] *over the fish of the sea, and over the fowl of the air, and over the cattle, and over all the earth, and over every creeping thing that creepeth upon the earth. So God created man in his own image, in the image of God created he him; male and female created he them (1:26–27).*

And God blessed them, and God said unto them, Be fruitful, and multiply, and replenish the earth, and subdue it: and have dominion over the fish of the sea, and over the fowl of the air, and over every living thing that moveth upon the earth (1:28).

By those words Moses declared it was the Creator's plan for the man and woman and their offspring to rule over the earth and its creatures. They were not under the authority of nature; the man and the woman were to *rule* over nature, having dominion over everything on earth.

God's evaluation of the six days

And God saw every thing that he had made, and, behold, it was very good. And the evening and the morning were the sixth day. Thus the heavens and the earth were finished, and all the host of them (1:31–2:1). According to these verses, what was good? Everything!

Day seven

By the end of day six creation was finished, so why was there a day *seven* (later called the *Sabbath*, which means to *cease* or *rest*)? In Moses' record of the seventh day he told what God did *after* the creation. *And on the seventh day God ended his work which he had made; and he rested on the seventh day from all his work which he had made. And God blessed the seventh day . . . (2:2–3b).* Moses made sure it was clear to his people that not all days were to be alike for them. The humans must have a day to rest from their labors, for they were no longer slaves; they were free.

My reflection on the creation account

A discussion came up on the meaning of the days. Some thought they were twenty-four hour days, some thought they represented long periods of time, and some thought the chapter was not dealing with time periods, but was a poetic way of saying that God made it all. Even though the class did not agree on those issues, we did agree that Moses gave no place for other gods, rather, that he was saying, "It was not Egypt's multitude of gods—it was the God of the Hebrews who made the world and all that's in it." I felt as if Moses was also saying, "Now enjoy this world, use its gifts, and bring forth good!"

Checking for understanding

1. Genesis 1:2 records that at first the earth was without form and void. What does that mean?

2. How do the objects made on day four relate to the first day of creation?

3. How do the creatures made on day five relate to day two?

4. How do the creatures made on day six relate to what was created on day three?

5. According to the Genesis 1 description, were both male and female created on the sixth day or only the male? Support your answer, telling why you answered as you did.

6. In Genesis 1:28 what responsibilities (or perhaps rights) did the humans have?

7. For at least two thousand years, some have taught that *matter*—anything physical or material—is evil. Prove from Genesis 1 that Moses looked at the universe, the earth, and physical life as valuable, worthwhile, and pleasurable.

8. Explain the benefit of the Sabbath day.

9. Compare the Genesis belief versus the ancient Egyptian belief about the relation of humans and nature.

The Garden of Eden

Based on Genesis 2:4–25

My first thoughts

OUR ASSIGNMENT WAS TO read Genesis 2, harmonize it with Genesis 1—see how the two chapters fit together—and write a report. After reading both Genesis 1 and 2, they seemed to me like two different creations.

Next, we were to read our reports aloud. The class would decide which seemed like the best resolution to the problem—the best answer for how the two chapters could be so different and yet be related. After we all had read our reports, we agreed that sophomore Sheila's was the best.

My notes on the teacher's lesson and our class discussion

Reminder before today's study

Before the lesson, our teacher reminded us that some see the early accounts in Genesis as legends about the past, while others see them as historical events about real people. Since these involve religious issues that the teacher may neither affirm nor deny, the goal for the class must be to see what is on the pages, seeking to discover what the writer wanted his readers to see. We understand that though we are still free to bring up our views in class, the teacher will not be the referee.

Sheila's story harmonizing
Genesis 1 and Genesis 2

"Suppose you have an older sister soon to be married. Your mother has made arrangements with a bridal coordinator to take charge of the preparations. The coordinator hovers over every part of the planning—the wedding site, the flowers, the invitations, the rehearsal arrangements, the ceremony, the reception, the picture taking, and everything else involved to be sure all goes without a hitch. She is very, very good. On each visit to your house, she advances the plans with an orderly perfection to make sure the wedding is all that your sister has hoped for and more. After all is over, the coordinator leaves all her notes in a scrapbook, every step she took to build that perfect wedding.

"When your sister and her new husband return from their honeymoon, one of your aunts gives them another scrapbook. It has pictures of the apartment they have leased. It has your sister's emails to the groom's family about what they would like in the wedding ceremony. It has a framed announcement and invitation, pictures of the showers, letters from those who could not come, the beautiful ceremony, the departure for the honeymoon, and the pile of thank-you notes to be written.

"Does that second album mean she was married twice? Or could it mean it was another person's wedding? The books are so different! These questions, of course, are foolish. The books are about the same perfect wedding and the same bride and groom, but each book is made from a different perspective, grouped with different themes in mind, giving a richer memory of the wedding."

The similarities and differences
between Genesis 1 and 2

I could see how Sheila's story related to Genesis 1 and 2. The wedding coordinator's organization was like the Genesis 1 organization; each step was in a precise order moving forward to perfection. The aunt's scrapbook, though, was much more personal, just as Genesis 2 is—the warm and fuzzy side.

The teacher added a difference that no one else would have known—a point that went along with Sheila's story. That difference is the Creator's name. In Genesis 1 his name in English is God, which in Hebrew is a more general name. In Genesis 2 his name in English is the LORD God, which in the Hebrew language is a name that expresses a personal closeness and care for the creation.

I thought to myself that in Genesis 1 God seems to be seated on a throne above the world, giving out his kingly orders, telling idol worshipers that he alone made it all and it was his—no disagreement allowed. In Genesis 2, though, he is right there in the garden, hands covered with dirt, lovingly forming a clay body.

The Genesis 2 description of the man and his home

And the LORD *God formed man of the dust of the ground, and breathed into his nostrils the breath of life and man became a living soul (2:7).*

After God created the man, but before he created the woman, he made a home for them. *And the Lord God planted a garden eastward in Eden and there he put the man whom he had formed (2:8).*

And out of the ground made the LORD *God to grow every tree that is pleasant to the sight, and good for food (2:9a).* Those ground-produced trees would satisfy the needs of their senses and bodies. Two other trees grew in the center of the garden—*the tree of life . . . and the tree of knowledge of good and evil (2:9b).* The man did not yet know their purposes.

And a river went out of Eden to water the garden; and from thence it was parted, and became into four heads [rivers] *(2:10).* Moses gave names to the four rivers (some familiar today) and told of treasures within the earth. *The name of the first is Pison: that is it which compasseth* [circles] *the whole land of Havilah* [Arabia?]*, where there is gold. And the gold of that land is good: there is bdellium* [perhaps a fragrant perfume] *and the onyx stone (2:11–12).*

And the name of the second river is Gihon: the same is it that compasseth [circles] *the whole land of Ethiopia. And the name of the third river is Hiddekel* [Tigris]*: that is it which goeth toward the east of Assyria. And the fourth river is Euphrates (2:13–14).*

There was good not only above the ground—the trees, plants, and rivers, but there was also good within the ground—precious metals.

The man's responsibilities in the garden home

In Genesis 1:28 God had commanded the humans to subdue the earth. In Genesis 2 he told the man how to begin that work. *And the LORD God took the man, and put him into the garden of Eden to dress it and to keep it (2:15).*

The man had two assignments. First, he must develop the garden. Second, he must *keep* it. The word *keep* has the idea of guarding the garden against dangers, but what danger could there be?

The danger in the garden

And the LORD God commanded the man, saying, Of every tree of the garden thou mayest freely eat: but of the tree of the knowledge of good and evil, thou shalt not eat of it: for in the day that thou eatest thereof thou shalt surely die (2:16–17).

The man faced the danger of death—death if he ate from the tree, but did he understand what death meant? He would have known nothing yet of death's sicknesses, pains, doctors, and hospitals; but he at least should have known that death meant separation from his Creator—a rift created by his intentional disobedience. Since he didn't need the tree's fruit and knew that eating it would bring death, why would he eat from it? It would be as reckless as drinking poison.

The man's need of the woman

Chapter 1 recorded that on day six God created male and female. So far, chapter 2 had spoken only about the creation of the male, but that was about to change. *And the LORD God said, It is not good that the man should be alone; I will make him an help meet for him* [someone matching him, or suitable for him] *(2:18).*

Some resent the idea that the woman is called a *helper*, thinking it makes her inferior, but the Hebrew word for *help* is *ezer*, a word used to describe God himself. The word *ezer* presents God, not as inferior, but as aiding and giving help where others need it. That threw a new light on our understanding of the woman's position.

The inability of any creature to be the man's equal

The search began—the search to determine if any living creature would be a proper mate for the man. *And out of the ground the LORD God formed every beast of the field, and every fowl of the air and brought them unto Adam to see what he would call them: and whatsoever Adam called every living creature, that was the name thereof.*

And Adam gave names to all cattle, and to the fowl of the air, and to every beast of the field, but for Adam there was not found an help meet for him (2:19–20).

The creation of the woman

And the LORD God caused a deep sleep to fall upon Adam, and he slept: and he took one of his ribs, and closed up the flesh instead thereof. And the rib, which the LORD God had taken from man, made he a woman, and brought her unto the man (2:21–22).

And Adam said,

This is now bone of my bones,

and flesh of my flesh:

she shall be called Woman,

because she was taken out of Man (2:23).

Moses used Adam's words to teach the Hebrews about marriage— teachings which he wove into many of his writings. The Hebrews were to see their own marriages in the light of being *one flesh.* Moses went on with his writing: *Therefore shall a man leave his father and his mother, and shall cleave unto his wife: and they shall be one flesh. And they were both naked, the man and his wife, and were not ashamed (2:24–25).*

Moses was saying that she who had come, not from a mother's womb, but from the man himself, was one flesh with him. The two had a perfect relationship with each other, a perfect relationship to the world, and a perfect relationship with the Creator. Everything was still *very good.*

My reflections on Genesis 2

Perfect as this chapter seems, something in it bothers me. I have the feeling we are watching a stage crew setting up for a play. The props and characters are in place—many trees, two special trees in the center, the man, the woman, and the animals nuzzling up to them for a scratch. The scene seems ideal, but I sense a dark cloud hanging over the stage—the warning. And then the stage director suddenly calls out, "Wait, we have one more character." That's the next chapter.

Checking for understanding

1. Since humans, birds, and animals all have to eat, it is obvious the trees that were *good for food* had an important benefit for earth's creatures; but why, in your opinion, would there be trees that seemed to have no value except for being pleasant to the sight; in other words, how would the pleasant-to-the-sight trees be a benefit to the humans?

2. In what part of the earth does Genesis 2 place the beginnings of human life? (Note the rivers.)

3. Explain what it meant that Adam was responsible to *keep* the garden.

4. In your opinion, what was the purpose of having the tree of the knowledge of good and evil in the garden?

5. How does the word *ezer* show, not a woman's inferiority, but rather a woman's likeness to God?

6. Was there any reason at all for the humans to be unhappy with their lives? Explain your answer.

Death in Eden: Part I

Based on Genesis 3:1–13

My first thoughts

THE TITLE FOR TODAY'S study, *Death in Eden*, troubles me. Eden was a paradise—a place where everything was *very good*. If, as Moses wrote, the only way evil could come would be by eating from the forbidden tree, why would the man and woman *want* to eat from it? What could make them take the death route? As our class talked together about what we had read, we began to see that it all began with their minds. Something had to come into their minds that would make the fruit desirable and seemingly right. Something had to convince them that disobedience to the command would bring personal joy and fulfillment. It began with the entrance of a serpent—a reptile—into the garden.

My notes on the teacher's lesson

The enemy and his attacks

Now the serpent was more subtile [crafty] *than any beast of the field which the LORD God had made (3:1a).* For some unexplained reason, the serpent seemed to hold a hidden hatred for both God and the humans, a hatred carefully hidden behind a simple question.

The enemy's first attack and the woman's overzealous response

The serpent asked a question that the woman was too quick to answer. *And he said unto the woman, Yea, hath God said, Ye shall not eat of every tree of the garden (3:1b)?* Perhaps the question implied to her that the serpent knew nothing of Eden's riches and privileges. She quickly corrected him, explaining that, except for one tree, they could eat from any and every tree they desired. In correcting the serpent, however, she made an overzealous response, a response with grave results.

And the woman said unto the serpent, We may eat of the fruit of the trees of the garden: but of the fruit of the tree which is in the midst of the garden, God hath said, Ye shall not eat of it neither shall ye touch it, lest ye die (3:2–3).

She seemed so anxious that God be respected that she added her own words. God had only said they could not eat of that one tree lest they die, but the woman added, *neither shall ye touch it.*

When she added those words, she was creating a different command— a command not given to Adam. Those added words, as we would shortly see, would make it easier for her to give in to temptation.

The enemy's second attack and the woman's response

And the serpent said unto the woman, Ye shall not surely die: for God doth [does] *know that in the day ye eat thereof, then your eyes shall be opened, and ye shall be as gods, knowing good and evil (3:4–5).*

"God knows," the serpent seemed to imply, "that by eating of this tree you will know what God is holding back from you. Are you sure he has your best interests in mind?"

The serpent's words brought new ideas. Perhaps she could, in some way, become an equal of God, perhaps a god herself. After all, God knew all about evil and it didn't hurt him! So she decided to take a step; simply think about the tree and its fruit and enjoy the thoughts. Thinking about the tree, however, led her to her second step—desire.

When the woman saw that the tree was good for food, and that it was pleasant to the eyes, and a tree to be desired to make one wise (3:6a), evidently her desire for the fruit became an overwhelming yearning, a longing for something she had come to believe she needed.

The desire for the fruit then led to her third step, touching without eating. She reached out her hand and *she took of the fruit thereof (3:6b)*, and what happened? Nothing! Contrary to the words she had added to God's words, she did not die! She was still alive.

So, free of fear, she made her choice and took her fourth step—*she . . . did eat (3:6c)*. Then we read the startling news that her husband was with her—silent, passive, doing nothing to safeguard either her or the garden. And she *gave also unto her husband with her; and he did eat (3:6d)*. He apparently wanted the serpent's promises as much as she did, the promises that they would be as gods, knowing good and evil.

The first effects of the choice to rebel—a new knowledge

And the eyes of them both were opened, and they knew . . . (3:7a). What did they know? They knew, now by experience, shame, guilt, fear, and self-justification.

The knowledge of shame

And the eyes of them both were opened, and they knew that they were naked; and they sewed fig leaves together, and made themselves aprons (3:7). They wanted a covering. For the first time, their nakedness made them ashamed.

The knowledge of guilt and fear

And they heard the voice of the LORD God walking in the garden in the cool of the day: and Adam and his wife hid themselves from the presence of the LORD God amongst the trees of the garden (3:8).

And the LORD God called unto Adam, and said unto him, Where art thou?

And he said, I heard thy voice in the garden, and I was afraid, because I was naked; and I hid myself (3:9–10).

The knowledge of self-justification

And he said, Who told thee that thou wast naked? Hast thou eaten of the tree, whereof I commanded thee that thou shouldest not eat? And the man said, The woman whom thou gavest to be with me, she gave me of the tree, and I did eat (3:11–12). In other words, "I couldn't help it, and God, don't forget, it was you who gave the woman to me."

Ignoring Adam's attack, the LORD God turned to the woman. *And the LORD God said unto the woman, What is this that thou hast done? And the woman said, The serpent beguiled* [deceived] *me, and I did eat (3:13).* Like her husband, she made an excuse—helplessness—as if to say, "How could I help it? The serpent made me do it."

God's response

God paid no attention to her defense. There would be no discussion, no response to the *innocent-victim* maneuverings. The verdicts followed.

[The man, the woman, and the serpent will hear the verdicts with the consequences and the effects on their lives in the next lesson.]

My reflections on their choices

To think they had all they needed, not just survival needs, but beauty needs, work needs, and love needs. To think that instead of wanting to be mature, perfected images of their Creator, they wanted to be gods themselves and ended up being just like the gods of the Egyptians—quarrelsome, unloving, and self-important. What sorrow!

Checking for understanding

1. According to the serpent, how would life be better for the man and woman if they ate from the forbidden tree?

2. Before the woman had her conversation with the serpent, she would have defined *good* as whatever her Creator said was good. After she ate from the tree, how do you think she would have defined the word *good*? Explain your answer.

3. Describe how the man and woman felt about their Creator after they ate from the tree.

4. As Adam tried to justify himself—in other words, as he tried to look innocent—in what two places did he lay the blame for his wrongdoing?

5. Compare the difference between what the woman thought she would get from eating of the tree and what she actually *did* get.

6. List the steps by which the woman and the man entered the world of death.

Death in Eden: Part II

Based on Genesis 3:14–24

My first thoughts

IN THE LAST LESSON, we saw Adam and Eve, in spite of God's warning of death, eat from the Tree of the Knowledge of Good and Evil. I thought they were supposed to die, but there they stood, very much alive, very fearful, and in some way each looking lost and alone.

As I reflected, I saw that some things truly *had* died—guilt-free peace, a loving relationship, truth, and respect for their Creator. They were speaking to him as if he were the cause of their problems by not being clear enough and by allowing temptation to enter the garden. Yes, in some sense they were already dead.

Perhaps as they stood waiting for the verdict, they hoped their not-so-subtle attacks would shame God and force him to go easy on them.

My notes on the teacher's lesson

The verdicts

Sentence on the serpent

The serpent was the first to receive his verdict. *And the LORD God said unto the serpent, Because thou hast done this, thou art cursed above all cattle, and above every beast of the field; upon thy belly shalt thou go, and dust shalt thou eat all the days of thy life (3:14)*. He was to become the lowest of creatures—a cursed, crawling reptile.

The sentencing continued: *and I will put enmity between thee and the woman . . . (3:15a)*. *Enmity* means ill will, hatred, and hostility. Had he expected the woman to be his partner in rebellion? That would not be for it seems, according to Moses, that God was wrenching her mind and her heart away from the serpent. Her heart was *not* in the serpent's hands.

The words of the curse continued, *I will put enmity between . . . thy seed and her seed*. By those words both the woman and the serpent learned that they would have seed, or offspring, and that their offspring would also be separated by *enmity*.

That enmity between the woman's seed and the serpent and his seed would become a battle. In that battle, *it* [the seed of the woman] *shall bruise thy* [the serpent's] *head, and thou* [the serpent] *shalt bruise his heel (3:15c)*. The word *bruise* is often translated *crush*. Clearly, the one with the crushed head—the serpent—not the one with the crushed heel, was the loser in the battle. The serpent would be crushed and defeated by a human.

But who, or what, was the seed of the serpent, and what was the hostility that would lie between the serpent's seed and the woman's? The teacher gave us several views.

- One view sees the serpent's seed as physical serpents (snakes) that the woman's seed (humans) despise, fear, and fight. In that fight even though the humans may be hurt, they successfully crush and defeat the despised snake.

- A second view sees the serpent's seed as humans who follow the serpent's example. They hate the Creator and do all in their power to destroy God and his followers.

- A third view holds that the seed of the woman is Jesus and that crushing the head of the serpent means that Jesus will completely defeat Satan and all his evils.

- Another of the numerous views, holds that the serpent and his temptations were actually good, because the only way, they say, for the man and woman to gain knowledge was to eat from the forbidden tree.

A point of likeness in most views is that even though evil fights that which is good and sometimes inflicts great pain on the innocent, in the end, evil will be crushed. In story after story in the Bible, warfare breaks out between two people, two sides, two countries, two brothers—the unrighteous against the righteous—beginning even with the first two sons born to Adam.

Sentence on the woman

The woman was next to receive her sentence. *Unto the woman he said, I will greatly multiply thy sorrow and thy conception; in sorrow thou shalt bring forth children (3:16a).* Having the children, though, was not a consequence of her disobedience. In Genesis 1:28 before they rebelled against God, he had commanded them, *Be fruitful and multiply.* Genesis 3:16 simply describes the sorrow and pain she would have in the carrying and in the delivery of the children.

Results in the marriage relationship

The words to the woman continue: [T]*hy desire shall be to thy husband, and he shall rule over thee (3:16b).* Perhaps Adam and his wife would each battle to dominate the marriage relationship.

Sentence on the man

And unto Adam he said, Because thou hast hearkened [listened] *unto the voice of thy wife, and hast eaten of the tree, of which I commanded thee, saying, Thou shalt not eat of it: cursed is the ground for thy sake; in sorrow shalt thou eat of it all the days of thy life; thorns also and thistles shall it bring forth to thee; and thou shalt eat the herb of the field; In the sweat of thy face shalt thou eat bread (3:17–19a).*

The cursed ground would produce what the man did not want: thorns, thistles, sweat, and suffering in the difficult work of getting food from the soil.

Sentence on both

In the sweat of thy face shalt thou eat bread, till thou return unto the ground; for out of it wast thou taken: for dust thou art, and unto dust shalt thou return (3:19).

Just as they had been warned, death had begun and was already leading them on their long and certain march to the grave. In the grave their
bodies, made from dust, would decay and return again into that dust.

Three mercies in spite of their rebellion

The human race to continue

When God spoke about children, Adam understood they would not die at
once. His wife would have children. *And Adam called his wife's name Eve;
because she was the mother of all living (3:20).*

Shame covered

Unto Adam also and to his wife did the LORD *God make coats of skins, and
clothed them (3:21).*

Protected from the tree of life

Moses wrote that a new danger confronted them, so catastrophic that the
LORD God stopped himself in the middle of its description.

Genesis 3:22 records his words: *And the* LORD *God said, Behold, the
man is become as one of us, to know good and evil: and now, lest* [to prevent
the risk that] *he put forth his hand, and take also of the tree of life, and eat,
and live for ever*—the statement does not even finish. With death already at
work in their bodies, action had to be taken at once. If they were to eat from
the tree of life and continue to live forever in the same bodies, they would
be always dying, but never dead.

Therefore the LORD *God sent him forth from the garden of Eden, to
till the ground from whence he was taken. So he drove out the man; and he
placed at the east of the garden of Eden cherubim* [angels], *and a flaming
sword which turned every way, to keep the way of the tree of life (3:23–24).*
When farming was difficult, Adam would long for life in the garden, but
cherubim would meet him with flaming swords, keeping him exiled east
of Eden.

Effects on their descendants

According to Genesis, their children, not yet conceived, and their children's children for all generations were born outside of Eden, banished from the garden. Genesis traces one generation after another battling with evil desires from within and evil forces from without, struggling, toiling, growing weary, and finally returning to the dust.

My reflections on Genesis 3

When I first read this story, I felt that eating a piece of fruit was not that serious. After all, people get hungry. But then I realized that Adam and Eve were not hungry. They lacked nothing. Their hunger was for something else.

And I also considered that the consequences of eating could never be called a punishment. If a boat's captain warns his passengers that they must put neither hands nor feet into the water—that deadly snakes are in it—a snake-bitten passenger would never accuse the captain of being cruel-hearted and unfair. The passenger's sure death was by his own choice. So was death for Adam and Eve. I felt that by dismissing their Creator—their life-giver—they had dismissed life; and by dismissing life, they had embraced death.

Checking for understanding

1. According to Genesis what were the physical consequences on the serpent for its part in causing the humans to turn against God?

2. If the seed of the serpent and the seed of the woman represent two different kinds of people, what would it mean that enmity exists between them?

3. Does Genesis 3:16 teach that having children was a punishment for the woman? Support your answer.

4. What would cause the man's work to be filled with weariness and sorrow?

5. Explain the meaning of the words, *for dust thou art, and unto dust shalt thou return.*

6. Since the man and woman were told they would die if they ate from the forbidden tree, why was it an act of hope and faith for Adam to give his wife the name Eve?

7. The expression *The Fall of Man* is a belief (not held by all) that in Genesis 3 the humans fell away from God and lost their original greatness. Because the term *Fall of Man* shows up frequently in English literature, you need to be familiar with the concept. List everything you can think of that the humans lost in Genesis 3.

Cain and Abel

Based on Genesis 4:1–16

My first thoughts about Cain

TODAY WE ARE TO discuss Cain, Eve's firstborn son. Before class began, several of us talked about whether Cain received a fair deal. I thought he hadn't. He and his brother Abel were hardworking, religious men. If, in the account, God had not rejected Cain's offering, might he have turned out to be a different person? Shouldn't you encourage people and give them a chance to be accepted? In this lesson the teacher said that Cain himself, by his own words, would answer these questions.

My notes on the teacher's lesson

The Bible's first children

And Adam knew Eve his wife; [which means they had sexual relations] *and she conceived, and bare Cain, and said, I have gotten* [or acquired] *a man from the LORD (4:1).* The birth of that child must have comforted Eve, assuring her that the entrance of death had not ended humanity.

And she again bare his brother Abel (4:2a). Abel's name means *breath* or *vapor* or *nothing.* Why name a child for something unimportant or that quickly disappears? Was it an indication of his future or of what they felt about him as a person? The verse does not say.

When grown, both brothers worked with nature: Abel as *a keeper of sheep*—a shepherd—and Cain as *a tiller of the ground*—a farmer (4:2).

The two offerings

The brothers also had spiritual interests. *And in process of time it came to pass, that Cain brought of the fruit of the ground an offering unto the* LORD (*4:3*). The fruit of the ground would be some kind of vegetation. *And Abel, he also brought of the firstlings of his flock and of the fat thereof (4:4a).* The firstling would be a firstborn from the sheep or goats. The fat (strange to most modern readers) was the choicest, most desirable part of the sacrifice.

For certain situations and purposes, each of their offerings would have been acceptable to God. Their gifts could have been to show God their gratitude or perhaps to show their dedication to him or perhaps to express repentance for their sins. The passage does not tell us their reasons.

The LORD's *responses to the offerings*

The two brothers then waited for the LORD's response to their gifts. His response was not what Cain expected. *And the* LORD *had respect unto Abel and to his offering, but unto Cain and to his offering he had not respect (4:4b–5a).*

Genesis 4 does not tell how God revealed his responses, but it was very clear to Cain that God was displeased. *And Cain was very wroth* [angry] *and his countenance* [face] *fell (4:5b)* showing his angry thoughts. He was infuriated, seeing nothing wrong either with himself or with his offering. Apparently, in Cain's mind, God was not fair.

The LORD's mercies to Cain

God's offer

And the LORD *said unto Cain, Why art thou wroth? and why is thy countenance fallen?* He went on with encouraging words, *If thou doest well, shalt thou not be accepted? (4:6–7a).* God was offering Cain a second chance. The gift of acceptance could be Cain's if he would take correction. If Cain decided to take the second chance and perhaps even bring the very same type of offering his brother Abel had brought, would he have been accepted? That depended. No offering would be accepted until Cain turned from whatever it was in his life that God did not respect. Cain's further actions revealed what it was.

The warning

In the warning the LORD used a specific word—the word *sin*. He said to Cain, *If thou doest not well,* [if you do not take the second chance] *sin lieth at the door (4:7b).* This is the first time the word *sin* appears in the Bible. The teacher asked us to write down what we thought *sin* means. Most of us gave *examples* of what we thought sin was, like intentionally killing an innocent person or stealing something valuable or abusing someone, the type of acts that would make it into the newspaper.

Then she explained to us what the Israelites would say *sin* was. A sincere Israelite, after receiving the Ten Commandments, would say that sin included every failure to love and obey the LORD their God, as well as every unloving act against their neighbors.

The acts against the neighbors would include far more than theft, abuse, and murder. Those acts would include the thoughts forbidden in the tenth commandment, the command forbidding coveting. To covet is to think with great desire about having what you cannot have now or what you *can* have now, but only by breaking another commandment. Coveting can lead to jealousy, bitterness, hatred, and even wishing the person who has what you want would die. Those exact sins were lying in wait at Cain's *door.*

Our teacher keeps a Hebrew–Greek concordance in the room. She had one of us look up the Hebrew word for *lieth* from the phrase *sin lieth* (lies) *at the door.* The concordance showed that the English word *lieth* could be translated as *crouches.* Cain was to understand that sin, like a beast, was crouching at the door of his thoughts and desires, waiting to enter and rule over him.

The LORD went on with the merciful warning. The beast, or sin, desired to destroy Cain, but Cain should *rule over him (4:7c)*—rule over his angry, covetous desires. But tragically, he had no desire to do that.

Cain's response to the warning

If Cain still thought he had no sin—that nothing was wrong within him— soon his own actions would prove he was self-deceived. *And Cain talked with Abel his brother: and it came to pass, when they were in the field, that Cain rose up against Abel his brother, and slew [killed] him (4:8).*

And the LORD said unto Cain, Where is Abel thy brother? And he said, I know not: Am I my brother's keeper? (4:9). Those words, *Am I my brother's keeper?* rang a bell with me. I had heard them from time to time in other books and in movies, but I hadn't known the background. Knowing the background brings it to life.

The punishment on Cain

And [God] said, What hast thou done? the voice of thy brother's blood crieth unto me from the ground. And now art thou cursed from the earth, which hath opened her mouth to receive thy brother's blood from thy hand; When thou tillest [when you farm] *the ground, it shall not henceforth* [any more] *yield unto thee her strength; a fugitive and a vagabond shalt thou be in the earth (4:10–12).*

In Genesis 3, after Adam and Eve ate from the forbidden tree, God had cursed the ground, yet with hard work it still brought forth crops. For Cain, God pronounced a further curse on the ground. When he farmed in the future, the ground he had successfully cultivated would not produce those crops, and he would wander over the earth as an outlaw and a drifter.

Cain's response to his punishment

And Cain said unto the LORD, *My punishment is greater than I can bear (4:13).* Evidently he felt neither shame nor sorrow for his hate-filled list of sins—his refusal to take God's second chance, his murder of innocent Abel, his lying about where his brother was, and his arrogance when confronted with his crimes!

Cain went on to add self-pity to his list of shame, letting God know that he was not being at all fair. *Behold, thou hast driven me out this day from the face of the earth; and from thy face shall I be hid; and I shall be a fugitive and a vagabond in the earth; and it shall come to pass, that every one that findeth me shall* [try to] *slay me (4:14).* According to some commentaries, to be hidden from the face of God meant to Cain that God would not be with him as he wandered on the earth.

Further mercy to Cain

Cain deserved the dangers he feared; nevertheless, to take away his fear, the LORD continued with even more mercy. *And the* LORD *said unto him, Therefore whosoever slayeth Cain, vengeance shall be taken on him sevenfold*

(4:15a). In other words, if anyone tried to give Cain what he deserved, the LORD himself would punish that person seven times more severely.

To make sure everyone knew about the protection for him, *the LORD set a mark upon Cain* [so that no one] *finding him should kill him (4:15b).* Some have wrongly interpreted that mark as a punishment, but it was not. Instead, it was a warning to any who might want to bring justice against Cain, a warning of great punishment on them if they tried.

In spite of that promise of protection, Cain would not humble himself; he would not admit he was wrong. *And Cain went out from the presence of the LORD, and dwelt in the land of Nod, on the east of Eden (4:16)* departing with not a word of sorrow for what he had done.

My reflections on Cain's attitude and losses

I realize now that when I first read this chapter, I was wrong. I thought Cain should have had another chance to do right, not realizing that Cain not only had a second chance—but also many, many, many chances. The problem lay in his proud hatred of being told he was wrong. Cain dealt with correction by the following:

- sulking at the disapproval of his deeds (4:5)

- murderous hatred toward the one who did receive approval (4:8)

- lying about his wrongdoing (4:9a)

- arrogance toward being questioned (4:9b)

- self-pity for deserved punishment (4:13)

- lack of gratitude for kindness offered (4:16a)

- proudly walking away from reconciliation (righting wrongs) (4:16b).

All of Cain's behavior came from inside him—the jealousy, murder, dishonesty, and arrogance came from his own idea of what was right, and of what he thought he deserved. Cain's attitude about himself —thinking he could do whatever he wanted—was the heart of the savage beast seeking to overpower him. I believe if it hadn't been the rejection of his offering, it would have been something else making Cain spill out his own self-worship—his own idea that he was a god.

He reminds me of an elegant mansion with a rotting corpse in the living room.

Checking for understanding

1. Give the names and occupations of the first two sons.

2. Explain how Abel's name was appropriate for him.

3. What was God offering to Cain when he said, *If thou doest well, shalt thou not be accepted?*

4. Cain's question *Am I my brother's keeper?* was not really a question. It was an attack meant to close God's mouth. Although that question *Am I my brother's keeper?* frequently arises in literary works, that question might not be what Moses intended as the main point of the story—the main point that he wanted his readers to ponder. In your opinion if that question *Am I my brother's keeper?* is the main point, what does it mean, and if it is *not* the main point, what is that point? Explain your answer.

5. Since Cain was a farmer, why would the punishment on him have been especially painful?

6. Tell how the mark on Cain was a protection, not a punishment.

7. Even though Genesis 4 does not define the word *sin*, list all of Cain's behaviors that his mother Eve, after God turned her heart away from the serpent, might have called *sin*.

Where Did Cain Get His Wife?

Based on Genesis 1–5

My first thoughts

I WAS GLAD TO see the plan for today. From Genesis 4 we all have questions—two in particular: "Where did Cain get his wife?" and "Who were the people Cain feared?" We've only met four people so far. The teacher told us that our questions are two of the most commonly asked questions about the Bible. She put us into groups to seek the answers.

The teacher's guidelines for our work

Before explaining our assignment, the teacher reminded us that in our study she will stay within the Court guidelines. We must remember that the answers could involve deeply held religious beliefs and interpretations, and the Supreme Court does not allow public school teachers to criticize or tear down the religious views of their students.

Also, our conclusion for what Genesis is saying must be honest to all of Moses' other writings whether we agree with them or not. The teacher didn't want Moses rushing back from the dead—not that he could—coming into the classroom, and scolding us for ignoring or twisting parts of his story.

For our assignment we are to search through the first five chapters of Genesis (and any other place in the Bible we would like) to find the best answers to the questions, "Where did Cain get his wife?" and "Who were the people Cain feared?" In answering the questions, we must also decide whether or not Moses was consistent in what he said. Did he ever contradict himself?

These were our group's notes to the questions: "Where did Cain get his wife?" and "Who were the people Cain feared?"

Our group decided we would first make a list of every verse or insight that we thought might relate to these issues of a wife for Cain and of the people Cain feared. After making that list, we would try to fit the pieces together.

1:27–28a; 3:20; 4:1–2; 4:14; 4:16–17; 4:25; 5:3–31.

Fitting the verses together

The plan for more people begins in Genesis 1. *So God created man in his own image . . . ; male and female created he them. And God blessed them, and God said unto them, Be fruitful, and multiply, and replenish* [fill] *the earth . . . (1:27, 28a).* Adam and Eve were supposed to have children—lots of them. Does the Bible say they did?

To start with, Genesis 3:20 reads, *Adam called his wife's name Eve, because she was the mother of all living.* Obviously, to have that name, she did have children.

Chapter 4 starts out with the births of Cain and Abel, sons of Adam and Eve. Only after they were grown men and after Cain murdered Abel, do we have any mention of Eve's having more children. *And Adam knew his wife again; and she bare a son, and called his name Seth: For God, said she, hath appointed me another seed instead of Abel, whom Cain slew (4:25).*

Did that announcement mean he was the only other child Adam and Eve had, or was it announcing that God was replacing Abel with this particular son? Soon we realized we needed to read further.

We had been automatically assuming Moses was writing about people as if they were just like us. Since Genesis 4 had no mention of their ages when Cain and Abel offered sacrifices, we all imagined them as young men in their twenties. But Genesis 5 changed that picture in our minds. Genesis 5 has clues. It tells Adam's age when the son named Seth was born. *And Adam lived a hundred and thirty years, and begat a son . . . and called his name Seth (5:3).* (We left the question of such long ages (130 years) for the end of our study.)

Was Moses saying that until Seth was born, 130 years after Adam and Eve were created, they had only had the two boys Cain and Abel? Genesis 5:4–5 says that *after he* [Adam] *had begotten Seth . . . he begat sons and daughters.* Was that saying there were none before the birth of Seth? Was it saying that for 130 years they were too busy and too tired to have more children?

If Adam and Eve had only two children for the first 130 years of their lives, would that not have been a failure to obey the command in Genesis 1—*Be fruitful, and multiply, and replenish* [fill] *the earth . . . (1:28a)?* That would mean for 130 years they had just ignored the command, content to have a tiny little world of Mother, Daddy, and two boys—Mother and Daddy not giving any thought to marriages for their sons. The silence about more births in those years, we all decided, did not necessarily mean there were no other children. In fact, all the clues seem to say there *were* more. Cain's fears were a large clue in our decision.

When Cain heard his punishment, he said, *Behold, thou hast driven me out this day from the face of the earth; and from thy face shall I be hid; and I shall be a fugitive and a vagabond in the earth; and it shall come to pass, that every one that findeth me shall slay me (4:14).* Since Cain thought others would try to kill him, it seemed to us that the people he feared must have already been living when he murdered Abel. Would Cain have feared yet-unborn babies?

Cain's marriage also seemed to say Adam and Eve had more children before Seth was born. If there were no other children until after Cain murdered his brother, then before he could have a wife, Eve would have to have a daughter, the little girl would have to grow up, and, at last, Cain could have a wife. But in a normal reading of Genesis 4, it seemed that there were women available to marry right away. It reads, *And Cain went out from the presence of the LORD, and dwelt in the land of Nod, on the east of Eden. And Cain knew his wife; and she conceived, and bare Enoch* [not the same Enoch as in Genesis 5] *(4:16–17a).* We ended up feeling Eve had been changing many diapers in those 130 years.

Then something gross struck us. Cain would be marrying his own sister! Not only did that sound gross, but it also sounded dangerous, at least it would be for us. According to what we studied in our biology classes, marriage to a close relative increases the chance of passing genetic weaknesses on to children. But then we remembered in the Genesis story Moses said, *God saw everything that he had made, and, behold, it was very good (1:31).* It seemed to us that it would be inconsistent for Moses to say that *everthing* (at first) *was very good,* and then to assume that Adam and Eve immediately had many damaging physical genetic defects to pass on to their children. So in these chapters, to be consistent with everything else Moses wrote, marrying a sister (who should have had no, or few, genetic weakness) would be fine—in fact, it *had* to be fine; there would have been only *sisters* available.

The question of the long lives

So far, we feel we have been true to Moses' account, but we couldn't figure out what he meant by saying people lived so long. Chapter 5 swept us away with the long lives. Why would he write something so (to us) preposterous?

The life-spans of Adam and his descendants through Seth:

Adam lived . . nine hundred and thirty years: and he died (5:5).

Seth [lived] *. . . nine hundred and twelve years: and he died (5:8).*

Enos [lived] *nine hundred and five years: and he died (5:11).*

Cainan [lived] *nine hundred and ten years: and he died (5:14).*

Mahalaleel [lived] *eight hundred ninety and five years: and he died (5:17).*

Jared [lived] *nine hundred sixty and two years: and he died (5:20).*

Enoch [lived] *three hundred sixty and five years. And Enoch walked with God: and he was not; for God took him (5:23, 24).*

Methuselah [lived] *nine hundred sixty and nine years: and he died (5:27).*

Lamech [lived] *seven hundred seventy and seven years: and he died (5:31).*

And all the days of Noah were nine hundred and fifty years: and he died (9:29).

I asked the teacher if any cultures apart from the Bible ever claimed that people lived long lives. She said that the ancient Sumerians (people who once lived in the area between the Tigris and Euphrates Rivers) claimed that their kings had long lives. Their records list a king who lived 36,000 years and another who lived over 46,000 years—far longer than biblical Methuselah's "short life" of 969 years. So Moses' readers probably didn't have any problem with the Genesis record.

We had a lively discussion trying to make those ages reasonable to the twenty-first century. We speculated that perhaps in the list of biblical life spans, Moses was *not* really talking about years like today's years. Maybe he meant a year was really only the length of a month. Twelve years then would be only twelve months, one of our years. That way, when Moses wrote that Methuselah lived 969 years, he meant only 81 real years. That solution, though, only raised a different problem.

Moses gave the ages of each man when a particular son was born. Enoch was sixty-five when his son Methuselah was born (5:21). If the number of years were really only the number of months, then Enoch could only have been about five years old when his wife gave birth to Methuselah! We crossed that idea off—the idea that those years really meant just months.

A student who had already read the chapters on Noah and the flood remembered that the flood narrative talked about days, months, and years. After our group skimmed chapters 7 and 8, we all agreed that the lengths of months and years in those chapters looked pretty much the same as today's lengths. We had to conclude that when Moses wrote *years,* he meant years like our years today.

One of the girls in our group suggested we go back again to Genesis 1:31. Earlier we had argued that you would not expect *very good* bodies to pass on a lot of weaknesses, at least not right away. We're not doctors, but we thought it was more consistent for the Bible to say that the life spans of the first generations of people would probably be a long, slow shortening over time, rather than the same as our own life spans.

In our conclusions all we could do was present what Moses wrote. We couldn't find any inconsistencies in his writings; we couldn't find contradiction in anything that he wrote no matter how strange or impossible it was to us. It seemed that he, or the last editor of the Genesis scroll, must have gone over it with a fine-tooth comb before writing it down for us to read.

My reflections on our study

The teacher gave us a good grade for our answers. She didn't say we were right or wrong in our conclusions—just said we showed thoroughness in our thinking. Tomorrow we will finish this study of the early biblical man.

We will see Moses' record of what people were like and of what their lives were like. I figure it must have been a paradise.

Checking for understanding

1. According to Genesis 1, why would it have been wrong for Adam and Eve to produce only a few children?

2. Since according to Genesis, Eve was the *mother of all living*, what person would Cain have to have married?

3. Give evidence that might indicate Moses was not claiming that Seth was just the third child born to Adam and Eve.

4. How would the long lives of the people in Genesis be consistent with Genesis 1:31?

Civilization Outside of Eden

Based on Genesis 1:1–6:8

My first thoughts

YESTERDAY WAS A FUN kind of class. We all liked combing so carefully through strange ideas. Our assignment for today was to examine the same chapters again—especially chapters 3 through 6—and tell what we would have liked about living in such a world. After that we were to decide what made it go bad.

Right from the start I thought I would have loved living in such a world. They had plenty of smart people and plenty of time to experiment, explore, and enjoy their lives. If we had lived that long our great grandparents would be out playing basketball with us and probably winning, and if the inventor Thomas Edison had lived that long, think of how many other wonderful inventions he might still be making. I didn't really know why the world would go downhill.

My notes on the teacher's lesson

Moses' record of life outside of Eden

Our teacher led us in comparing Cain's family with Seth's family, showing their admirable qualities and successes, as well as their failures and problems.

The successes of early Genesis people

The successes of Cain's descendants
as seen in the family of Lamech

Genesis 4 traces Cain's family seven generations to Lamech, the Bible's first bigamist. He had three sons by Adah and Zillahall, all clearly industrious, intelligent, and creative. *Adah bare Jabal: he was the father of such as dwell in tents, and of such as have cattle (4:20).* Dwelling in tents would enable them to move their flocks and find good pasture as they wished. *And [Jabal's] brother's name was Jubal: he was the father of all such as handle the harp and organ,* bringing to their world the joys of music. *And Zillah* [Lamech's other wife], *she also bare Tubal-cain, an instructer of every artificer* [craftsman, working] *in brass and iron (4:21–22a)*—men benefiting the world with the earth's hidden treasures.

The lives of Lamech's sons sounded comfortable, providing time not merely for survival, but also for donning their fine clothes and jewels and spending the evening at a concert.

The successes of Seth's descendants
as seen in the family of Enos

The family of Cain's brother Seth was different—different in a way Moses would have liked. *And to Seth . . . there was born a son; and he called his name Enos: then began men to call upon the name of the LORD (4:26).* Seth's family evidently saw a need for help from the LORD that Cain's family did not.

Seth's descendant Enoch, seven generations from Adam, was like no other man in Genesis. Enoch not only *walked with God (5:22),* but he also had such a close relationship with God that at age 365 *he was not, for God took him (5:23–24).*

Some interpret this to mean that he had a death especially fitting for such a good man. The New Testament book of Hebrews also speaks of him: *Enoch was translated* [taken away] *that he should not see death, and was not found, because God had translated him (Hebrews 11:5).* In other words, according to this verse, he went to heaven without dying! No matter how a person interprets Enoch's life, he was clearly an unusual man who had an unusually short life—short life, that is, compared to others of his time!

The failures and problems of early Genesis people

The failures of Cain's descendant Lamech

Cain's descendant Lamech knew about the lives of his ancestors. Evidently Great-great-great-grandfather Cain was one of his heroes—a man protected from all enemies by the mark God had placed upon him. Lamech also knew that the mark on Cain was a warning that if anyone tried to hurt him, God would take vengeance seven times worse (4:15)! Lamech liked those words so much that he changed them a little and wrote a poem for himself. Perhaps he sang it as a song to his two wives.

> *Adah and Zillah, Hear my voice;*
>
> *ye wives of Lamech, hearken* [listen] *unto my speech:*
>
> *for I have slain a man to my wounding* [for wounding me],
>
> *A young man to my hurt* [for hurting me].
>
> *If Cain shall be avenged sevenfold,*
>
> *truly Lamech seventy and sevenfold* [seventy-seven times worse]
> *(4:23b–24).*

It was a poem of vengeance. A young man had wounded him. Not letting this injury pass, Lamech boasted, "Since God would have punished a person seven times more severely if he had slain Grandfather Cain, I will get vengeance seventy-seven times worse on anyone who dares to wrong me." When the mark was put on Cain the murderer, he received undeserved mercy and less punishment than he deserved, but toward the young man who had only wounded him, Lamech showed no mercy—only death. He was vengeful, violent, and proud of it.

The problems of another Lamech, nine generations from Adam through Seth

Seth's Lamech, who was in the ninth generation from Adam, wrote despondent words. The words were not about Cain's family; they were words about the difficulties of working with the ground: *And Lamech* [from Seth's line] *. . . begat a son: And he called his name Noah, saying, This same* [son] *shall comfort us concerning our work and toil of our hands, because of the ground which the* Lord *hath cursed* (5:28–29). Lamech had hopes that newborn

Noah would bring relief for the earth, but by the time Noah was grown, getting food was not the worst problem. The worst problem had to do with what God was seeing.

God's judgment on what he saw

And God saw that the wickedness of man was great in the earth, and that every imagination of the thoughts of his heart was only evil continually (6:5).

The earth also was corrupt before God, and the earth was filled with violence. And God said unto Noah, The end of all flesh is come before me; for the earth is filled with violence through them; and, behold, I will destroy them with the earth (6:11, 13). He was through giving warnings and extra chances. The end was at hand.

The causes behind the violence

Before moving into the rest of Genesis 6 where the plans for destruction are laid out, our teacher had questions for us.

"What do you believe is the cause of violence today?" We all thought that the main causes of violence were broken homes, bad neighborhoods, and drugs. She asked if we had considered pride as a cause of violence, not the self-respect pride that might make you work hard to succeed, but the self-centered kind that makes you angry with people who don't treat you as you wish. When we didn't understand, she assigned us to be in groups to look at three men—Adam, Cain, and Cain's descendant Lamech. We were to describe their pride and see pride's connection to violence.

The pride of Adam, Cain, and Lamech

We decided that with our descriptions, we would have each of the three men make a statement.

- Adam's was an excuse-making pride: "I want everyone to know I am perfect; and if I do wrong or make a mistake, it is someone else's fault."

- Cain's was a jealousy kind of pride: "I hate those who are more popular than I, and I will do all I can to knock them off their high horses."

- Lamech's was a boasting pride: "I think it is a mark of honor to pay back anyone who hurts me, no matter how I have to do it."

Pride's connection to violence

Next, we connected their pride to violence. Obviously Cain's pride and Lamech's pride both led to murder. We thought Adam's pride didn't lead to violence until a boy who never says a word surprised us. He said Adam's was the beginning of violence. Adam knew he was in deep trouble with God and due for some kind of "death" for his disobedience, so he tried to shift the blame and its penalty (and whatever the pain might be) on to his wife. He wanted "death" for Eve, but not for himself. Our group all agreed with him that Adam's pride had violence in it too. (Because of this answer, the teacher gave us bonus points.)

We considered what was common in each of these cases and realized that their behavior came from the same impulse within them. Evil came from a self-focused desire—maybe even a demand—that others reverence them and stand in awe of them. They wanted to rule their own world, have all their wishes fulfilled, escape any correction, and always find someone else to blame for problems. It seemed to us that all three wanted to be gods themselves.

My reflections on Moses' accounts of ancient life

As I thought on these issues I was struck by how the Bible's picture of humanity seems to cut right inside us and inside all the problems around us. We had thought broken homes, bad neighborhoods, and drugs were the main causes of violence. But now I'm not so sure. I'm thinking that if everyone stopped trying to be gods themselves, maybe we wouldn't have any violence at all. I know the opposite of self-centered pride is humility. I also know that humility, to many, looks like weakness. Yet, I believe it probably takes a lot more strength to overlook an insult than it does to pay someone back; it takes a lot more strength to accept a put-down than it does to get into a fight.

Checking for understanding

1. In the description of Lamech's family, what gives the impression of intelligent, creative, well -to-do lifestyles?

2. What was it about Seth's family line that Moses would have admired?

3. Do you look on the account of what happened to Enoch when he was 365 years old as something good or as something sorrowful? Explain your answer (5:23–24).

4. In what way was the Lamech of Genesis 4:23–24 like his ancestor Cain?

5. Explain what Seth's Lamech (Genesis 5:29) hoped for from his new-born son Noah.

6. Based on Genesis 1 through 6, which do you think is worse, pride or poverty? Explain your answer.

Noah and the Flood

Based on Genesis 6:1–9:17

My first thoughts

THE COVER OF MY favorite childhood storybook, *Noah and the Flood*, pictured a large boat with a small red-roofed house built on top. Two crows sat on the roof, two yellow snakes draped themselves over the bow, two monkeys chased around on the deck, and a little old lady was lining up pairs of dogs, bears, lions, and mice. I didn't know the story was based loosely on the Bible.

A senior who wanted extra credit, learning that other ancient cultures also had stories of a massive flood, prepared a report on one of them. It came from *The Epic of Gilgamesh* [GIL-guh-mesh], a story in some ways like the biblical account. Before the class studied the biblical flood, the teacher had him give his report. These are the notes I took.

The Epic of Gilgamesh

Records outside the Bible tell of a king named Gilgamesh who, ruled in Sumer about 4700 years ago; Sumer lay between the Tigris and Euphrates Rivers. Years after his reign, a poet took the records of Gilgamesh and wrote a popular epic—a long poem about his life. Over the years other writers reworked, revised, and recorded it on clay tablets. Because of the permanence of the clay tablets, copies of that story survive to this day.

In this account, dreading the thoughts of growing old and dying, Gilgamesh went on a journey to find Utnapishtim [oot-na-PISH-tim], the man to whom the gods were supposed to have granted eternal life. Gilgamesh did not get eternal life from Utnapishtim, but he did get something else—a story of a great flood.

The Gilgamesh flood story

"According to the beliefs of some of the people living long before the time of Gilgamesh, the many gods that ruled the world decided they couldn't stand the noisiness of the swarms of humans. They decided to get rid of the human pests by drowning them in a great flood.

"The ancient author of this story wrote that the gods did send a flood, but not before one of the gods, Ea [AY-ah], interfered. He secretly revealed the plans to Utnapishtim and warned him to build a large boat. He must make a six-deck boat (ten decks in some versions), one hundred eighty feet in length, breadth, and height—a huge cube. He must also waterproof the boat inside and outside with bitumen, a substance something like tar.

"Utnapishtim did as Ea told him and built the boat. He brought into it plenty of food, gold, silver, animals, family and relatives, and also the workmen who helped in the building. When all were in, he sealed the door making it watertight.

"Torrents of rain fell, drowning all living creatures outside the boat and utterly terrifying the gods. At the end of six days, the rain stopped and the boat lodged on a mountain. Utnapishtim waited six more days and then sent out a dove. The dove, not finding a place to perch, came back. Next he sent out a swallow; it, too, came back. Last he sent out a raven that did not return; deciding the ground was dry, Utnapishtim sent out all the boat's occupants.

"According to some of the versions of this epic, the humans were created to provide food for the gods, so for the week of the flood and the week of waiting for dry land, the terrified gods had eaten nothing. Utnapishtim's first act after the flood was to offer a lamb as a sacrifice—a sacrifice that the hungry gods gathered on like flies.

"Then the god Enlil [EN-lil], who evidently was the chief god in the efforts to destroy the humans, found out some were still living. At first he was furious, but after the other gods shamed him for his lack of compassion, he changed his mind, touched Utnapishtim and his wife on their foreheads, and made them gods also."

I wrote in my notes on the Gilgamesh Epic the words, "Strangely similar to the Genesis flood in my childhood storybook, yet weirdly different."

My notes on the teacher's presentation of the Genesis flood

The teacher began this study with the reason for the flood—the reason we saw at the end of our last lesson. It had to do with what God was seeing.

The reason for the Genesis flood

And God saw that the wickedness of man was great in the earth, and that every imagination of the thoughts of his heart was only evil continually . . . and the earth was filled with violence (6:5, 11). And the LORD *said, I will destroy man whom I have created from the face of the earth; both man, and beast, and the creeping thing, and the fowls of the air; for it repenteth me that I have made them (6:7).*

Terrible as the plan might sound, according to the rest of the story, God was not planning to wipe out humanity; rather, he was planning to give humanity a new start. That makes this a survival story, the survival of the human race.

The way of escape—the ark

Eight people would escape—Noah, his wife, their three sons, *Shem, Ham, and Japheth,* and their wives. They would be saved because *Noah found grace* [or favor] *in the eyes of the* LORD. . . . *Noah was a just man and perfect in his generations, and Noah walked with God (6:8–9).*

And God said unto Noah . . . Make thee an ark of gopher wood. An *ark* is another name for a box, particularly a protective box. That ark would be a giant protective ship made not to take a journey, but to keep living creatures alive on the earth. *Rooms shalt thou make in the ark, and shalt pitch it within and without with pitch* [which would waterproof the boat] *(6:13a, 14).*

The ark had similar proportions to modern ocean liners. *The length of the ark shall be three hundred cubits* [450 feet], *the breadth of it fifty cubits* [75 feet], *and the height of it thirty cubits* [45 feet] *(6:15b).*

Knowing that a football field is 300 feet long, I realized that, unlike the picture on my childhood storybook, Noah's ark would need the space of a football field and a half!

A window shalt thou make to [in] *the ark, . . . and the door of the ark shalt thou set in the side thereof; with lower, second, and third stories shalt thou make it (6:16).*

And, behold, I, even I, do bring a flood of waters upon the earth . . . and every thing that is in the earth shall die (6:17).

The ark's occupants and provisions

Noah had exact instructions for the ark's occupants. *Thou shalt come into the ark, thou, and thy sons, and thy wife, and thy sons' wives with thee. And of every* [other] *living thing of all flesh, two of every sort . . . male and female . . . of fowls . . . and of cattle . . . of every creeping thing of the earth . . . to keep them alive (6:18–20).*

Chapter seven enlarges on the number of animals and birds. *Of every clean beast* [those that have a split hoof and chew the cud] *thou shalt take to thee by sevens,* [either seven pairs or seven of each kind] *. . . of fowls also of the air by sevens, the male and the female; to keep seed alive upon the face of all the earth (7:2–3).*

How would Noah gather them to the ark? The instructions included an answer: *Of fowls . . . of cattle . . . of every creeping thing . . . two of every sort shall come unto thee, to keep them alive (6:20).* Noah would not have to go out seeking them; according this verse the animals and birds would come to him.

And take . . . of all food that is eaten . . . for thee, and for them. Thus did Noah; according to all that God commanded him, so did he (6:21–22). And they went in unto Noah into the ark . . . and the LORD shut him in (7:15a, 16b).

The flooding

In the six hundredth year of Noah's life, in the second month, the seventeenth day of the month, the same day were all the fountains of the great deep broken up [water coming up from the earth], *and the windows of heaven were opened* [water coming from the sky] *(7:11).*

And the flood was forty days upon the earth [almost six weeks]: and the waters increased, and bare up the ark, and it was lift [lifted] up above the earth. And the waters prevailed exceedingly upon the earth; and all the high hills, that were under the whole heaven, were covered (7:17, 19).

And all flesh died that moved upon the earth . . . (7:21). Noah only remained alive, and they that were with him in the ark. And the waters prevailed upon the earth an hundred and fifty days (7:23b–24) [which would have included the forty days of rain]. At last, after five months, the flooding had peaked.

The turning point of the flood

In Genesis 8:1 there was a pause; the flood stood still, waiting to turn backwards. Into that pause Moses wrote, And God remembered Noah (8:1a). By the word remembered, Moses did not mean that God, for a while, had forgotten Noah's family; rather, he meant it was time for the next step—a change of direction of the floodwaters.

The end of the flood

It was time for the removal of the floodwaters. And God made a wind to pass over the earth, and the waters assuaged [subsided]. . . . And the waters returned from off the earth continually: and after the end of the hundred and fifty days the waters were abated (8:1b–3).

And the ark rested in the seventh month [the fifth month in the boat] on the seventeenth day of the month, upon the mountains of Ararat (8:4).

And the waters decreased continually until the tenth month: in the tenth month on the first day of the month, were the tops of the mountains seen (8:5).

The birds sent to find dry land

And it came to pass at the end of forty [more] days, that Noah opened the window of the ark . . . . And he sent forth a raven, which went forth to and fro, until the waters were dried up from off the earth. Also he sent forth a dove from him, to see if the waters were abated . . . (8:6–8). But the dove found no rest for the sole of her foot, and she returned unto him into the ark . . . (8:9).

And he stayed yet other seven days; and again he sent forth the dove out of the ark; And the dove came in to him in the evening; and, lo, in her mouth *was an olive leaf plucked off: so Noah knew that the waters were abated from off the earth. And he stayed yet other seven days; and sent forth the dove; which returned not again unto him any more (8:10–12).*

And it came to pass in the six hundredth and first year, in the first month, the first day of the month, the waters were dried up from off the earth: and Noah removed the covering of the ark, and looked, and, behold, the face of the ground was dry. And in the second month, on the seven and twentieth day of the month [a year and ten days after entering the ark], *was the earth dried (8:13–14).*

The new genesis—the new beginning

A command came: *Go forth of the ark . . . . Bring forth with thee every living thing . . . that they may . . . be fruitful, and multiply upon the earth (8:16–17). And Noah* [and all with him] *went forth out of the ark (8:18a, 19c).*

The covenant

And Noah builded an altar unto the LORD; and took [some] *of every clean beast, and of every clean fowl, and offered burnt offerings on the altar (8:20).* To the Israelites, that would have meant that Noah was offering thanks and perhaps confessing that he and his family needed cleansing themselves, just as the earth had been cleansed.

According to Genesis, not only did the LORD accept Noah's offering but he also followed it with a covenant [a promise]. *I will establish my covenant with you, neither shall all flesh be cut off any more by the waters of a flood; neither shall there any more be a flood to destroy the earth (9:11).*

With the covenant the LORD gave a sign, a permanent reminder that he would keep his promise. He said, *I do set my* [rain]*bow in the cloud, and it shall be for a token* [sign] *of a covenant between me and the earth (9:13). While the earth remaineth, seedtime and harvest, and cold and heat, and summer and winter, and day and night shall not cease (8:22).* They were to count on it. The earth and its cycles, in spite of human evil, would continue as long as the earth stood.

My reflections on the two flood stories

To me, even though I saw similarities in the two flood stories, I saw huge differences. In the Gilgamesh flood the problem was noisy humans. In the biblical flood, the problem was violent humans. The biblical flood gave a new start. I saw it, not as a *cruel* story as some said, but as a story of *mercy*— an unearned kindness for the future world.

Checking for understanding

1. If a camel is an unclean animal and a sheep is a clean animal, how many camels would have been in the ark? How many sheep?

2. Considering what Noah did after they left the ark, explain why Noah had to bring seven (or seven pairs) of clean animals into the ark rather than only one pair of each.

3. Based on Genesis 7:11, give the two sources from which the floodwater came.

4. Explain Noah's purpose in sending out the two birds.

5. In what way did Moses' record show that Noah's flood was a kindness to the future world?

6. In two parallel columns, compare and contrast the epic of the Gilgamesh flood with the Genesis flood in the following four areas:

   - the reasons for the floods;

   - the approximate length of time the people stayed in the boat, or ark;

   - the size and probable safety and security of each boat;

   - the difference between God as he is seen in Genesis and the gods as they are seen in the Gilgamesh Epic.

New Restraints on Evil

Based on Genesis 11:1–25

My first thoughts

I WAS INTERESTED IN the title of today's study, *New restraints on evil.* Moses wrote that following the flood Noah's family walked out of the ark into a changed world—a world freed from corruption, bloodshed, and violence; all evil buried under great flood deposits. As good as that sounded, I sensed the story would not stay that way; I remembered reading in Genesis 8:21 that *the imagination of man's heart is evil from his youth.* If Moses was going to be consistent, if the *source* of the corruption was *not* gone, it only makes sense that restraints had to come.

My notes on the teacher's lesson

Restraints after the flood:
Case 1—The tower of Babel

Time passed; the population was growing *and the whole earth was of one language, and of one speech (11:1).* There was no need of a United Nations, no need of interpreters, and no need of language classes. They all understood each other.

The descendants of Noah had left the high mountains of Ararat for Shinar, the land between the Tigris and Euphrates Rivers. And *they found a plain in the land of Shinar; and they dwelt there* (11:2), and just as they had been commanded in Genesis 8:17, they were multiplying and increasing.

There was one command, however, that they were not attempting to obey; they had what seemed to them better plans.

The world's plan and the plan's progress

And they said one to another, Go to, let us make brick, and burn them thoroughly. And they had brick for stone, and slime [tar] *had they for mortar (11:3).* While they energetically made their bricks, they would have discussed their plans, plans that would change their lives forever. They wanted to build a city and a tower.

And they said, Go to, let us build us a city and a tower, whose top may reach unto heaven; and let us make us a name, lest we be scattered abroad [to make sure we are not scattered] *upon the face of the whole earth (11:4).*

The city and tower would bring them, they imagined, three benefits. First, they would reach into the heavens; second, they would be a generation praised as long as the tower stood; and third, they would have the safety and security of staying together. The words had a happy ring.

Unfortunately, either they forgot God's command to fill the earth (Genesis 9:1) which would have meant scattering and spreading out, or they intentionally rebelled against it. They based their plan on pride—not the pride of self-respect that leads to noble works, but another kind. They had a goal, a goal of making great names for themselves. They wanted to be remembered, praised, and adored by all future generations, and they planned on happily working toward that goal no matter what anyone else might say.

Satisfied to reject the command to spread out, they continued collecting slime and making bricks quite unaware just as the pre-flood people had been, that someone was watching.

The center of the story—the pause

The last lesson, Noah's flood, had a turning point in it where the whole direction of the flood changed. In the same way, the tower building in Genesis 11 also has a turning point where the whole direction of the tower work changes. We are now at this turning point.

Moses used irony (the opposite of what is expected) to explain what happened. *And the LORD came down to see the city and the tower, which the children of men builded (11:5).* It was as if the LORD was making fun of them. The impressive tower was so puny that he had to come down from heaven to see it!

The LORD then went on with his evaluation of the people. (It wasn't an evaluation of the tower; he had no law against towers. It was an evaluation of the people and their desires.) He said, *Behold, the people is one, and they have all one language; and this they begin to do: and now nothing will be restrained from them which they have imagined to do (11:6).* That was an extremely troubling statement. Unless something changed the people, they could unite in every rebellion they might wish, no matter how evil the plans might be.

It was time for the change, the change of direction. The LORD spoke again, *Go to, let us go down, and there confound* [throw into confusion] *their language, that they may not understand one another's speech (11:6b–7).* Imagine going to school one morning being greeted by confused, irritated classmates, no one making sense, no one cooperating—no one even *able* to cooperate.

It would have been that way for the workers on the tower. The work was hopeless! Unable to understand each other, Moses wrote that their plans and their work came to a halt—their hopes and dreams dashed.

So the LORD scattered them abroad from thence [there] *upon the face of all the earth: and they left off to build* [building] *the city (11:8).*

Therefore is the name of it [the city] *called Babel* [meaning confusion, or jumble]; *because the LORD did there confound the language of all the earth: and from thence did the LORD scatter them abroad upon the face of all the earth (11:9).* [From the word *Babel* comes the name *Babylon*, an infamous city remembered throughout both the Hebrew Bible and the New Testament book of Revelation for its pride and arrogance.]

The purpose of the tower story

My classmates and I agreed that on our first reading of this account, building the tower sounded like a good idea. With one language and united dreams, the sky was the limit, but after we looked at the center—the turning point in the story—we understood. The central words were—*now nothing will be restrained from them which they have imagined to do (11:6).* There it was again, the *imagination*, the thought-life with its dreams and desires, and we remembered Moses' depressing description of human imagination—*The imagination of man's heart is evil from his youth . . . (8:21).*

To most of the class, the purpose of the story seemed to be that humanity, with its united abilities and goals, with one common language, and with proud, unrestrained imaginations, would quickly return to its violent, pre-flood state.

We thought it was interesting that no one forced them to scatter. They did not do it against their own will or desire. They scattered from the tower to escape its confusion and frustration. The need and desire for order and peace made them (out of their own free choice or free will) choose to do what earlier they had refused to do—spread out and fill the earth.

Restraint after the flood:
Case 2—Changing life spans

Scattering to unsettled, unknown areas might have brought fear into the lives of these people, but there was another even worse fear. Moses' record showed they were aging faster than their parents. Genesis 5 records age spans *before* the flood of more than 900 years, but Genesis 11 records age spans *after* the flood continually dropping. Just as the tower plans crumbled, their life spans were crumbling, getting as low as the one hundreds. The table below from Genesis 11 charts those drops.

Noah	lived 950 years
Noah's son Shem	lived 600 years
Shem's son Arphaxad	lived 438 years
Arphaxad's son Salah	lived 433 years
Salah's son Eber	lived 464 years
Eber's son Peleg	lived 239 years
Peleg's son Reu	lived 239 years
Reu's son Serug	lived 230 years
Serug's son Nahor	lived 148 years
Nahor's son Terah	lived 205 years

The teacher gave us three different interpretations for these ages. One interpretation views these ages as just a good story. Another interpretation views the ages as records of family dynasties. A third views them as actual ages of the people during the deterioration from Eden's perfection. All agree, though, that no matter how those long lives and the shortening of them might be interpreted, a short life limits all that a human can do whether for good or whether for evil.

My reflections

Because we are at the end of the biblical account of the world's ancient history, the teacher asked us to discuss what we thought was the theme, or dominant strand of thought, that runs throughout the first eleven chapters of Genesis. I thought the dominant theme was pride, the vain kind that wants to be a god (the kind that Adam and Eve, Cain, Lamech, and the builders of the tower also seemed to have). Maybe Moses wanted us to see that wishing to be greater and more important than others (and also wanting to be above correction) messes up life for ourselves and for everyone else. (I wonder if that's why my neighborhood basketball team is falling apart.)

Checking for understanding

1. Explain the reasons the people of Genesis 11:1–9 wanted to build a city and tower.

2. Since people were not forbidden to build cities and towers, why did God stop the building of the city and tower in Genesis 11?

3. Were the people of Babel forced by the LORD to obey him and spread out, or did they obey because they chose to? Explain your answer.

4. By the lifetime of Serug's son, Nahor, how low had the life span dropped?

5. Explain how the second restraint, shorter lives, would limit the increase of evil in the world.

6. Take a page out of a newspaper. With a colored felt pen, make a mark across every article, picture or advertisement that speaks of or reflects the idea of *human greatness* or *human strength*.

7. Using the same newspaper page, with a different colored felt pen, mark across every article, picture or advertisement that speaks of or reflects the idea of *human evil* or *human weakness*. (Some articles, pictures or advertisements may need both colors.)

A New Direction: Abram (Abraham) and His Family

Based on Genesis 11:27–12:9

My first thoughts

THE SUBJECT ON THE board notes that today in Genesis we reach a dividing line—a change of direction from the focus on the whole world in Genesis 1–11 to the focus on one man and his family. A student who seems to know the Bible well proudly declared, "That is *my* family!" I was amazed. The record of his own family, he claims, goes all the way back to the name on the board—Abram—later re-named Abraham. Realizing this was a significant chapter, I took careful notes of the teacher's presentation.

My notes on the teacher's lesson

Abram's background

Those who see Abram as a historical figure disagree about the dates of his life. Most conclude that he lived either several hundred years *before* 2000 BC or several hundred years *after* 2000 BC or sometime in between. Roughly speaking, he lived about 4000 years ago.

Abram's family

The story starts with Abram's father Terah, [TAY-ruh], who had three sons. *Now these are the generations* [descendants] *of Terah: Terah begat* (fathered) *Abram, Nahor* [NAY-hor], *and Haran* [HAR-ran. rhymes with Karen]; *and Haran* [Abram's brother who died young] *begat Lot (11:27).*

Nahor married and eventually had twelve sons (22:20–24). Abram also married, but had neither sons nor daughters for *Sarai* [his wife] *was barren; she had no child (11:29–30).*

The family lived in Ur [ER as in her] of the Chaldees [KAL-deez], an ancient city on the Euphrates River. According to *Joshua* the sixth book of the Bible, Abram's family worshipped and *served other gods* (Joshua 24:2). At some point in Abram's life, though, if he ever did serve other gods, by Genesis 12 he had turned away from those beliefs to worship the LORD God alone.

The family's travels

Moses tells that sometime after the death of his son Haran, Abrams' father, Terah, migrated northwest from Ur of the Chaldees with his family, hoping eventually to go to the land of Canaan (11:31).

They traveled 700 miles northwest along the Euphrates River as far as the city of Haran (not the same name in the Hebrew language as the name of Abram's brother). At Haran, perhaps liking what they saw or perhaps just weary of travel, the family decided to put down their roots and make that city home; but for Abram, Haran was not to be the end of his journey. He would soon leave his relatives behind.

The plan for Abram's future

Genesis 12:1 says that *the Lord had said unto Abram, Get thee out of thy country, and from thy kindred, and from thy father's house, unto a land that I will show thee.* Acts, the fifth book in the New Testament, says that before the family left their home in the Chaldees, God appeared to Abram, and gave him that command to leave his country and kindred and land *(Acts 7:2, 3).*

So Abram left his relatives in Haran, and though he did not know where he was to go, he did know the reason. He knew that the LORD GOD, the God in whom he believed, had spoken to him and given him a command—a command that included great promises.

The story of Abram is a story about promises and hope—promises of what the LORD said he would do for Abram, what he would do in the future with Abram's yet-unborn descendants, and what he would do in the world because of him.

The first promise

This first promise would have thrilled Sarai. *I will make of thee a great nation . . . (12:2a).* That was a promise of something Abram could *not* do, have enough descendants to become a nation, for his wife was barren. According to that promise, however, Sarai would have at least one son and then, from that one son, would come a multitude of descendants—a nation.

The second promise

I will bless thee (12:2b), . . . The word *bless* means to give favor, kindness, and benefits. (That promise, I thought, would be far better even than having great riches.)

The third promise

And make thy name great (12:2c), . . . Three major world religions—Judaism, Christianity, and Islam—all look to Abram (Abraham) as a major figure in their histories. The New Testament refers to Abram more times than to any other person in the Old Testament (the Hebrew Bible). Many people have had their *hour of fame* only to fall into an abyss of obscurity, but these three religions would agree that Abram has had his own *hour of fame* for forty centuries.

The fourth promise

And thou shalt be a blessing (12:2d). His life would greatly benefit others.

The fifth promise

And I will bless them that bless thee (12:3a), . . . Any who blessed him would receive blessings themselves.

The sixth promise

I will curse him that curseth thee (12:3b), . . . A wall of protection and security, says Genesis, encircled Abram. He must not be afraid in his travels, and he must not be afraid in the new home awaiting him.

The seventh promise

And in thee shall all families of the earth be blessed (12:3c). That meant blessings from him would wrap around the world.

The command

What directions did Abram have? Almost none—only the words, *Get thee out of thy country, and from thy kindred, and from thy father's house, unto a land that I will show thee (12:1).* So believing those words and promises, *Abram departed* [from Haran], *as the* LORD *had spoken unto him; and Lot went with him: and Abram was seventy and five years old when he departed out of Haran (12:4).*

And Abram took Sarai his wife, and Lot his brother's son, and all their substance that they had gathered, and the souls [servants] *that they had gotten in Haran; and they went forth . . . (12:5a).*

If Abram truly believed his descendants would become a nation, he must also have believed they would have a land to settle in, but he did not yet know which land that would be. Apparently he at least knew to go south toward Canaan, the land possessed by the descendants of Noah's cursed grandson (9:25). Traveling 400 miles from Haran, they arrived at the northern edge of Canaan, *and into the land of Canaan they came (12:5b).* The land measured about one hundred and fifty miles from north to south and fifty miles from the Jordan River on the east to the Mediterranean Sea on the west. *And the Canaanite was then in the land (12:6b).*

And the LORD *appeared unto Abram, and said, Unto thy seed* [descendants] *will I give this land*—the land of Canaan *(12:7a).*

A test of Abram's faith

If Abram and Sarai anticipated settling in a peaceful land, they must have been quite disappointed. The land of Canaan and its surrounding area was a war zone, some of it under the control of powerful kings from the Euphrates (14:1–16). Also disappointing, many of the occupants of the land, the Canaanites, had beliefs and practices that would have been shameful to Abram (See Genesis 13:13). There is no record that Abram and Sarai ever talked about it, but I wondered if they ever thought about how hard it could be to raise a good family with neighbors like the Canaanites.

Abram's response

Despite the problems in the land, Abram showed no disappointment, made no complaints, and never wavered. Instead, *there builded he an altar unto the LORD, who appeared unto him. And he removed from thence* [from there] *unto a mountain on the east of Bethel, and pitched his tent . . . and there he builded an altar* [a second altar] *unto the LORD, and called upon the name of the LORD (12:7b–8).*

One of our classmates asked the teacher why Abram would build those altars. She said that Genesis doesn't say why, but that some scholars say he was staking out a claim on the land, perhaps claiming it for the LORD his God.

My reflections on the study of Abram

So here was a seventy-five year old man leaving his home and relatives all because the LORD God promised him that the world would become a better place through his future family. Was it hope for the troubled world that made him willing to go out, not knowing where he was going? What kindness! I'm guessing he was one of those ancient super-hero types—never wavering, no challenge too big for him, always trusting and faithful. At least it seemed that way.

Checking for understanding

1. Give the names of Abram's father, Abram's two brothers, and Abram's nephew.

2. Even though Sarai's husband loved her, what unhappiness could he not take from her?

3. Explain how the formation of Abram's nation would be different from the formation of a nation like the United States or Canada.

4. Considering the definition given of the verb *to bless*, how is a life of *being blessed* different from merely having great power?

5. Name the three major world religions that look to Abram as a major figure in their history.

6. Which of the promises meant Abram's life would cause the world to be better?

7. Explain why settling in Canaan would be a test of Abram's faith, of his certainty that the LORD God could fulfill his promises.

Abram Scandalizes His Own Name

Based on Genesis 12:10–20

My first thoughts

THE TOPIC WRITTEN ON the board surprised me. I thought that Abram, one of the most important men in Genesis, would be a hero-type man. How could it be that with the kind of faith and obedience Abram had shown earlier—leaving Ur, traveling amidst dangers, and going out he-knew-not-where—that he turn around and disgrace himself, if he really did? And even if he did, why would Moses include it in his family's record? Shouldn't such a good man be protected? Why tell all the secrets? I would think family scrapbooks would leave out scandals and failures, but here was Moses about to expose their ancestor's shame.

My notes from the teacher's lesson

The problem in Canaan

Before looking at Abram's failure, the teacher explained that from this chapter and throughout the rest of Genesis, Moses structured his writings on four significant characters —Abram, his son Isaac, Isaac's son Jacob, and Jacob's son Joseph. The first three, Abram, Isaac, and Jacob, had the flaws and failures of all humanity. Abram's failure appeared early in his journeys.

This is the account of problems that brought great regrets to Abram, and great shame to his name. *There was a famine in the land (12:10)* evidently brought on by drought since the solution seemed so clear—go down to Egypt. There the Nile River provided crops for food and abundant vegetation for livestock. So *Abram went down into Egypt to sojourn there; for the famine was grievous in the land (12:10b)*.

The problem in Egypt

Though Abram would see the ancient pyramids when he entered Egypt, his mind was evidently elsewhere. He knew ahead of time he could face danger there, but he and Sarai had made plans for that—plans to protect him.

He knew that powerful kings married any women they wished. He also knew that if a woman the king desired had a husband, conveniently for the king, the husband might suddenly die, and the king could then take that woman for his own wife. Abram also knew that his wife Sarai was very, very beautiful.

He might have hoped Pharaoh (the title for Egyptian kings) would neither see nor hear about their entrance into Egypt, but a man with Abram's wealth, coming with large flocks and herds, could hardly escape notice. Neither could his wife. (From what I remember of the lengthy, but diminishing, age spans of Genesis 11, Sarai's great beauty at age sixty-five—ten years younger than seventy-five year old Abram—didn't seem so strange. It fit right in with the earlier Genesis accounts.)

Abram's solution to the problem in Egypt

On entering Egypt Abram reminded his wife of their plan. *And it came to pass, when he was come near to enter into Egypt, that he said unto Sarai his wife, Behold now, I know that thou art a fair* [beautiful] *woman to look upon: therefore it shall come to pass, when the Egyptians shall see thee, that they shall say, This is his wife: and they will kill me, but they will save thee alive 12:11–12)*.

Before Abram and Sarai began their travels, Abram had asked his wife to tell a half-truth wherever they went. *Say, I pray thee, thou art my sister: that it may be well with me for thy sake; and my soul shall live because of thee (12:13)*. (According to Genesis 20:12, Abram and Sarai had the same father but different mothers.) Sarai agreed to the deception.

The failure of Abram's plan

And it came to pass, that, when Abram was come into Egypt, the Egyptians beheld the woman that she was very fair. The princes also of Pharaoh saw her, and commended her before Pharaoh. The princes did such a good job that Pharaoh wanted Sarai immediately *and the woman was taken into Pharaoh's house (12:14–15).*

The cost of the deception on Pharaoh and his family

They did not just grab Sarai and take her away. Pharaoh, believing she was Abram's sister, gave him costly gifts in order to have her as his wife: *sheep, and oxen, and he asses, and menservants, and maidservants, and she asses, and camels (12:16).* And Abram didn't take one step to correct his scam.

That was not the only cost to the unaware Pharaoh. Abram was supposed to be a blessing to all nations, but instead, his dishonesty brought a plague on Pharaoh and on his household, for *the LORD plagued Pharaoh and his house with great plagues because of Sarai Abram's wife (12:17).* [Whatever the plagues were, they should not be confused with the plagues Moses describes in Exodus.]

The cost of the deception on Abram and Sarai

Not only had Abram brought grief on Egypt, but what grief and fear their half-truth (for she was a part of it) would have brought on Sarai—actually a lie to which she had agreed!

Genesis does not tell how Pharaoh connected the plagues to the truth about Sarai, but clearly he was furious. He *called Abram, and said, What is this that thou hast done unto me? Why didst thou not tell me that she was thy wife? Why saidst thou, She is my sister? so I might have taken her to me to wife. Now therefore behold thy wife, take her, and go thy way And Pharaoh commanded his men concerning him: and they sent him away, and his wife, and all that he had (12:18–19).* When the teacher had us read these verses, I thought of the shame I would feel if I myself one day rose to a place of honor, only to be exposed as a liar.

Abram's lie—for that was what his deception was—brought them much wealth, but that wealth did not make up for his losses. Instead of bringing a blessing to Egypt, he brought a curse, and instead of having a great name in Egypt, surely to the Egyptians his name became a symbol of shame.

As he departed from Egypt, evidently Abram knew what he had to do. Our teacher gave us a heads-up on that—it would be Abram's first act back in Canaan. I am guessing that whatever it was, it would be the only way he could live with himself.

A possible reason for the lie

Was Abram's trouble in Egypt a proof that he should not have gone there, or was it proof that he did not yet fully believe the promises? If he had believed that he and Sarai would eventually have a son, wouldn't he have believed that Pharaoh could neither kill him nor marry Sarai? If Abram had truly believed the promises, then why did he lie and deceive? Later the Bible calls Abram the father of the faithful, but obviously, this far into his story, he was not yet worthy of that name.

My reflections on Abram's behaviors

I asked myself, "Why did Moses include this stain on the father of his nation?" He certainly wasn't telling the freed slaves, "Be like your father Abram." He was not setting him up as an example. When another student raised that question, the teacher said that ancient people usually did *not* record their nation's failures, but unlike the rest of the world, the Hebrews *did* over and over again.

I wondered if maybe they included the stains so that those coming later would learn from them. Perhaps, also, the truths of shame might be better to hear than a whitewash, a version that kept the family picture impossibly and discouragingly perfect.

Checking for understanding

1. Explain why Sarai's beauty was so dangerous for Abram.

2. Give at least two particular promises that the LORD gave Abram (see Genesis 12:1–3) that would have kept him from fear and from lying if he had been convinced of them.

3. How did Abram justify his lie, in other words, how did he convince himself that his lie was not wrong?

4. Describe the suffering that the deception of Abram and Sarai brought upon her own life.

5. Because of Abram, what losses came upon Pharaoh and his household?

6. How might hearing the story of Abram's failure bring benefit to his descendants?

Nephew Lot's Choices

Based on Genesis 13–14

My first thoughts

THE PLAN ON THE board had a question. "Suppose when Abram, Sarai, and Lot were staying temporarily in Egypt, an Egyptian asked Lot about his background, about his relationship to Abram, about what Abram was like, and about what he, Lot, hoped for in his own future. What might Lot have answered?" The teacher put us into groups to write an answer. This is what my group wrote.

"I am Lot. I was born in Ur, the great city on the Euphrates. After my parents died my uncle and aunt, Abram and Sarai, made me a part of their family. That's why I am with them here in Egypt. The LORD God, whom Uncle Abram worships, promised to make a great nation from him, a nation that would live in Canaan and bring blessing to the world; but he has a problem. My uncle must have a son from whom that nation will come, but so far, Aunt Sarai is barren—so how can my uncle have a child? I haven't told anyone yet, but I'm wondering if one day I will be chosen as the adopted son from whom my uncle will have his nation."

We didn't have Lot saying anything about Abram's failures because all of us felt he would say nothing that might shame his family.

My notes on the teacher's lesson

Abram and his first act back in Canaan

Evidently humiliated and shamed because of his lies in Egypt, Abram knew exactly where he wanted to go in Canaan. Directing the caravan back to his altar in Bethel, an altar he had built when he entered the land, he *called on the name of the LORD (13:4b)*. Moses does not tell what Abram said in his prayers. Perhaps he spoke words of sorrow, confessing that he was wrong, asking not to be rejected. After going to that altar to meet with the LORD, Abram returned to his work.

Abram and his work

Life must always have meant work for Abram and Lot, for *Abram was very rich in cattle, in silver, and in gold (13:2). And Lot also . . . had flocks, and herds, and tents (13:5)*. (Clearly Abram had far more than Lot. Abram was *very rich in cattle* and he had silver and gold. Moses only speaks of Lot's animals.) Their flocks continually increased until the land was not large enough for all of their flocks and herds. *And there was a strife* [quarreling] *between the herdmen of Abram's cattle and the herdmen of Lot's cattle* because of the limited amount of grass and water *(13:7a)*.

Abram's generosity toward Lot

And Abram said unto Lot, Let there be no strife, I pray thee, between me and thee, and between my herdmen and thy herdmen; for we be brethren [we are family]. *Is not the whole land before thee? separate thyself, I pray thee, from me: if thou wilt take the left hand, then I will go to the right; or if thou depart to the right hand, then I will go to the left (13:8–9)*.

Offering his nephew whatever part of the land he wanted was a great step of faith on Abram's part. Moses wrote that God had promised Abram the land of Canaan for his descendants, but here he was offering Lot whatever part of the land he wanted with no concern for his own loss. (Could it have been that Abram himself wondered if one day it would all be Lot's anyway?)

Lot's choice

The teacher pointed out that to understand the choice Lot made, readers must first understand the Israelite view of the map; otherwise, they will think Abram made either an unkind offer, or a foolish offer. In the world today, left on a map means west and right means east. That makes it seem that Abram was offering either the mountains of Canaan on the left or the fertile plain on the right alongside the Jordan River.

In those days, however, people faced east toward sunrise when giving directions. The left hand would then be toward the northern mountains of Canaan, and the right toward the southern mountains. Lot might have looked north, and he might have looked south, the directions his uncle had wisely and generously offered; but then he looked eastward toward the plain along the Jordan River, a direction Abram had *not* suggested at all. *And Lot lifted up his eyes, and beheld all the plain of Jordan, that it was well watered every where . . . even as the garden of the* LORD, *like the land of Egypt . . . (13:10).*

To Lot, the beautiful Jordan plain looked just as he would have imagined the Garden of Eden. In addition to its beauty, he might have seen plenty of room for his family, his flocks, his herds, and his many servants. Perhaps he also saw that on the plain he could become a wealthy man. *Then Lot chose him all the plain of Jordan; and Lot journeyed east: and they separated themselves the one from the other. Abram dwelt in the land of Canaan, and Lot dwelt in the cities of the plain, and pitched his tent toward Sodom. But the men of Sodom were wicked and sinners before the Lord exceedingly (13:11–13).*

Lot probably knew about the problems, the wickedness of the land's inhabitants, but perhaps he envisioned himself as becoming an honorable and valuable influence on them for their good.

Encouragement to Abram

Abram had good reason to be discouraged. His nephew Lot had made a troubling choice—what might that do to Lot's future? Even worse, he himself, had made a troubling choice, a choice to lie to the king of Egypt and thus bring a plague on the king's household. How could Abram know for sure whether or not he had lost God's promises for his future? Immediately he had his answer.

And the LORD *said unto Abram, after that Lot was separated from him, Lift up now thine eyes, and look from the place where thou art northward,* and southward, and eastward, and westward: For all the land which thou seest, to thee will I give it [which included the very land Abram had offered to his nephew] . . . (13:14–15). The promise of the land of Canaan still stood!

The LORD spoke again, this time about his seed, his descendants. And I will make thy seed as the dust of the earth: so that if a man can number the dust of the earth, then shall thy seed also be numbered (13:16). Abram knew then that the promise of many descendants also still stood.

Then Abram removed his tent, and came and dwelt in the plain of Mamre, which is in Hebron [in the southern part of Canaan]. There, perhaps to show his gratitude, he built an altar [his third altar] unto the LORD (13:18).

How Lot was faring on the Jordan plain

Lot, no doubt, had traveled to the Jordan plain with high hopes for success. Ignoring the known reports that the men of Sodom were wicked and sinners before the LORD exceedingly (13:13), he settled near their city. He must have imagined the benefits of the Jordan plain as far greater than the risks he might face there.

Lot also seemed to ignore the troubling history of the area. Twelve years earlier four kings from the north had come down and conquered the kings of the five cities along the Jordan River. Sodom was one of the five. Ever since that defeat, year after year the southern kings paid taxes to the north (14:1–4). By choosing the plain of the Jordan, Lot had chosen a land occupied by corrupt men, and ruled by foreign conquerors.

The southern rebellion

According to Genesis 14, Lot arrived on the plain just before the southern rebellion, the southern refusal to continue paying taxes to their conquerors (14:4). The northern kings, having no intention of letting the southern kings get by with this rebellion, headed back south. By the time they arrived, Lot had moved into Sodom's walled-safety. The move did not help. In the fourteenth year, the four kings attacked. And they took all the goods of Sodom and Gomorrah, and all their victuals [pronounced vitls, an old word for food], and went their way. And they took Lot, Abram's brother's son, who dwelt in Sodom, and his goods, and departed (14:11–12). Lot had exchanged the hoped-for robes of prosperity for chains and a shameful march toward poverty and slavery.

Abram's continued generosity

And there came one that had escaped, and told Abram. . . . And when Abram heard that . . . [Lot] *was taken captive, he armed his trained servants, born in his own house, three hundred and eighteen, and pursued them. . . . And* . . . [by a surprise attack in the night, Abram defeated them]. . . . *And he brought back all the goods, and also brought again . . . Lot, and his goods, and the women also, and the people (14:13–16).* No doubt that victory encouraged Abram that despite his deceit, he would still bless his world. Unlike the curse that he had brought upon Egypt, Abram had brought stunning blessing upon the people from the five cities of the Jordan.

Two kinds of kings

As Abram returned from the battle, two kings met him. The first was Melchizedek [mel-KIZ-eh-dek], the king of Salem, a city the northern kings had not attacked. The second was the king of Sodom, Lot's ransacked, plundered home.

Melchizedek had trekked eastward to meet Abram and had *brought forth bread and wine: and he was the priest of the most high God. And he blessed him and said: Blessed be Abram of the most high God, possessor of heaven and earth: and blessed be the most high God, which hath delivered thine enemies into thy hand. And he* [Abram] *gave him tithes* [ten percent] *of all (14:18–20).* Clearly, this king was a great man, far superior to Abram.

The second king, the surly king of Sodom, met Abram with the demanding words, *Give me the persons* [the people you have rescued], *and take the goods to thyself (14:21),* as if the king of Sodom had any right to offer anyone or anything to Abram that Abram had rescued in battle. But Abram answered, *I have lift* [lifted] *up mine hand unto the* LORD, *the most high God, the possessor of heaven and earth, that I will not take from* [you so much as] *a thread even to a shoe-latchet* [shoe strap], *and that I will not take any thing that is thine, lest thou shouldest say, I have made Abram rich (14:22–23).*

Lot's continued choice

No doubt Abram's success could have given Lot an opportunity for new decisions. What better time to leave Sodom, find a place in Canaan, and come back into his uncle's circle of blessing? If it was a second chance for

Lot, he did not choose to take it, but instead chose to return and remain in Sodom, the city where he evidently was placing his future hopes.

My reflections on Lot's choices

Since it was Lot's uncle who rescued the cities, perhaps Lot expected that his own approval ratings would skyrocket in Sodom. Perhaps he would gain an increase of respect and influence. Our class schedule shows that we will meet him again in later chapters. I wonder if by then Lot might be a leader, influencing all of Sodom for good.

Checking for understanding

1. Explain why Abram and Lot needed to separate from each other.

2. Describe the plain of the Jordan, showing how Lot felt about it.

3. What new and surprising information does Genesis 14:14 reveal about Abram's life and work?

4. What made Abram's victory over the kings from the north so astounding?

5. One of the two kings who met Abram on his return from the battle held the same beliefs about God that Abram held. What was the name of that king, and what were the beliefs that he shared with Abram? (See the words of the king and of Abram in Genesis 14:18–20 and Genesis 14:22–23.)

6. Contrast the way Abram felt about the king of Salem with the way he felt about the king of Sodom.

7. Tell how nephew Lot was like Eve. (See Genesis 3 as a reminder of her thinking.)

8. Compare Abram's motivation for leaving his relatives in the north and moving to Canaan (Genesis 12:1–3) with Lot's motivation for leaving his uncle in Canaan and moving to Sodom (Genesis 13:10–11).

9. If Abram had ever wondered if his nephew would have to be the son from whom his nation would come, how might Genesis 13 and 14 have settled that question for him?

Great Rewards and Great Failures

Based on Genesis 15 and 16

My first thoughts

ABRAM HAD JUST COME off a few good days. He and his servants had defeated four kings from the Euphrates area, he had rescued Lot and all the people of the cities of the plain, and the greatest man in Canaan—the priest-king Melchizedek—had given his blessings to him. So why then does the title to this lesson bring up failures? I thought we were through with that kind of business.

My notes on the teacher's lesson

Reward, promises and gifts

Though Abram must have received many praises for his daring rescue of the captives taken in battle, surely his friends warned him: "Those humiliated armies will return." That was probably why *the word of the LORD came unto Abram in a vision, saying, Fear not, Abram: I am thy shield and thy exceeding great reward (15:1)*. What a wonderful picture to his mind— God, like a great shield encircling and protecting him from his enemies!

The words *exceeding great reward* might not have meant a lot to Abram. He wasn't looking for a reward: he was already a wealthy man. He just wanted to have the son that God had promised him ten years earlier.

As the years passed with no child in sight, Abram had thought long and hard about who would inherit all that he had, including the promises of a great nation and of blessings to the world. Who would be his heir if he didn't have a son? Perhaps there was another way—adoption. *And Abram said, LORD God what wilt thou give me* [for a reward], *seeing I go childless, and the steward of my house is this Eliezer of Damascus (15:2)* who, evidently, Abram was deciding would have to be his heir by adoption.

In the midst of those thoughts, *behold, the word of the LORD came unto him, saying, This shall not be thine heir; but he that shall come forth out of thine own bowels* [body] *shall be thine heir (15:4).* Those words meant Abram himself would be the physical father of the promised heir.

The LORD added a visible sign for Abram. *And he brought him forth abroad* [outside], *and said, Look now toward heaven, and tell* [count] *the stars, if thou be able to number them*—the words continued—*So shall thy seed be* [for number]. *And he believed in the LORD (15:5–6a).* According to the Genesis account, never again did Abram doubt he would father a son. Every night he could go out and look at the stars and confidently say, "Our family reunions will look just like that!" But that wasn't all.

Abram's new record

Because Abram believed that promise the *LORD counted it to him* [Abram] *for righteousness* (15:6). In other words because Abram believed the promise that God would give him the son, the LORD wrote on his account, or on the record of his life, *righteous, or upright.* For Abram that promise of a cleansed record would give him nights of peaceful sleep.

The land promise

The second part of chapter 15 talks about possessing the land of Canaan, a gift that could not come at that time, and a possession that Moses told his readers would be for Abram's sake, not because they deserved it (Deuteronomy 9). It could not come at that time for two reasons: first, Abram didn't yet have a multitude of his descendants to live in it; second, it would not be an act of justice to take it away from its present inhabitants.

According to Moses' writings, when it would be time for Abram's descendants to possess the land, removing Canaan's inhabitants must be an act of justice. In 400 more years (or four one-hundred-year generations) the Canaanites, also called *Amorites,* would fall so low into evildoings that justice would demand their removal.

To keep Abram's descendants from being corrupted in Canaan, they would live somewhere else during those 400 years (15:13–14, 16).

Sarai's thoughts

Abram might have been walking around with a huge smile after those promises, but if poor *Sarai* was smiling, she probably didn't feel like it. In her own eyes, she had failed. Even though she herself said *the LORD hath restrained me from bearing* [children] (16:2)—that God was the reason for her barren womb—Sarai decided she was the real problem. With a heavy heart, she made her decision, a decision she later wished Abram had rejected. That decision changed the whole family pattern and removed its household peace.

Sarai's handmaid

Sarai . . . had an handmaid, an Egyptian, whose name was Hagar (16:1). A handmaid (sometimes called a bondmaid, or bondservant) was a household servant, the property of that household—a household that was responsible to meet all her needs. Since Hagar was an Egyptian and probably had no family in Canaan, I wondered how she had come into Abram's household. Then I remembered the humiliating events of ten years earlier—how Abram let the king of Egypt think he could marry Sarai (12:15–16). I remembered how the king loaded Abram with gifts, gifts that included maidservants and menservants. Maybe she was one of those gifts.

For Hagar to be Sarai's own personal handmaid, Sarai must have been pleased with her, liking her strength, her abilities, and her good work. Perhaps Hagar showed sympathy for Sarai, grieving with her over her inability to give Abram a son.

Sarai's solution

Evidently Sarai was unaware of the marriage pattern given in Genesis 2:24, the pattern that describes a husband and wife as "one flesh." If she had seen herself as one flesh with Abram, she would have assumed that for Abram to be a father, then she had to be a mother—the mother of his child. Having lost all hope, she took matters into her own hands. *And Sarai said unto Abram, Behold now, the LORD hath restrained me from bearing* [children]. *I pray thee, go in unto my maid* [to sleep with her]; *it may be that I may obtain children by her (16:2).* She wanted Hagar to bear a son for Abram!

In the world of Abram's day, no one would say it was wrong for him to have a child by the maid. Hagar was Sarai's personal property. That meant anything Hagar possessed was also Sarai's, including any children. "In that way," thought Sarai, "Abram can have the promised nation."

Hagar must have heard the news of Sarai's plan in complete shock. Sarai wanted her to bear a son for Abram. Hagar understood what it was all about. She would sleep with Abram, give birth (hopefully) to a son, and thus Abram could have a nation of his own descendants. Evidently Hagar did not object. She might have hoped that possibly she would no longer be a servant but rather a wife, even if only a second-class wife.

Just as Adam had listened to Eve, *Abram hearkened to the voice of Sarai. And Sarai Abram's wife took Hagar her maid the Egyptian, after Abram had dwelt ten years in the land of Canaan, and gave her to her husband Abram to be his wife. And he went in unto Hagar, and she conceived (16:2b–4a).* The plan had worked.

Sarai's change of mind

Sadly for Sarai, though, it did not turn out as she had expected for Hagar's attitude dramatically changed. *When she saw that she had conceived, her mistress* [Sarai] *was despised in her eyes (16:4b).* Hagar's newly contemptuous attitude infuriated Sarai.

In anger and frustration, Sarai went to Abram and poured the blame upon him. *And Sarai said unto Abram, My wrong be upon thee: I have given my maid into thy bosom; and when she saw that she had conceived, I was despised in her eyes: the LORD judge between me and thee (16:5)*—as if to say, "Husband, this is all your fault!" and since Abram ruled their home, maybe it *was* his fault; maybe he himself *was* to blame.

Perhaps not knowing how to respond to Sarai's attack, he said to her, *Behold, thy maid is in thy hand; do to her as it pleaseth thee. And when Sarai dealt hardly* [harshly] *with her, she fled from her face (16:6).* Abram had only let matters get worse.

The kindness of the angel of the Lord to Hagar

And the angel of the Lord found her [Hagar] by a fountain of water in the wilderness, by the fountain in the way to Shur [the route back to Egypt]. And he said, Hagar, Sarai's maid, whence camest thou [where have you come from]? and whither wilt thou go [where are you going]? And she said, I flee from the face of my mistress Sarai. And the angel of the Lord said unto her, Return to thy mistress, and submit thyself under her hands (16:7–9). Hagar must go back and submit to Sarai no matter how Sarai received her, even if Sarai treated her, not as a second wife, but as a despised slave.

The next verse shows what made her agree to go back to Sarai. And the angel of the Lord said unto her, I will multiply thy seed exceedingly, that it shall not be numbered for multitude (16:10). Through her unborn child, Hagar would have more descendants than could be counted. The angel of the Lord continued, Behold, thou art with child and shalt bear a son, and shalt call his name Ishmael; because the Lord hath heard thy affliction (16:11b). Though Hagar did not deserve it, the angel was promising to bless her anyway.

Description of Ishmael

The angel of the Lord went on to describe what her son would be like. And he will be a wild man; [the Hebrew language says, a wild donkey of a man, in other words, as untamable as a wild donkey] his hand will be against every man [in opposition], and every man's hand against him; and he shall dwell in the presence [midst] of all his brethren (16:12). Independent like his mother, evidently he would sharply oppose any relative or neighbor who might disagree with him.

Perhaps Ishmael's name, the Lord hears, became a warning and a security for both Sarai and Hagar remembering that the Lord heard every word each of them spoke. And Hagar bare Abram a son: and Abram called his son's name, which Hagar bare, Ishmael (16:15).

At last Abram had a son, a son whom he loved, a son who would become the father of a multitude of descendants, but for Sarai, life had lost its joy. Year after year nothing changed for her until unexpected visitors came with an unexpected and overwhelming message for Abram, a message that included Sarai.

My reflections on Abram's unhappy home

I tried to picture Hagar's return to Sarai: I wondered what Hagar would have said about her running away, about the angel who appeared to her, and about the angel's words. I wondered if it frightened Sarai that the LORD had heard and was hearing her hate-filled words to Hagar.

What were Sarai's benefits with the birth of Ishmael? Since Abram at last had his own son, she didn't need to worry anymore about her barrenness. I wondered what kind of relationship Sarai could have had with the boy—whether she would have just left him to his mother and had little to do with him, or whether she welcomed him into the family. When Sarai met other people who asked if she had children, since technically Hagar's child belonged to Sarai, I wondered how she would have answered.

Checking for understanding

1. For what reasons did Abram need to hear the words, *I am thy shield*?

2. Explain why the stars in the sky would always encourage Abram.

3. According to Genesis 15:6, the LORD accounted Abram as righteous. Describe Abram's part in receiving that promise.

4. How long would it be before Abram's descendants would possess Canaan?

5. Why did Hagar and Sarai come to despise each other?

6. Based on what the angel told Hagar in 16:12, describe what it would have been like to have Ishmael as your relative.

7. Tell how the name *Ishmael* might have helped the relationships in Abram's family.

Visitors, Promises, Beliefs, and Fears

Based on Genesis 17:1–27 and 18:1–15

My first thoughts

AT THE END OF Genesis 16, *Abram was fourscore and six years old.* Knowing that one score is twenty, I figured he was eighty-six. In the first verse of the next chapter, though, his age is *ninety years old and nine.* That means thirteen years had passed in silence.

Our teacher told us the fourteenth year makes up for it. It is a year so alive with visitors, promises, horrors, doubts, and joys that it covers four chapters and seven verses. She also said no other one-year period in Genesis takes up that much written space, and that this chapter in particular is the turning point in the lives of Abram and Sarai. I'm wondering what's so important.

My notes on the teacher's lesson

A theophany

The fourteenth year opens with a theophany [thie (as in thief)-AHH-fan-ee]. Frequently in Genesis Moses wrote that God *appeared.* Since Bible writers say that God cannot be seen, how then could they say he *appeared*? Theologians (people who study about God) have a name for this. They call such an appearance a *theophany,* a visible manifestation or appearance of God. Sometimes biblical theophanies came in objects of nature as in the *smoking furnace, and burning lamp* of Genesis 15. At other times they came in the appearance of an angel, as the angel who appeared to Hagar. Today in Genesis 17 and 18 we see another theophany where he came as a man. *When Abram was ninety years old and nine, the LORD appeared to Abram, and said unto him, I am the Almighty God (17:1a).* What did he look like? We are not told.

A covenant

The words continued, *Walk before me, and be thou perfect. And I will make my covenant between me and thee (17:1–2a).* In Genesis 12 God had made promises to Abram. In this chapter he will enlarge on certain of the promises and call the promises a covenant—an agreement that would be ratified by a sign.

The covenant's enlarged promise

In Genesis 12, God had promised to make from Abram a nation, but in this chapter he said, *I will . . . multiply thee exceedingly . . . and thou shalt be a father of many nations (17:2b, 4b)*—not just one nation but many nations! That great increase of offspring required a new name. *Neither shall thy name any more be called Abram* [meaning exalted father], *but thy name shall be Abraham; for a father of many nations have I made thee. And I will make thee exceeding fruitful, and I will make nations of thee, and kings shall come out of thee (17:5–6).*

Sarai's part in that promise

God continued: *As for Sarai thy wife, thou shalt not call her name Sarai, but Sarah shall her name be (17:15).* Both names, Sarai and Sarah, mean *princess.* Instead of giving an explanation for that name change, God spoke words about Sarah's future: *And I will bless her, and give thee a son also of her: yea, I will bless her, and she shall be a mother of nations; kings of people shall be of her (17:16).* Those words so shocked Abraham that he fell to the ground laughing as if he had just heard a hugely funny and absurd joke. *And Abraham said unto God,* [apparently doubting that Sarah could possibly have a child] *O that Ishmael might live before thee! (17:18).*

The name of Sarah's son

And God said, Sarah thy wife shall bear thee a son indeed; and thou shalt call his name Isaac (17:19a). The name for the child Isaac, about whose birth Abraham was laughing, is the Hebrew word for *laughter*. That name would become a witness about Abraham's God to all who met him. All through Isaac's life, explaining his name to strangers would lead to the explanation that his mother was ninety years old and his father one hundred when he was born. And that would lead to surprise, more explanations, awe, and even more delighted laughter.

The sign of the covenant

This covenant included many people. God said to Abraham, *I will establish my covenant with him* [Isaac] *for an everlasting covenant, and with his seed after him (17:19b);* thus, it included both Isaac and his descendants. And then God gave more information that would have helped friends plan baby showers for Sarah. Her son would be born . . . *at this set time in the next year (17:21b).*

The covenant also included a sign to remind all the males that the promises would surely be kept. The sign would be worn in the body and would plunge Abraham, his son Ishmael, and every one of the males into a week of pain. It was, by command of God, surgery on the male sexual organ. The LORD said to Abraham, *This is my covenant* [sign] . . . *every man child among you shall be circumcised (17:10).* Circumcision meant taking a knife and removing the foreskin of the male organ, a painful procedure.

That act of obedience required faith in the promise of protection, for the pain would immobilize them for up to a week. It would leave Abraham's family, his treasury, his flocks, and his herds with no male protection during the healing process.

About twenty-five years earlier, Abraham had had 318 male servants old enough to go to battle (14:14). Our class did some math. We assumed many of those servants had their own sons. We also assumed that as his flocks and herds increased, Abraham would have acquired even more servants. How many males might there have been by Genesis 17? We figured there could have been hundreds more, and every one of them, according to the command, had to be circumcised!

The directions continued. *And he that is eight days old shall be circumcised . . . he that is born in the house, or bought with money . . . which is not of thy seed* [not a physical descendant] . . . *my covenant shall be in your flesh for an everlasting covenant (17:12–13).*

What circumcision might have meant to the servants

A classmate then asked if Abraham's servants would have resented having to go through this painful surgery. The teacher said the book of Genesis doesn't tell us. The servants who understood the covenant with God, though, might have seen the sign of circumcision, even though painful, as a wonderful privilege. In the book of Genesis, circumcision made a great statement. It declared to them that they too—not just Abraham and his family—had a special relationship to Abraham's God. The servants would know that they were no longer outsiders; they and their own children, no matter what their race, shared in the blessings included in the covenant with Abraham's God.

Abraham's obedience

Immediately, that very day (the day of the appearance of the LORD), even as Abraham might still be grinning over the announcement about Sarah (17:15–19), he set out to obey the new command: *Abraham took Ishmael his son, and . . . every male among the men of Abraham's house; and circumcised the flesh of their foreskin in the selfsame day, as God had said unto him (17:23).* What a job! Our class decided that every woman on Abraham's compound would have been drafted into medical duty. What a painful, bloody day! We hoped they had some kind of painkiller.

And Abraham was ninety years old and nine, when he was circumcised in the flesh of his foreskin. And Ishmael his son was thirteen years old, when he was circumcised in the flesh of his foreskin (17:24–25).

Abraham receives another visit

A short time later, at least long enough for Abraham to heal from the circumcision, company appeared—no ordinary company. *And the LORD appeared unto him* [another theophany] *in the plains of Mamre* [MAM-ree]: *and he* [Abraham] *sat in the tent door in the heat of the day; and he lift* [lifted] *up his eyes and looked, and, lo, three men stood by him (18:1–2a).* As soon as Abraham saw them, he concluded that one of them was the LORD himself.

And when he saw them, he ran to meet them from the tent door, and bowed himself toward the ground, and said, My Lord, if now I have found favor in thy sight, pass not away, I pray thee, from thy servant (18:2b–3).

Let a little water, I pray you, be fetched, and wash your feet, and rest yourselves under the tree: and I will fetch a morsel of bread, and comfort ye your hearts; after that ye shall pass on . . . . And they said, So do, as thou hast said (18:4–5).

And Abraham hastened into the tent unto Sarah, and said, Make ready quickly three measures of fine meal, knead it, and make cakes upon the hearth. And Abraham ran unto the herd, and fetched a calf tender and good, and gave it unto a young man; and he hasted to dress it. And he took butter, and milk, and the calf which he had dressed, and set it before them; and he stood by them under the tree, and they did eat (18:6–8).

News for unbelieving Sarah

And they said unto him, Where is Sarah thy wife? And [Abraham] *said, Behold, in the tent. And he* [the LORD] *said, I will certainly return unto thee according to the time of life; and, lo, Sarah thy wife shall have a son.* [All that time Sarah had been eavesdropping] *and Sarah heard it in the tent door, which was behind him (18:9–10).*

Now Abraham and Sarah were old and well stricken in age; and it ceased to be with Sarah after the manner of women. Therefore Sarah [perhaps with a tinge of bitterness] *laughed within herself, saying, After I am waxed* [grown] *old shall I have pleasure* [the pleasure of bearing a child]*, my lord* [Abraham] *being old also? (18:11–12).* Perhaps Abraham had not told Sarah about the promise of a child made at least a week earlier.

And the LORD said unto Abraham, Wherefore [why] *did Sarah laugh, saying, Shall I of a surety bear a child, which am old? (18:13).*

Then he asked Sarah a question: *Is any thing too hard for the LORD?* When no answer came from her, he went on speaking: *At the time appointed I will return unto thee, according to the time of life, and Sarah shall have a son (18:14).*

Then Sarah denied, saying, I laughed not; for she was afraid. And he said, Nay; but thou didst laugh (18:15). How humiliating to be caught eavesdropping on the guests and also to be caught telling a falsehood! If anyone else had accused Sarah of lying, she could have hidden behind many seemingly sincere and pure excuses, but with one who seemed to hear the silent words in her mind, she had no way to hide.

Immediately after that rebuke to Sarah, the three guests arose to leave, heading for another appointment in a city in the valley.

My reflections on the promises

I'm thinking a keyword or theme in Abraham's story is *believe* or maybe *faith*. All of his hopes were for a future that was humanly unattainable—having children in old age, possessing a land occupied by Canaanites, and bringing blessing to the world. His hopes were based only on promises. I suspect that will be true for all of Abraham's descendants throughout the rest of Genesis.

Checking for understanding

1. Define the word covenant.

2. What is a theophany?

3. What is the difference in the meaning of *Abram* and of the new name, *Abraham?*

4. Explain what circumcision, the sign of God's covenant with Abraham, said about a circumcised boy, whether the boy was Abraham's descendant or a child born to one of his servants.

5. How old will Abraham and Sarah be when Sarah gives birth to Isaac?

6. Why was the name *Isaac*, an appropriate name for Sarah's son?

7. Describe what Ishmael's thoughts might have been that day when he and his mother heard that Sarah was supposed to have a child the next year.

Lot's Rewards in Sodom

Based on Genesis 18:16—19:38

My first thoughts

I WAS PLEASED TO see the words, *Lot's rewards in Sodom*. The Jordan plain, as Genesis 13 described it, was like the Garden of Eden, a place of beauty and a place to gain wealth. Lot's home, Sodom, was on that plain. I was confident that the people of Sodom must appreciate Lot. After all, it was his uncle Abraham who rescued them from the northern kings (Genesis 14). Perhaps part of Lot's acceptance included sitting in the gate of the city—the "town hall"—where influential leaders carried out legal and civic business.

My notes on the teacher's lesson

The LORD and Abraham discuss Sodom

Up in the hills of Canaan, Abraham has just entertained three guests. They had come with a message that Sarah, within a year, would give birth to the promised son. After a lavish noontime meal, *the men rose up from thence, and looked toward Sodom (18:16a).*

It looks as if we will now find out how Lot is doing. *And Abraham went with them to bring them on the way. And the LORD said, Shall I hide from Abraham that thing which I do; seeing that Abraham shall surely become a great and mighty nation, and all the nations of the earth shall be blessed in him? (18:16b–18).*

And the Lord said, Because the cry of Sodom and Gomorrah is great, and because their sin is very grievous, I will go down now, and see whether they have done altogether according to the cry of it, which is come unto me; and if not, I will know. (18:20–21). The prayers of Sodom's victims crying out for vengeance had reached the heavens, and the men were going down to confirm those cries. This was not what I expected!

And [two of] *the men turned their faces from thence, and went toward Sodom: but Abraham stood yet before the Lord (18:22).* He correctly understood that the Lord planned judgment upon Sodom.

Abraham pleads with the Lord

And Abraham drew near, and said, Wilt thou also destroy the righteous with the wicked? (18:23). The word *righteous*, as Abraham used it, would have meant those people who were good, honorable, and morally upright.

He knew if the Lord wiped out wicked Sodom, he would also destroy any good people there; he must have been sure this would have included Lot and his family. In the next ten verses, Abraham presented arguments for why the Lord should spare Sodom.

Peradventure [suppose] *there be fifty righteous within the city: wilt thou also destroy and not spare the place for the fifty righteous that are therein? That be far from thee to do after this manner, to slay the righteous with the wicked: and that the righteous should be as the wicked, that be far from thee: Shall not the Judge of all the earth do right? (18:24–25).*

And the Lord said, If I find in Sodom fifty righteous within the city, then I will spare all the place for their sakes. And Abraham answered and said, Behold now, I have taken upon me to speak unto the Lord, which am but dust and ashes (18:26–27).

Peradventure there shall lack five of the fifty righteous: wilt thou destroy all the city for lack of five? And he said, If I find there forty and five, I will not destroy it. And he spake unto him yet again, and said, Peradventure there shall be forty found there. And he said, I will not do it for forty's sake (18:28–29).

And he said unto him, Oh let not the Lord be angry, and I will speak: Peradventure there shall thirty be found there. And he said, I will not do it, if I find thirty there (18:30).

And he said, Behold now, I have taken upon me to speak unto the LORD: Peradventure there shall be twenty found there. And he said, I will not destroy it for twenty's sake (18:31).

And he said, Oh let not the LORD be angry, and I will speak yet but this once: Peradventure ten shall be found there. And he said, I will not destroy it for ten's sake (18:32).

And the LORD went his way, as soon as he had left communing with Abraham: and Abraham returned unto his place [perhaps confident the city had at least ten righteous people] *(18:33).*

The wickedness of Sodom proved

And there came two angels to Sodom at even; and Lot sat in the gate of Sodom: and Lot seeing them rose up to meet them; and he bowed himself with his face toward the ground; and he said, Behold now, my lords, turn in, I pray you, into your servant's house, and tarry all night, and wash your feet, and ye shall rise up early, and go on your ways. And they said, Nay; but we will abide in the street all night. And [Lot] *pressed upon them greatly; and they turned in unto him, and entered into his house; and he made them a feast, and did bake unleavened bread, and they did eat (19:1–3).*

But before they lay down, the men of the city, even the men of Sodom, compassed [or circled] *the house round, both old and young, all the people from every quarter: And they called unto Lot, and said unto him, Where are the men which came in to thee this night? bring them out unto us, that we may know them (19:4–5).*

The biblical word *know* does not always mean getting acquainted. In the Bible the word can mean having sexual relations. The men of the city wanted to rape the two angels who appeared to them to be humans.

And Lot went out at the door unto them, and shut the door after him, and said, I pray you, brethren, do not so wickedly. Behold now, I have two daughters which have not known man; let me, I pray you, bring them out unto you, and do ye to them as is good in your eyes: only unto these men do nothing; for therefore came they under the shadow of my roof (19:6–8).

And they said, Stand back. And they said again, This one fellow [Lot] *came in to sojourn* [live], *and he will* [wants to] *be a judge: now will we deal worse with thee, than with them. And they pressed sore upon the man, even Lot, and came near to break the door (19:9).*

But the men put forth their hand, and pulled Lot into the house to them, and shut to the door. And they smote [struck] the men that were at the door of the house with blindness, both small and great: so that they wearied themselves to find the door (19:10–11).

And the men said unto Lot, Hast thou here any besides? son in law, and thy sons, and thy daughters, and whatsoever thou hast in the city, bring them out of this place: for we will destroy this place, because the cry of them is waxen [grown] great before the face of the LORD; and the LORD hath sent us to destroy it (19:12–13).

And Lot went out, and spake unto his sons in law, which married his daughters, and said, Up, get you out of this place; for the LORD will destroy this city. But he seemed as one that mocked unto his sons in law (19:14).

And when the morning arose, then the angels hastened Lot, saying, Arise, take thy wife, and thy two daughters, which are here; lest thou be consumed in the iniquity of the city. And while he lingered, the men laid hold upon his hand, and upon the hand of his wife, and upon the hand of his two daughters; the LORD being merciful unto him: and they brought him forth, and set him without [outside] the city (19:15–16).

And it came to pass, when they had brought them forth abroad, that he said, Escape for thy life; look not behind thee, neither stay thou in all the plain; escape to the mountain, lest thou be consumed (19:17).

Lot's losses

Then the LORD rained upon Sodom and upon Gomorrah brimstone and fire from the LORD out of heaven; And he overthrew those cities, and all the plain, and all the inhabitants of the cities, and that which grew upon the ground (19:24–25).

All was gone—his flocks and herds, his home, and all his possessions except the few he could carry, and tragically, he was about to lose even more.

When the angels dragged Lot and his family out of the city, one of the angels had given the family an urgent warning. He had said, *Escape for thy life; look not behind thee, neither stay thou in all the plain; escape to the mountain, lest thou be consumed (19:17).* Perhaps hearing the sounds of destruction, thinking of all she was losing, or not believing the angel's words, *his wife looked back from behind him, and she became a pillar of salt (19:26).*

And Abraham gat up early in the morning to the place where he stood before the Lord: and he looked toward Sodom and Gomorrah, and toward all the land of the plain, and beheld, and, lo, the smoke of the country went up as the smoke of a furnace (19:27–28).

And Lot went up out of Zoar, and dwelt in the mountain, and his two daughters with him; for he feared to dwell in Zoar: and he dwelt in a cave, he and his two daughters (19:30). Living in the isolated cave, however, brought more sorrow.

Fearful of living in any city below, and seeing no way of finding husbands, the daughters considered how they could have children. *And the firstborn said unto the younger, Our father is old, and there is not a man in the earth to come in unto us after the manner of all the earth: come, let us make our father drink wine, and we will lie with him, that we may preserve seed of our father. And they made their father drink wine that night: and the firstborn went in, and lay with her father; and he perceived not when she lay down, nor when she arose (19:31–33).*

And it came to pass on the morrow, that the firstborn said unto the younger, Behold, I lay yesternight with my father: let us make him drink wine this night also; and go thou in, and lie with him, that we may preserve seed of our father. And they made their father drink wine that night also: and the younger arose, and lay with him; and he perceived not when she lay down, nor when she arose (19:34–35).

The people who came from Lot and his daughters

According to Moses' record in Genesis 19, each girl conceived a son by Lot, and each son grew up to become the father of a small nation. Those two nations, Moab and Ammon (19:37–38), had the same ancestors as Abraham and Lot, but by the time of Moses, Lot's descendants had no affection for Abraham's people—their own relatives—instead, they saw them as enemies.

My reflections on Lot

All of us remembered Lot's excitement when almost twenty-five years earlier the Jordan plain looked to him like the Garden of Eden, and we remembered his eagerness to stay there despite its wicked reputation. It seemed to the class that Lot and his wife might have loved riches too much. A student who knows the Bible pretty well said there was another side to Lot. She said the New Testament calls Lot a righteous man who was greatly distressed by the wickedness of Sodom (II Peter 2:7–8). (I now wonder if his wife had something to do with his staying there.) As we reflected, we could think of several times when his behavior was righteous, or upright, but we could also think of other times when he was terribly foolish.

Checking for understanding

1. Judging from the location in Sodom at which the guests first met Lot, what indicates that he had become a leader in Sodom?

2. Prove that hospitality to his guests was of utmost importance to Lot.

3. How did the men of Sodom make it clear to Lot that, even though he had become a leader in the city, he was not respected?

4. In the New Testament in Luke 17:32 and 33, Jesus said, *Remember Lot's wife. Whoever seeks to keep his life will lose it, and whoever loses his life will preserve it.* Based on those words, what might Jesus have been saying about the reason Lot's wife looked back at Sodom?

5. List everything about Lot that might be called righteous.

6. In what way was the purpose of the destruction of Sodom by fire like the purpose of the destruction of the world in Noah's flood (Genesis 6–8)?

Challenges to Sarah's Son in Gerar

Based on Genesis 20:1–18—21:1–7

My first thoughts

IN PREPARING FOR TODAY'S lesson, we were to read Genesis 20, keeping Sarah's promised son Isaac in mind. The teacher told us that sometimes after the death of a very wealthy person, all kinds of supposed heirs rise up claiming they are the legal offspring—the rightful inheritors. We were to look for any situation that might make it appear that Isaac was neither Abraham and Sarah's rightful son nor Abraham's rightful heir.

The first potential challenge would come before Isaac was even conceived. The second would arise at *a great feast* about two or three years later. (We will study the second potential challenge in the next lesson.)

I decided to draw a one-year timeline to make sense of the first challenge. My timeline year begins when the LORD promised that Sarah would have a son at that same time the next year (17:21; 18:10). The timeline continues through the destruction of Sodom and ends at Isaac's birth.

My notes on the teacher's lesson

The first potential challenge to Sarah's son

For some unknown reason, Abraham and Sarah decided to move away from their home in Mamre near the Dead Sea. *And Abraham journeyed . . . toward the south country . . . and sojourned in Gerar* [GEE rahr] a small kingdom within Canaan *(20:1)*. Perhaps the sight of smoke still rising from distant Sodom brought too much distress. Moving from Mamre, however, did not remove distress from their lives. In that new location, Gerar, they faced what could have become a life-long question about their future son's legitimacy—a question about the identity of his true father.

Abimelech, king of Gerar

In Gerar an old fear came back to Abraham—fear that the king of that land might kill him in order to take Sarah for his own wife. Evidently not certain that God could protect him, Abraham resorted again to his half-truth that he had told in Egypt years earlier. *Abraham said of Sarah his wife She is my sister: and Abimelech king of Gerar,* [no doubt after giving gifts to Abraham] *sent, and took Sarah* [as his wife] *(20:2).*

Newly married to the king, Sarah never knew from night to night when he might call for her to sleep with him. So far, he had not. Time passed. We readers do not know until the last verses of the chapter why the king never called for her. He had a problem and needed healing of some kind. All the females in his household also had a problem; they were unable to conceive children. Since it can take one or two months for a woman to realize she has not conceived, probably at least two months had passed on my timeline.

No one was connecting the king's problems with Sarah; they had no reason to—not until Abimelech, one night, had a terrifying experience. *God came to Abimelech in a dream by night, and said to him, Behold, thou art but a dead man, for the woman which thou hast taken; for she is a man's wife (20:3).*

Abimelech, who *had not come near her,* responded; *and he said, LORD, wilt thou slay also a righteous nation? Said he not unto me, She is my sister? and she, even she herself said, He is my brother: in the integrity of my heart and innocency of my hands have I done this (20:4–5).* The king rightly claimed to be innocent. He did not know he had taken a married woman.

And God said unto him in a dream, Yea, I know that thou didst this in the integrity of thy heart; [I know you are innocent, and I] *withheld thee from sinning against me:* [I did not allow you to touch her]. *Now therefore restore the man his wife; for he is a prophet, and he shall pray for thee, and thou shalt live: and if thou restore her not, know thou that thou shalt surely die, thou, and all that are thine (20:6–7).*

Abimelech's righteous behavior

Therefore Abimelech rose early in the morning, and called all his servants, and told all these things in their ears: and the men were sore [greatly] afraid. Then Abimelech called Abraham, and said unto him, What hast thou done unto us? and what have I offended thee, that thou hast brought on me and on my kingdom a great sin? thou hast done deeds unto me that ought not to be done (20:8–9). Canaanite Abimelech was showing more integrity than Abraham. *And Abimelech said unto Abraham, What sawest thou, that thou hast done this thing? (20:10).*

Abraham then made a pathetic excuse: *I thought, Surely the fear of God is not in this place; and they will slay me for my wife's sake. And yet indeed she is my sister; she is the daughter of my father, but not the daughter of my mother; and she became my wife.*

He went on with his excuse: *And it came to pass, when God caused me to wander from my father's house, that I said unto her, This is thy kindness which thou shalt show unto me; at every place whither we shall come, say of me, He is my brother (20:11–13).*

And Abimelech took sheep, and oxen, and menservants, and womenservants, and gave them unto Abraham, and restored him Sarah his wife (20:14). Then Abimelech spoke directly to Sarah (perhaps sarcastically) using the words of her lie. *And unto Sarah he said, Behold, I have given thy brother* [which she had claimed he was] *a thousand pieces of silver behold, he is to thee a covering of the eyes, . . . thus she was reproved (20:16).* The reason for giving her such a huge sum of money, or even any money at all doesn't make sense in our culture, but evidently, somehow it was to demonstrate that she had not slept with him and that he was repaying her for her grief.

After that Abraham prayed for Abimelech, *And God healed Abimelech, and his wife, and his maidservants; and they bare children. For the LORD had fast closed up all the wombs of the house of Abimelech, because of Sarah, Abraham's wife (20:17–18).*

Abimelech, who had been so greatly wronged, again demonstrated his integrity and kindness. He sent Abraham and Sarah away from Gerar with rich gifts and a kind offer. *Abimelech said, Behold, my land is before thee: dwell where it pleaseth thee (20:15).* That meant Abraham was free to live anywhere he chose in Abimelech's territory.

How these events protected Sarah's son

Abraham's actions could have supplied Gerar with a great gossip question—
the question of Isaac's true father. It could have followed Isaac throughout
his whole life, but as far as the records go, that question never arose. Probably after the fright of Abimelech's dream, none of the king's household
would have dared speak falsely against Abraham and Sarah. They would
have trembled at the power of Abraham's God who could arrange to have
Sarah tucked away in a harem where no man but the king could get near
her and then to strike that man with sickness so that he never slept with her.
In addition to that, all the women of the king's household had their own
stories to tell. They themselves needed healing. With their stories whisper-
ing around Gerar, that town had enough excitement to last a long time. The
reports of those events would have protected Abraham and Sarah's future
son from any suggestion that he was the son of another man—of Abimelech the king of Gerar.

On my timeline of their lives, marking off the two months it would
take for the women of Gerar to know they had not conceived children, I
figured that would have left a good nine or ten months in that year, enough
time for Sarah to carry a little boy in her womb, and bring him to birth *at
the set time of which God had spoken . . . (18:10; 21:2).*

Isaac's birth

And the LORD *visited Sarah as he had said, and the* LORD *did unto Sarah
as he had spoken. For Sarah conceived, and bare Abraham a son in his old
age, at the set time of which God had spoken to him. And Abraham called
the name of his son that was born unto him, whom Sarah bare to him, Isaac
(21:1–3).*

*And Abraham circumcised his son Isaac being eight days old, as God
had commanded him. And Abraham was an hundred years old, when his
son Isaac was born unto him. And Sarah said, God hath made me to laugh,
so that all that hear will laugh with me. And she said, Who would have said
unto Abraham, that Sarah should [nurse children]? for I have born him a son
in his old age (21:4–7).*

My reflections on both Abraham and Sarah

Years earlier God had promised Abraham that he would bless him, but I wonder whether Abraham sometimes thought he had to manipulate people to get those blessings. Apparently he did think that; apparently he believed that the gift of blessings sometimes required deceit—maybe telling white lies and half-truths to get a good life. How ironic—the only *gift* his lies ever gave him was humiliation. But maybe humiliation actually *was* a blessing all by itself—a removal of any pride in his own goodness.

Checking for understanding

1. How does Genesis 20 demonstrate that Abraham was not yet a heroic figure?

2. What kept King Abimelech from sleeping with Sarah?

3. If you had been a resident of Abimelech's territory during the time Abraham and Sarah lived there, explain why you might have treated the two with great humility and respect.

4. Explain how the difference between the men of the Canaanite city of Sodom (Genesis 19) and the men of the Canaanite city of Gerar (Genesis 20) proved that all the people living in Canaan (often called Amorites) had not yet become hopelessly evil (as Genesis 15:16 said they would).

5. Since Hagar and Ishmael would have been in Gerar with Abraham's household, why would they, above all people, have wanted absolute certainty that Isaac was the son of Abraham, not of Abimelech.

Challenges to Isaac from Within the Family

Based on Genesis 21; 25:7–18

My first thoughts

IN OUR LAST STUDY, we looked at a possible challenge to Isaac's rights. In our study today, we are looking at a second possible challenge to his rights. It comes from *within* Abraham's family—a potential challenge from Ishmael. After I had read the story, even though Ishmael was the cause of the problems, I felt a little sorry for him. I also felt sorry for Abraham.

My notes on the teacher's lesson

I had to use my dictionary for this chapter—it had a word I didn't know. *And the child grew, and was weaned (21:8a).* I've never been around babies much so I didn't know that mothers have to *wean* their children—in other words, train them to eat food other than their mother's milk.

The second potential challenge to Sarah's son

And the child [Isaac] *grew, and was weaned,* perhaps anywhere from ages one to three. *And Abraham made a great feast the same day that Isaac was weaned (21:8).* Evidently surviving infancy was a great cause of celebration. I don't remember any celebration when Ishmael was weaned though—probably because he was the son of what Sarah called a slave woman and because Sarah so resented him. It's hard to believe that Hagar and Ishmael were enjoying Isaac's party knowing what it meant for Ishmael's future.

Genesis tells us that in the midst of the revelry, Sarah noted an alarming scene. *Sarah saw [Ishmael] the son of Hagar the Egyptian, which she had born unto Abraham, mocking* his half-brother (21:9). She drew her own conclusions. For fourteen years Ishmael was the only heir. In those fourteen years, it seems his mother would have often told him of the greatness awaiting him, but with Isaac's birth everything had changed.

Sarah's demand

Looking into the future and envisioning conflict between Abraham's two sons, Sarah anticipated jealousy, more mockery, and battles. Perhaps she was remembering the words of the angel to Hagar about her son, words spoken before Ishmael was born: *And he will be a wild man; his hand will be against every man, and every man's hand against him (16:12a).* Sarah was already seeing Ishmael's personal challenge to the son who had replaced him.

In anger and no doubt in fear, Sarah went to Abraham with a demand. *Cast out this bondwoman and her son: for the son of this bondwoman shall not be heir with my son, even with Isaac (21:10).* Sarah wanted to be rid of them both.

And the thing was very grievous in Abraham's sight because of his [great love for Ishmael his] *son (21:11).* According to scholars, the word *grievous* shows that Abraham was extremely angry at the thought of removing Ishmael. Perhaps he had hoped the two sons would share in the promises for the future. *And God said unto Abraham, Let it not be grievous in thy sight because of the lad, and because of thy bondwoman; in all that Sarah hath said unto thee, hearken unto her voice; for in Isaac shall thy seed be called (21:12).* God agreed with Sarah. Ishmael should leave. God had no intention, however, of forsaking Ishmael. He went on speaking: *And also of the son of the bondwoman* [Hagar] *will I make a nation, because he is thy seed (21:13).* Isaac's "first-place" would not keep teenage Ishmael from God's blessings.

Ishmael's departure

Believing that God would keep his promise to bless Ishmael, *Abraham rose up early in the morning, and took bread, and a bottle of water, and gave it unto Hagar . . . and sent her* [and Ishmael] *away: and she departed (21:14a).*

If Hagar had intended to return to Egypt, she was not headed in the right direction. She was lost and wandering *in the wilderness of Beersheba. And the water was spent in the bottle, and she cast the child under one of the shrubs. And she went, and sat her down over against him a good way off, as it were a bow shot: for she said, Let me not see the death of the child. And she sat over against him, and lift* [lifted] *up her voice, and wept (21:14b–16).*

And God heard the voice of the lad; and the angel of God called to Hagar out of heaven, and said unto her, What aileth thee, Hagar? fear not; for God hath heard the voice of the lad where he is (21:17). What did God hear the boy saying? Certainly, growing up with Abraham as his father, Ishmael would have understood prayer. Surely he would also have understood what repentance for wrongdoing was; he would have seen that in Abraham's life. Perhaps he was admitting his mockery of Isaac and was pleading with God to forgive him and give him help.

The words of the angel to Hagar continued: *Arise, lift up the lad, and hold him in thine hand; for I will make him a great nation (21:18).* What encouraging words for both Hagar and Ishmael. Abraham's God was not rejecting them.

And God opened her eyes, and she saw a well of water; and she went, and filled the bottle with water, and gave the lad drink. And God was with the lad; and he grew, and dwelt in the wilderness, and became an archer. And he dwelt in the wilderness of Paran: and his mother took him a wife out of the land of Egypt (21:19–21).

Ishmael's future

With that, Ishmael's story fades out of the picture. About seventy years later, the brothers came together to bury their father Abraham in the cave where he had years earlier buried his wife Sarah (25:7–10). At no time did Ishmael make any move to claim any inheritance rights over Isaac.

Moses briefly concluded the story of Ishmael's family, showing that the separation worked out well for him. It separated him to live his own life as a prosperous hunter with a large and influential family. Moses listed his sons and said of them, *These are the sons of Ishmael, and these are their names, by their towns, and by their castles; twelve princes according to their nations (25:12–16).* Islam teaches that Ishmael became the father of the Arabs—at least some groups of Arabs. Many in the religion of Islam believe Mohammed descended from Ishmael.

The record ends with the words *And these are the years of the life of Ishmael, an hundred and thirty and seven years: and he gave up the ghost* [spirit] *and died; and was gathered unto his people (25:17).*

My reflections on Ishmael

The seniors in our class said they wished they had known more about the biblical Ishmael when they were reading *Moby Dick*. One of the main characters in Herman Melville's *Moby Dick* was also named Ishmael, a spin-off on Abraham's son.

To me, the irony of the half-brothers, Ishmael and Isaac, is that the Arab's claim Ishmael as their father and Jewish people claim Isaac as their father, and both Ishmael and Isaac are sons of the same man, Abraham.

Checking for understanding

1. Why would Ishmael and Hagar probably resent Isaac?

2. Explain Sarah's reason for wanting Ishmael permanently out of the home.

3. Would you have felt sorry for Ishmael? Why or why not?

4. What great promise did God make for Ishmael's future?

5. Ishmael lived in the desert wilderness for his adult life. What was it about Ishmael that made the desert wilderness a suitable or appropriate dwelling place for him?

Abraham's Worst Test

Based on Genesis 22:1–19

My first thoughts

THE PLAN WRITTEN ON the board reads, *Abraham's worst test*. That title put a lot of questions into my mind. Why would God test him again? He's already had what I think would be the hardest test of all—believing Sarah would have a baby in her old age. Why would he need any more tests? I'm also confused about the first verse of Genesis 22. It says God *tempted* Abraham. That doesn't sound fair—trying to get someone to do wrong. And on top of that, what was so important about a burnt offering? What was its purpose? This chapter shocked me.

My notes on the teacher's lesson

The word *tempt*

Even before reading the chapter as a class, the teacher gave us a heads-up on the troubling words, *God did tempt Abraham (22:1)*. No one in our class knows Hebrew; that was why we had a problem. Our teacher told us that the Hebrew word translated here as *tempt* may also be translated *try, prove* or *test*. Each word is talking about an examination of a person or object. You *try on* clothes to *prove* whether or not they fit. You *test* the brakes of a car so you won't wreck. Colleges give exams to *test* whether you can make it in their school. Most translations use *God did test Abraham*.

She reminded us that all by themselves, any tests we face cannot make changes in us; they only show us where we *need* to change or to *be* changed. The coach looks at your tennis swing. He's testing you. The test does nothing to your swing. It only shows him yours is dreadful. After that, perhaps he can teach you how to become a good player. This chapter is a test of Abraham—it tests what is most important in his life, and shows him whether or not he needs changing

The command

Terrible words had come to Abraham in the night, words that made the LORD appear harsh, cruel, and unfaithful, just like the gods of the Canaanites. *And it came to pass after these things, that God did tempt* [or test] *Abraham, and said unto him, Abraham: and he said, Behold, here I am. And he said, Take now thy son, thine only son Isaac, whom thou lovest, and get thee into the land of Moriah; and offer him there for a burnt offering upon one of the mountains which I will tell thee of (22:1–2).*

If Sarah had awakened early the next morning, she might have been surprised to hear Abraham, Isaac, and two servants preparing for a journey. Her husband's explanation would probably have been brief. He was taking young Isaac on a three-day journey to Mount Moriah where he would offer a burnt offering and worship God.

She would understand burnt offerings. Her husband would set up an altar made either of stones or earth, place wood on it, tie up the sacrifice, lay it upon the wood, take a knife, kill the sacrifice, and set it on fire. It was a way of saying to God, "I offer myself, all my hopes, desires, and loves to you. You are most important in my life." Since the test was only for Abraham, Sarah probably knew nothing of God's orders. She did not seem to notice that he left with no animal for the sacrifice.

Arguments against obeying the command

If on hearing this story, an Israelite boy turned to his father and said, "If God told you to sacrifice me, would you obey him?" How should the father answer? If the father said he would *not* sacrifice him, he would be teaching the child to obey only when the commands were pleasing to him. If the father said he *would* sacrifice him, what fears might the child have every time he saw his father with a knife? If the father said he didn't know what he would do, he would still be leaving the child in terror.

Hopefully, the father would say to his son, "My son, that will never happen. That command will never come. Immediately after we departed from Egypt (in Exodus), we went straight to Mount Sinai where God gave us his laws. One of those laws—strongly given—not only forbade the sacrifice of children, it demanded the death penalty for any parent who committed such a vile act (Leviticus 20:1–5). For Abraham, though, that law in Leviticus had not yet been given.

Abraham's obedience

And Abraham rose up early in the morning, and saddled his ass, and took two of his young men with him, and Isaac his son, and clave [cut] the wood for the burnt offering, and rose up, and went unto the place of which God had told him (22:3).

The trip to Mount Moriah

When they arrived three days later at the place commanded by God, Abraham gave orders to the two servants with them: *And Abraham said unto his young men, Abide ye here with the ass; and I and the lad will go yonder and worship, and [we will] come again to you (22:5).*

And Abraham took the wood of the burnt offering, and laid it upon Isaac his son; and he took the fire in his hand, and a knife; and they went both of them together (22:6).

And Isaac spake unto Abraham his father, and said, My father: and he said, Here am I, my son. And he said, Behold the fire and the wood: but where is the lamb for a burnt offering? And Abraham said, My son, God will provide himself a lamb for a burnt offering: so they went both of them together (22:7–8).

Preparing for the offering

And they came to the place which God had told him of; and Abraham built an altar there, and laid the wood in order . . . (22:9a).

It was time for the sacrifice, time to tell Isaac that it was he himself who was the sacrifice. It was time for binding him as all sacrifices were bound and for taking his life. Moses gives no clue as to how Abraham would have prepared Isaac for this horrifying command. Surely he would have reminded him over and over again that God had promised that a nation would come from him, which meant Isaac would one day marry and have at least one son in order to have that nation. Surely he would have assured Isaac that somehow obedience to this command would not wipe out the promises.

Yet what terrible grief would have been upon them as he *bound Isaac his son, and laid him on the altar upon the wood. And Abraham stretched forth his hand, and took the knife to slay his son (22:9b–10).*

God ends the test

And the angel of the LORD *called unto him out of heaven, and said, Abraham, Abraham: and he said, Here am I. And he said, Lay not thine hand upon the lad, neither do thou any thing unto him: for now I know that thou fearest God, seeing thou hast not withheld thy son, thine only son from me (22:11–12).* This test confirmed that Abraham trusted and loved the LORD God so completely that he would obey anything and everything he commanded.

The test was complete. Abraham had displayed what was within him. *And Abraham lifted up his eyes, and looked, and behold behind him a ram caught in a thicket by his horns: and Abraham went and took the ram, and offered him up for a burnt offering in the stead of his son (22:13).*

The reward for both Abraham and Isaac

And the angel of the LORD *called unto Abraham out of heaven the second time, and said, By myself have I sworn, saith the* LORD*, for because thou hast done this thing, and hast not withheld thy son, thine only son, that in blessing I will bless thee, and in multiplying I will multiply thy seed as the stars of the heaven, and as the sand which is upon the sea shore; and thy seed shall possess the gate of his enemies; and in thy seed shall all the nations of the earth be blessed; because thou hast obeyed my voice (22:15–18).*

Some of the promises, such as the many blessings and the many descendants, were repetitions of previous ones, but the promise *thy seed shall possess the gate of his enemies* was new. To possess the gate of their enemies included victory over the evil Canaanites and their practices.

So Abraham returned unto his young men, and they rose up and went together to Beersheba, their home *(22:19).*

My reflections after studying this test of Abraham

Our teacher had us conclude the study by writing a brief paragraph stating what the test revealed about Abraham. We all read our paragraphs to the class.

Some said it tested Abraham's belief that a nation would come through Isaac—his faith that Isaac would one day marry and have children. That meant Abraham had to believe that God would either stop the sacrifice or he would raise Isaac from the dead. (They had found a footnote in one of their Bibles to Hebrews 11:17–19 which says he believed that.)

Several others wrote that it proved that Abraham loved and trusted God so much that he would do whatever God said no matter what the cost to him.

I was thinking of a different angle. If Abraham had refused to obey the command, it would have proved that he was, at heart, a polytheist with more than one god—his son having the most important place of all.

Checking for understanding

1. Remembering the promise that Isaac would have a nation and considering verse 5, what do you think Abraham might have expected to happen after Isaac was offered up as a burnt offering?

2. For Isaac's sake, what would you expect Abraham to have talked about as they walked to Mount Moriah?

3. What do you think the Bible means when it says that Abraham "feared God"?

4. In what way was Isaac included in the rewards for Abraham?

5. You were to ask yourself what benefit Moses wanted the Israelites to receive from this account. In a brief paragraph, give your response to this question.

The Standards for Isaac's Wife

Genesis 24

My first thoughts

OUR TEACHER INTRODUCED THIS lesson by asking what standards most young people look for in the person they marry. For myself I thought good looks and a good personality. She then told us that in today's chapter, the longest chapter in Genesis, Moses set forth standards and guidelines that would go a long way in bringing happiness and success to a marriage—standards that Moses believed would strengthen the well-being of Abraham's descendants.

My notes on the teacher's lesson

Abraham's basic requirement for choosing a wife for Isaac

Isaac was forty years old, and his mother, whom he greatly missed (verse 67b), had died three years earlier. Abraham knew Isaac needed a wife, but where could he find one for his son who would follow the LORD his God? Having lived sixty-five years among the Canaanites, Abraham knew Canaanite lifestyles. He surely would have known how Lot's daughters—his own nieces— were affected by living in a Canaanite city (19:30–38). And he would remember the prophecy that the iniquity, or evil, of the Canaanite people (also referred to as Amorites) would grow worse and worse beyond any hope of change (15:16b). So he called for the servant that ruled over all that he had, and to him not to Isaac, Abraham assigned the task of finding a wife for his son.

And Abraham said unto his eldest servant of his house, that ruled over all that he had, Put, I pray thee, thy hand under my thigh [a way of making an unbreakable promise]: *and I will make thee swear by the* LORD, *the God of heaven, and the God of the earth, that thou shalt not take a wife unto my son of the daughters of the Canaanites, among whom I dwell (24:2–3).*

Where, though, would the servant search to find such a girl—a girl with high values who would be willing to follow the LORD God of Abraham and Isaac? Then he thought of his brother Nahor who lived five hundred miles north in Haran. Sometime earlier, news had come that Nahor, unlike Abraham, had twelve sons plus grandchildren (Genesis 22:20–24). Abraham had his answer. He decided that the best place to find the right girl would be from his own relatives in Haran, so he gave these orders to his servant: *Thou shalt go unto my country, and to my kindred* [my relatives], *and take a wife unto my son Isaac (24:4).*

As the servant began to think about his task, he had a question. *Peradventure* [what if] *the woman will not be willing to follow me unto this land: must I needs bring thy son again unto the land from whence thou camest?(24:5).* In other words, if the servant thought he found the right girl but she wanted to remain in her family's town, should he bring Isaac back to live there?

Shocked at the thought, *Abraham said unto him, Beware thou that thou bring not my son thither again (24:6).* My son is not to go there—Canaan is where our family is to live. *The* LORD *God of heaven . . . shall send his angel before thee, and thou shalt take a wife unto my son from thence (24:7).* He meant that an angel would go before the servant and lead him to the right girl. The servant did not have to worry.

The servant's search for a girl with high qualities

And the servant took ten camels of the camels of his master, and departed; for all the goods of his master were in his hand: and he arose, and went to Mesopotamia, unto the city of [Abraham's brother] *Nahor. And he made his camels to kneel down without* [outside] *the city by a well of water at the time of the evening, even the time that women go out to draw water. And he said O* LORD *God of my master Abraham, I pray thee, send me good speed this day, and show kindness unto my master Abraham (24:10–12).*

Behold, I stand here by the well of water; and the daughters of the men of the city come out to draw water. And let it come to pass, that the damsel to whom I shall say, Let down thy pitcher, I pray thee, that I may drink; and she shall say, Drink, and I will give thy camels drink also: let the same be she that thou hast appointed for thy servant Isaac; and thereby shall I know that thou hast showed kindness unto my master (24:13–14).

The servant could have prayed that the right girl would be dressed in a certain way or would be singing a song or perhaps carrying a lamb. Instead he asked that she volunteer to water the ten thirsty camels—animals that can go a week without water, but that will drink many gallons when they are thirsty. That would take a lot of hard work!

It was a shocking prayer. The servant had brought other servants with him who could water the camels—that would probably be one of their jobs. For a girl, though, not merely to give a stranger a drink, but also to water his camels (expecting nothing in return) was astounding. If she would make that offer, the servant would see a cluster of the qualities he wanted for Isaac's wife—kindness, friendliness, self-sacrifice, strength, energy, and a willingness to work hard.

And it came to pass, before he had done speaking, that, behold, Rebekah came out, who was born to Bethuel, son of Milcah, the wife of Nahor, Abraham's brother, with her pitcher upon her shoulder. And the damsel was very fair to look upon [beautiful], *a virgin, neither had any man known her: and she went down to the well, and filled her pitcher, and came up (24:15–16).*

The servant had no idea that the first girl who approached the well was the granddaughter of Abraham's brother.

And the servant ran to meet her, and said, Let me, I pray thee, drink a little water of thy pitcher. And she said, Drink, my lord: and she hasted, and let down her pitcher upon her hand, and gave him drink (24:17–18).

And when she had done giving him drink, she said, I will draw water for thy camels also, until they have done drinking. And she hasted, and emptied her pitcher into the trough, and ran again unto the well to draw water, and drew for all his camels. And the man wondering at her held his peace, to wit [to know] *whether the LORD had made his journey prosperous or not (24:19–21).*

And it came to pass, as the camels had done drinking, that the man [gave her] *a golden earring* [nose ring] *of half a shekel weight* [one-fifth of an ounce]*, and two bracelets for her hands of ten shekels* weight [four ounces] *of gold (24:22).*

Though the servant was looking for quality of character as one of the standards for Isaac's wife (and he was seeing in Rebekah what he was looking for) he still did not know enough about her to be sure she was the right girl. He did not know what the readers know, that she was from Abraham's family, so he asked, *Whose daughter art thou? tell me, I pray thee: is there room in thy father's house for us to lodge in? And she said unto him, I am the daughter of Bethuel the son of Milcah, which she bare unto Nahor (24:23–24).*

She added more words—words of enthusiastic hospitality, a standard or quality held high throughout the Bible. She was sure her family would be willing to accommodate unannounced men whom they had never seen before. She said, *We have both straw and provender enough, and room to lodge in (24:25b).*

When Rebekah said that she was from the family of Nahor (Abraham's brother), the servant *bowed down his head, and worshipped the LORD. And he said, Blessed be the LORD God of my master Abraham, . . . I being in the way, the LORD led me to the house of my master's brethren (24:26–27).*

Rebekah's family

And the damsel ran, and told them of her mother's house these things (24:28). Her brother Laban, seeing the jewelry on her, raced to the well and brought the servant and his men to their home. *And* [Laban] *said, Come in, thou blessed of the LORD; . . . I have prepared the house, and room for the camels. And the man came into the house: and he* [Laban] *ungirded* [unharnessed] *his camels, and gave straw and provender* [food] *for the camels, and water to wash his feet, and the men's feet that were with him (24:31–32).*

The servant presents the proposal

And there was set meat before him to eat: but [the servant] *said, I will not eat, until I have told mine errand. And he said, Speak on (24:33).*

The servant, believing that an angel was leading him, would not eat a bite until he had openly and honestly told the family everything. Wanting the family to know the security Rebekah would have as Isaac's wife, he told them about Abraham's great wealth (which his having costly camels would have proved). He wanted them to know that Isaac was the only heir. He told them of his prayer at the well and of how Rebekah did exactly what he had prayed the right girl would do. He hid nothing that they needed to know.

Unless he was open and honest, he would never have a clear conscience. He would never be sure he had found the right girl, and he would feel that any problems that arose later were because he had brought back the wrong person.

The decisions of the family and of Rebekah

After the servant had told all—the whole story of Abraham and Isaac—he made a request. Even though he believed that God had led him to Rebekah, he was not yet certain she was the right girl. He had one more standard. He needed something else—their willing consent.

And now if ye will deal kindly and truly with my master, tell me: and if not, tell me; that I may turn to the right hand, or to the left (24:49). For the servant, without the consent of the family—without that standard—Rebekah would not be the right girl for Isaac.

Then Laban and Bethuel answered and said, The thing proceedeth from the LORD: we cannot speak unto thee bad or good. Behold, Rebekah is before thee, take her, and go, and let her be thy master's son's wife, as the LORD hath spoken (24:50–51). They approved. No one, though, had asked Rebekah for her desire, but when they did, they asked only if she wanted ten days to get ready before she left, or if she would be willing to leave the next day. She chose the next day. Clearly, she too was convinced that this was the right marriage for her.

And the servant [after bowing to the earth to worship] *brought forth jewels of silver, and jewels of gold, and raiment, and gave them to Rebekah: he gave also to her brother and to her mother precious things (24:53).*

The blessings on her marriage

And they sent away Rebekah their sister, and her nurse (the woman who would have helped rear her), *and Abraham's servant, and his men. And they blessed Rebekah, and said unto her, Thou art our sister, be thou the mother of thousands of millions, and let thy seed possess the gate of those which hate them (24:59–60).*

Those blessings included sending with her, not only her nurse, but also her maids. It would be part of her home life going with her, giving her the comfort and courage of not being alone on the long journey south to a strange land. *And Rebekah arose, and her damsels, and they rode upon the camels, and followed the man: and the servant took Rebekah, and went his way (24:61).*

Isaac's confident choice

Down in southern Canaan, Isaac waited. A number of months would have passed since the servant left. *And Isaac went out to meditate in the field at the eventide: and he lifted up his eyes, and saw, and, behold, the camels were coming. And Rebekah lifted up her eyes, and when she saw Isaac, she lighted off the camel. For she had said unto the servant, What man is this that walketh in the field to meet us? And the servant had said, It is my master: therefore she took a veil, and covered herself (24:63–65).*

Confident of his choice, *the servant told Isaac all things that he had done (24:66),* and Isaac believed—without even seeing the beautiful face behind the veil—that she was the one he too would happily choose as his wife.

And Isaac brought her into his mother Sarah's tent, and took Rebekah, and she became his wife; and he loved her: and Isaac was comforted after his mother's death (24:67).

My reflections on the search for Isaac's bride

After our class finished reading Genesis 24, we all felt, "How could he do anything but *want* to marry such a girl?" It surprised me that in a book of covenants, kings, and nations forming, Moses would give such a lengthy description of a marriage choice. But then I realized, marriage is *also* a covenant, an agreement between two people and ideally, I suppose, between two families. I hope they will "live happily ever after," but even if they don't, I can't imagine anything that could bring this marriage covenant to an end.

Checking for understanding

1. Based on the plan for Abraham's life, why was it necessary for Isaac to marry?

2. Explain why it was so important that Isaac's wife be from the family in the north rather than from the neighborhood in which he lived.

3. What made Abraham confident that the servant would find a good wife for Isaac?

4. Explain the wisdom of the servant's prayer—his prayer that the right girl would volunteer to water the camels.

5. Find out the cost of gold today and estimate the value of the jewelry that the servant gave to Rebekah after she had watered his camels.

6. Explain how the family's consent to her marriage increased Rebekah's benefits and her future happiness.

7. Based on this chapter, in your own words list each quality that Moses would have wanted each Israelite family to set for the marriages of their children, qualities that would guide them in any culture in which they lived.

8. How was the servant's standards for Isaac's bride either the same or different from the standards you gave before this study began?

The Sons of Isaac Compete

Genesis 25:19–34; 26:34–35; 27:1–40

My first thoughts about inheritance

OUR TEACHER ASKED US a question: "Suppose your aunt and uncle have four sons who will inherit everything they own—it's in their will. In your opinion, how should the inheritance be divided?"

We all agreed it should be divided equally, so when the teacher told us how it would have been divided in Bible days, we were quite surprised. That is our study for today.

My notes from the teacher's lesson

In Bible days, firstborn sons usually had a special position in the family. When the father died, the firstborn son would receive special rights. His inheritance would be twice as much as each of the other brothers would receive, and he would *rule,* or have authority, over the family. All of those rights were included in what was called the *birthright.* (Girls in a family would have no inheritance unless the parents had no sons. If the parents did have sons, the girls would receive gifts, but not inheritance. *Wealth* for them usually had to come through their husbands.)

Our study for today is a *brother* story—an older brother in line for the birthright with its wealth, authority, and privileges, and the younger brother who wanted it.

Rebekah's glimpse into the future

In the last study, Isaac had just married and had immediately fallen in love with his beautiful wife, Rebekah. In today's study twenty years had passed, and though life was blissful for the two, they had one problem. Rebekah, just like Sarah earlier, had not yet conceived a child.

And Isaac entreated [pleaded with] *the* Lord *for his wife, because she was barren: and the* Lord *was entreated of him, and Rebekah his wife conceived (25:21).* As the pregnancy continued, however, Rebekah was troubled. Something was wrong—so wrong that *she went to enquire of the* Lord. *And the children struggled together within her; and she said, If it be so, why am I thus (25:22)* In other words, "What does this mean? Why is this happening to me?" The Lord gave her an answer: *And the* Lord *said unto her,*

> *Two nations are in thy womb,*
>
> *and two manner of people shall be separated from thy bowels;*
>
> *and the one people shall be stronger than the other people*
>
> *and the elder shall serve the younger (25:23).*

With those words she learned she was carrying two very different babies—babies struggling together in her womb. Those words also gave her a glimpse into their futures. Each would father a separate nation; the younger would be stronger and would rule over his brother. From this, Rebekah concluded that her younger son, contrary to custom, would have the birthright—which included all the great promises made to Abraham.

And when her days to be delivered were fulfilled, behold, there were twins in her womb. And the first came out red, all over like a hairy garment; and they called his name Esau. And after that came his brother out, and his hand took hold on Esau's heel [perhaps as if he were trying to get out first and obtain firstborn rights]; *and his name was called Jacob.* Jacob's name means, *he grasps the heel* or as some interpret, *he cheats*—quite a foreshadowing of Jacob's character. *And Isaac was threescore* [sixty] *years old when she bare them (25:24–26).*

The choices made by Esau and Jacob

And the boys grew: and Esau was a cunning [skillful] *hunter, a man of the field; and Jacob was a plain* [mild or civilized] *man, dwelling in tents (25:27).*

So far, Moses has written a beautiful picture of the marriage of Isaac and Rebekah. At this point, however, he reveals something else—a serious mistake they were making in rearing their sons—a foreshadowing of family division.

And Isaac loved Esau, because he did eat of his venison [the deer meat from his hunting]: *but Rebekah loved Jacob (25:28).* From events about to take place, it is clear that the brothers knew what was in the birthright their father would give. The boys also knew that unless for some reason their father chose differently, the birthright would go to Esau and not to Jacob, who evidently desperately wanted to have it.

Believing his father would certainly give the birthright to Esau, apparently Jacob began watching for a way to convince Esau to let him have it. Would Esau be willing to make a sale? How much would he want for a trade? One day an opportunity arose for Jacob to find out what the birthright meant to Esau.

And Jacob sod pottage [boiled stew]: *and Esau came from the field, and he was faint: and Esau said to Jacob, Feed me, I pray thee, with that same red pottage; for I am faint: therefore was his name called Edom* [which means red] *(25:29–30).*

And Jacob said, Sell me this day thy birthright. And Esau said, Behold, I am at the point to die: and what profit shall this birthright do to me?(25:31–32). Our class questioned whether Esau was really dying. It seemed he had returned to the home site on his feet, not crawling. The possibility of death, we all thought, might not have been Esau's real issue.

And Jacob said, Swear to me this day; and he sware unto him: and he sold his birthright unto Jacob. Then Jacob gave Esau bread and pottage [stew] *of lentils; and he did eat and drink, and rose up, and went his way: thus Esau despised his birthright (25:33–34).* That—according to this account—was Esau's real reason for the sale, or trade of the birthright. He despised it. Just like that—with merely the cost of a bowl of stew—Jacob had the promise of the birthright.

Perhaps the birthright carried too many responsibilities for Esau's liking or too much that had to do with the LORD God of his father—or perhaps the birthright promises were too far into the future, such as bringing blessings to the world (12:3b). Clearly, the birthright had less value to Esau than bread and a bowl of stew. (I thought Esau's contempt of it would probably convince a man like Jacob that he was right to take advantage of Esau's pathetic ambitions.)

Then, to make matters worse, Esau made two more disappointing choices. *And Esau was forty years old when he took to wife Judith the daughter of Beeri the Hittite, and Bashemath the daughter of Elon the Hittite.* Both girls were from the Canaanite culture, and neither of them worshipers of the LORD God. [They] *were a grief of mind unto Isaac and to Rebekah (26:34–35).* Esau's indifference toward Abraham's marriage standard (Genesis 24) must have given even more proof to Jacob's conscience that exploiting Esau was the right thing to do.

Isaac's blessing

Jacob wanted even more from his father. In the book of Genesis, fathers gave not only a birthright, but also blessings that shaped the futures of the sons. Once given, the blessings could not be taken back.

Years passed. Believing he might be close to death, Isaac called for Esau and gave him some instructions—instruction Rebekah, too, heard. *Now therefore . . . take me some venison; and make me savory meat, such as I love, and bring it to me, that I may eat; that my soul may bless thee before I die (27:3–4).* She was horrified. Rebekah was sure that Isaac would include in the blessings the birthright privileges—sure that Isaac would try to reverse the words of the prophecy made before the boys were born.

Since Isaac clearly planned to give the blessing to Esau, some in our class wondered whether he knew about the sale of the birthright, but most of us were sure he did. Would he not have known why people called Esau *Edom,* the name he received for exchanging stew for the birthright? Apparently, if Isaac knew about the sale, he did not consider it legitimate, had completely excused Esau's actions, and was not about to consider giving either the birthright or the blessing to Jacob.

Jacob's theft

And Rebekah spake unto Jacob her son, saying, Behold, I heard thy father speak unto Esau thy brother, saying, Bring me venison, and make me savory meat, that I may eat, and bless thee before the LORD before my death (27:6–7).

We all noted again that even though Isaac and Rebekah were a perfect match, they were not perfect people. Rebekah went on speaking to her favorite son Jacob.

Now therefore, my son, obey my voice . . . . Go now to the flock, and fetch me from thence two good kids of the goats; and I will make them savory meat for thy father, such as he loveth: and thou shalt bring it to thy father, that he may eat, and that he may bless thee before his death (27:8–10).

And Jacob said to Rebekah his mother, Behold, Esau my brother is a hairy man, and I am a smooth man: my father peradventure will feel me, and I shall seem to him as a deceiver; and I shall bring a curse upon me, and not a blessing (27:11–12).

And his mother said unto him, Upon me be thy curse, my son: only obey my voice, and go fetch me them. And he went, and fetched, and brought them to his mother: and his mother made savory meat, such as his father loved (27:13–14).

And Rebekah took goodly raiment [clothing] *of her eldest son Esau, which were with her in the house, and put them upon Jacob her younger son: And she put the skins of the kids of the goats upon his hands, and upon the smooth of his neck (27:15–16).*

A student who had goats remarked that goat hair feels like horse hair. The teacher said that was true with most of our goats, but Angora goats (raised in Turkey close to Genesis Bible lands) have soft, curly hair, so soft it is woven into a choice fabric called mohair.

The lies

And she gave the savory meat and the bread . . . into the hand of her son Jacob. And he came unto his father, and said, My father: and he said, Here am I; who art thou, my son?(27:17–18).

And Jacob said unto his father, I am Esau thy firstborn; I have done according as thou badest [told] *me: arise, I pray thee, sit and eat of my venison, that thy soul may bless me. And Isaac said unto his son, How is it that thou hast found it so quickly, my son? And he said, Because the LORD thy God brought it to me (27:19–20).* Not only was Jacob lying, he was lying about the LORD.

And Isaac said unto Jacob, Come near, I pray thee, that I may feel thee, my son, whether thou be my very son Esau or not. And Jacob went near unto Isaac his father; and he felt him, and said, The voice is Jacob's voice, but the hands are the hands of Esau (27:21–22).

Isaac kept questioning: *And he said, Art thou my very son Esau? And he said, I am. And he said, Bring it near to me, and I will eat of my son's venison, that my soul may bless thee. And he brought it near to him, and he did eat: and he brought him wine and he drank (27:24–25).*

Jacob receives the blessing

And his father Isaac said unto him, Come near now, and kiss me, my son. And he came near, and kissed him: and he smelled the smell of his raiment, and blessed him, and said (27:26–27a),

> *See, the smell of my son*
>
> *is as the smell of a field*
>
> *which the LORD hath blessed:*
>
> *therefore God give thee of the dew of heaven,*
>
> *and the fatness of the earth,*
>
> *and plenty of corn and wine:*
>
> *let people serve thee,*
>
> *and nations bow down to thee:*
>
> *be lord over thy brethren,*
>
> *and let thy mother's sons bow down to thee:*
>
> *cursed be every one that curseth thee,*
>
> *and blessed be he that blesseth thee (27:27b–29).*

Rebekah then knew for certain that her husband was ignoring the prophecy that said the birthright was to go to the younger son, Jacob. Isaac would have given not only the blessing to Esau, but also the birthright, for Isaac's blessing just pronounced on Jacob included nations bowing down to him and authority over the family—all parts of the birthright.

Esau's hopeless regrets

And it came to pass, as soon as Isaac had made an end of blessing Jacob, and Jacob was yet scarce gone out from the presence of Isaac his father, that Esau his brother came in from his hunting. And he also had made savory meat, and brought it unto his father, and said unto his father, Let my father arise, and eat of his son's venison, that thy soul may bless me (27:30–31).

And Isaac his father said unto him, Who art thou? And he said, I am thy son, thy firstborn Esau. And Isaac trembled very exceedingly, and said, Who? where is he that hath taken venison, and brought it me, and I have eaten of all before thou camest, and have blessed him? yea, and he shall be blessed (27:32–33).

And when Esau heard the words of his father, he cried with a great and exceeding bitter cry, and said unto his father, Bless me, even me also, O my father. And he [Isaac] *said, Thy brother came with subtilty* [deceit] *and hath taken away thy blessing* (27:34–35).

And he [Esau] *said, Is not he rightly named Jacob? for he hath supplanted me these two times: he took away my birthright; and, behold, now he hath taken away my blessing. And he said, Hast thou not reserved a blessing for me?* (27:36).

And Isaac answered . . . I have made him thy lord . . . . And Esau said unto his father, Hast thou but one blessing, my father? bless me, even me also, O my father. And Esau lifted up his voice, and wept (27:37–38), but in spite of Esau's tears and sorrow, Isaac could do nothing to give the blessing to his firstborn son.

Isaac had planned to pour all his favor on Esau, apparently intending to leave nothing for Jacob. Instead, he had left Esau with nothing except a sad glimpse into the future of his descendants (27:39–40).

Jacob's great need

Jacob was now in line to receive the promises to Abraham. He would have the promised nation, the land of Canaan, and descendants who were to bring blessing to the world. Even with all those blessings he still had a great need. He needed to be changed—humbled and stripped of his cold-hearted greed and dishonesty. That painful process would follow Jacob throughout the rest of Genesis.

My reflections on Jacob and Esau

The student who seems to know a lot about the Bible asked if she could read some verses from the New Testament that talk about Esau. Hebrews 12:15–17 says, *Looking diligently lest . . . there be any . . . person, as Esau, who for one morsel of meat sold his birthright. For ye know how that afterward, when he would have inherited* [wished to inherit], *the blessing he was rejected: for he found no place of repentance* [no possibility of his father's changing his mind], *though he* [Esau] *sought it carefully with tears.* She thought, and we all agreed with her, that Esau is a picture of people who want what they want when they want it, even if they are giving up future benefits to have that immediate, temporary satisfaction.

Checking for understanding

1. Explain why Rebekah suffered during her pregnancy.

2. What benefits would come to the son who received Isaac's birthright?

3. How was Jacob's name a foreshadowing of his character?

4. In two separate columns, contrast Esau and Jacob in their appearance, interests, relation to parents, and characters.

5. Of the four members in Isaac's family, which were to blame for their divisions and unhappiness?

6. Esau traded the birthright for something he convinced himself he had to have at once, even at the cost of the birthright. Write a modern day example of trading away the future for present, immediate desires.

Development of Jacob's Family

Genesis 27:41—30:24

My first thoughts

A BIBLE VERSE WAS on the board this morning—Galatians 6:7b: *"Whatsoever a man soweth, that shall he also reap."* It was pretty obvious what it meant: If you plant strawberries, you will, if you tend them, reap strawberries, not poison ivy. I didn't know what it had to do with Genesis until I understood that the verse was a metaphor for, *What you do comes back to you.* I suppose it means both good and bad.

We were to relate that verse, Galatians 6:7b, to Isaac's sons. Everyone could see how it related to Esau, shedding bitter tears over the lost blessings. For Jacob it was different. He had underhandedly and happily gotten everything he wanted, with no problems except for an angry brother. Perhaps Jacob was the exception to the rule that you reap what you sow.

My notes on the teacher's lesson

The teacher told us that many more blessings were coming to Jacob. Wouldn't that be like giving a selfish, deceitful child everything he wanted? Then again, since I remember that he needed to be made into a new person, I wonder if those blessings might be the very tools to change him.

More blessings in Jacob's life

Escape from Esau

Everything was going along perfectly for Jacob except for a little problem with Esau. *And Esau hated Jacob . . . and Esau said in his heart, The days of mourning for my father are at hand* [he is about to die]; *then will I slay* [kill] *my brother Jacob (27:41).* Hearing Esau's plans, Rebekah ordered Jacob to flee to her brother Laban's home up in Haran and stay there *a few days* until Esau cooled off *(27:44).*

Before Rebekah could send Jacob away though, she must make Isaac think it was all his own idea. So *Rebekah said to Isaac, I am weary of my life because of* [Esau's wives]: *if Jacob take a wife . . . such as these . . . what good shall my life do me? (27:46).*

And Isaac [who could not bear the thought of such a marriage] *called Jacob, and blessed him . . . and said unto him, Thou shalt not take a wife of the daughters of Canaan. Arise, go to Padan-aram . . . and take thee a wife from . . . the daughters of Laban thy mother's brother (28:1-2).*

More blessings from Jacob's father

Before Jacob left home, his father continued the blessings. *And God Almighty bless thee, and make thee fruitful, and multiply thee . . . and give thee the blessing of Abraham, to thee, and to thy seed with thee; that thou mayest inherit the land* [of Canaan] *. . . which God gave unto Abraham (28:3-4).*

His father gave no rebuke, just kindness, goodness, and assurance that the promises to Abraham were his. All was going very, very well for Jacob.

Blessings from God

Jacob began the long journey from Beersheba in southern Canaan to Haran five hundred miles north. *And he lighted upon* [came to] *a certain place, and tarried there all night, because the sun was set; and he took of the stones of that place, and put them for his pillows, and lay down in that place to sleep (28:11).*

And he dreamed, and behold a ladder set up on the earth, and the top of it reached to heaven: and behold the angels of God ascending and descending on it. And, behold, the LORD stood above it, and said, I am the LORD God of Abraham thy father, and the God of Isaac (28:12-13a).

Our teacher asked us, "If you were God, and you had Jacob lying at the bottom of that ladder, what would you do?" One student answered, "I would drop a rock on him." It seemed only right that Jacob would get justice—that he would receive the justice he deserved. What Moses wrote surprised us.

The LORD said to Jacob, *the land whereon thou liest, to thee will I give it, and to thy seed; and thy seed shall be as* [many as] *the dust of the earth, . . . and in thee and in thy seed shall all the families of the earth be blessed (28:13b–14).*

Those were the same promises made to Abraham and Isaac! How could they go to heartless Jacob? Yet even more promises came.

And, behold, I am with thee, and will keep thee in all places whither [where] *thou goest, and will bring thee again into this land; for I will not leave thee, until I have done that which I have spoken to thee of (28:15).*

And Jacob awaked out of his sleep, and he said, Surely the LORD is in this place; and I knew it not. And he was afraid, and said, How dreadful is this place! this is none other but the house of God, and this is the gate of heaven. . . . And he called the name of that place Bethel (28:16–17, 19a).

Blessings in Laban's home

In the strength of those undeserved promises and perhaps with the belief that he was a pretty good man, Jacob went on his way to his uncle's home. What a welcome! There were kisses, embraces, joyful tears, and more kisses and hugs. No one in that home to fear!

When, after a month, it was obvious to Laban that Jacob was staying, *Laban said unto Jacob, Because thou art my brother* [relative], *shouldest thou therefore serve me for nought* [nothing]? *tell me, what shall thy wages be? (29:15).* Jacob knew exactly what he wanted—and he wanted it so much he was willing to work seven years to get it.

Laban had two daughters: the name of the elder was Leah, and the name of the younger was Rachel. Leah was tender eyed [her eyes were weak]; *but Rachel was beautiful and well favored. And Jacob loved Rachel; and said, I will serve thee seven years for Rachel thy younger daughter. And Laban said, It is better that I give her to thee, than that I should give her to another man: abide with me (29:16–19).*

And Jacob served seven years for Rachel; and they seemed unto him but a few days, for the love he had to her. Life was a joy! And [at the end of the seven years] *Jacob said unto Laban, Give me my wife, for my days are fulfilled, that I may go in unto her (29:20–21).* Would the joys of love and marriage make him into a new man?

The unexpected, but necessary "reaping-blessings"

Reaping-blessings are benefits that teach us what we may have ignored, such as the differences between right and wrong, wisdom and foolishness, truth and falsehood, kindness and cruelty. Jacob had ignored these. He was due some of those "reaping-blessings."

The blessing of reaping in marriage

And Laban gathered together all the men of the place, and made a feast. And it came to pass in the evening, that he took Leah his [older] *daughter, and brought her to* [Jacob]; *and he went in unto her (29:23).* Even with a veil over her face and the marriage chamber no doubt a beautifully decorated, dark tent, none of us could understand how Jacob had not known it was Leah! Had he and the men at Laban's feast had too much wine?

And it came to pass, that in the morning [to Jacob's heartbreaking shock], *behold, it was Leah* [whom he had taken as a wife]: *and he said to Laban, What is this thou hast done unto me? did not I serve with thee for Rachel? wherefore then hast thou beguiled* [deceived] *me? And Laban said, It must not be so done in our country, to give the younger before the firstborn. Fulfill her week, and we will give thee this* [Rachel] *also for the service which thou shalt serve with me yet seven other* [more] *years (29:25–27).*

If Jacob would stay and work another seven years he could have Rachel, too. In a sham show of generosity, Laban said he could even marry Rachel in one more week, as long as he stayed and worked, of course, and continued being a husband to Leah.

For the first time, Jacob knew how it felt to be deceived and defrauded, knew in the most painful way imaginable. He accepted the offer; he had no other choice.

[One week later] *he went in also unto Rachel, and he loved also Rachel more than Leah, and served with him yet seven other years (29:30).*

The blessing of reaping in his family

Leah's first children

And when the LORD saw that Leah was hated, he opened her womb [and let her conceive]: *but Rachel was barren (29:31).*

And Leah conceived, and bare a son, and she called his name Reuben: for she said, Surely the LORD hath looked upon my affliction; now therefore my husband will love me. And she conceived again, and bare a son; and said, Because the LORD hath heard I was hated, he hath therefore given me this son also: and she called his name Simeon. And she conceived again, and bare a son; and said, Now this time will my husband be joined unto me, because I have born him three sons: therefore was his name called Levi. (29:32–34).

Pity Leah, longing to be loved—or at least not hated—hoping and praying Jacob would have some attachment to her, that she would not live in a world of contempt and scorn. *And she conceived again, and bare a son: and she said, Now will I praise the LORD: therefore she called his name Judah; and left bearing (29:35).*

Rachel's attempt to have children by Bilhah

And when Rachel saw that she bare Jacob no children, Rachel envied her sister; and said unto Jacob, Give me children, or else I die. And Jacob's anger was kindled against Rachel: and he said, Am I in God's stead, who hath withheld from thee the fruit of the womb? (30:1–2).

And she said, Behold my maid Bilhah, go in unto her [as Abraham did with Hagar] . . . *that I may also have children by her . . . . And Bilhah . . . bare Jacob a son. And Rachel said, God hath . . . given me a son: therefore called she his name Dan (30:3–6). And . . . Bilhah . . . bore Jacob a second son. And Rachel . . . called his name Naphtali (30:3–8).*

Leah's sons by Zilpah

When Leah saw that she had left bearing [was no longer conceiving], *she took Zilpah her maid, and gave her Jacob to wife. And Zilpah . . . bare Jacob a son. And* [Leah] *called his name Gad. And Zilpah . . . bare Jacob a second son. And Leah . . . called his name Asher (30:9–13).*

Everyone in our class agreed that this story beat every soap opera any of us had ever seen!

More children

And Reuben [Leah's firstborn] *. . . found mandrakes in the field, and brought them unto his mother Leah. Then Rachel said to Leah, Give me, I pray thee, of thy son's mandrakes (30:14).* Evidently women thought if they had the mandrake plant, they could conceive children. *And* [Leah] *said unto her, Is it a small matter that thou hast taken my husband? and wouldest thou take away my son's mandrakes also? And Rachel said, Therefore he shall lie with thee tonight for thy son's mandrakes (30:15).*

Obviously, since Leah was no longer getting pregnant, Jacob had not continued to sleep with her, but Rachel would let Leah have him that night in exchange for the mandrakes. Elated with the chance to have Jacob that night, Leah began praying—praying that God would let her conceive a child.

And Jacob came out of the field . . . and Leah went out to meet him, and said, Thou must come in unto me; for surely I have hired thee with my son's mandrakes. And he lay with her that night. And God hearkened [listened] *unto Leah, and she conceived, and bare Jacob the fifth son. And Leah . . . called his name Issachar (30:16–18).*

And Leah . . . bare Jacob the sixth son. And Leah . . . called his name Zebulun. And afterwards she bare a daughter, and called her name Dinah (30:19–21).

Rachel's sons

For the first years of marriage, Rachel might have gloried in her husband's great love just for her, perhaps never connecting her hatred toward Leah with her barren womb (Genesis 29:31). As time passed, though, and grief over her childlessness replaced her gloating, *God remembered Rachel . . . and opened her womb. And she . . . bare a son, . . . and she called his name Joseph . . . (30:24).* Years later, Rachel would have one more child, Benjamin (Jacob's last), giving him a total of twelve sons.

The future of Jacob and his twelve sons

The distant future

Grandfather Abraham's two sons, Isaac and Ishmael, would produce two separate nations. Father Isaac's two sons, Jacob and Esau, would also produce two separate nations. Jacob's sons, however, would not become separate nations. All of Jacob's young sons would become the fathers of tribes, or families, all making up one nation—the large nation Moses would bring out of Egypt 400 years in the future.

The immediate future

Jacob, the father of those twelve sons (one of them to be born later) wanted to return home. He had completed the fourteen years of "paying" Laban for his daughters, Rachel and Leah, but after he talked with his uncle, Jacob seemed to realize he wasn't ready. He needed more time in Haran.

My reflections on Jacob's reaping

I thought about Jacob's needing to stay longer in Haran. I wondered why until I remembered that his wages for the fourteen years had been just two wives—that was all. Everything except his wives belonged to his uncle. Jacob needed more time in Haran so he could support his family on his journey home.

I also suspected there were more reasons—that there were lessons Jacob had not yet learned. I am beginning to understand the idea that unseen blessings can be hidden within sufferings, blessings that might change Jacob as he saw for himself what it is like to be the victim of another.

Checking for understanding

1. Why did Jacob have to leave home?

2. List three surprising promises God made to Jacob at the site of the ladder to heaven (28:13–15).

3. Jacob had an unpleasant surprise the morning after his wedding. How was that surprise similar to the surprise he gave to Isaac and Esau seven years earlier? (See Genesis 27).

4. Name Leah's first four sons.

5. What did Leah hope the births of her sons would do for her relationship with Jacob?

6. Explain why both Rachel and Leah gave their maids as wives to Jacob.

7. Name Bilhah's two sons.

8. Name Zilpah's two sons.

9. Name Leah's last three children.

10. Name Rachel's two sons.

11. How many tribes would make up Jacob's nation?

12. What were Jacob's "reaping blessings" in his service to his uncle?

Jacob Faces Enemies

Genesis 30:25—33:20

My first thoughts

IN OUR READING OF Genesis, I've been struck with how much those people
are like lots of people in my town—even in my school. The biblical people
sound like characters in the grocery store magazine racks—same loves and
hates, same feelings and feuds, and same successes and scandals. When one
of the boys in the back of the room said he felt as if he himself were Jacob,
the teacher said most of us, before we finish studying Jacob's life, will probably get at least a glimpse of ourselves also.

My notes on the teacher's lesson

Review of Jacob's miseries

Two impossibilities kept Jacob from returning to his father's home in Canaan. The first was his brother Esau, who might meet him with vengeance
and murder. The second was Laban whose deceptions had trapped Jacob
into continuous slave-type obligations.

Uncle Laban (who was also Jacob's father-in-law) had an enviable life.
His two daughters were married, maybe not happily, but at least married.
He had eleven healthy grandsons and a granddaughter, and best of all and
thanks to Jacob his finances had increased from almost nothing to great
wealth (30:30).

Nephew Jacob, however, had a depressing life. We were sure he knew he was reaping the same pain he had poured out upon his father and brother. He knew his own wrongdoings had put him under Laban's control and kept him in the north. Yet he also knew that the LORD God, the God of his father, Isaac, and of his grandfather, Abraham, had promised to bless him and bring him back to his father's home. He hung on to that hope.

Freedom from Laban

New wages for Jacob

Jacob finally completed the fourteen-year price for his wives and wanted to leave Laban, but he realized he could not. He had no way of knowing how Esau felt, for his mother (if she were still living) had not sent for him. Additionally, he had no way to support his large family. He would be going back with nothing but wives and children—the payment for his years of service.

If Jacob chose to leave, would his uncle outfit him with all he would need for that journey? Never! Laban wanted Jacob to stay, not for love of his nephew, but for love of himself, admitting surprisingly, *I have learned by experience that the LORD hath blessed me for thy sake* [or because of you] (*30:27b*). So, just as fourteen years earlier Laban had asked Jacob to set his own wages, Laban again asked him to set them, knowing, of course, he would twist every term of the agreement to keep Jacob trapped under his thumb.

And he said, What shall I give thee? And Jacob said, Thou shalt not give me any thing: if thou wilt do this thing for me, I will again feed and keep thy flock. I will pass through all thy flock to day, removing from thence all the speckled and spotted cattle, and all the brown cattle among the sheep, and the spotted and speckled among the goats: and of such shall be my hire (*30:31–32*).

Only the animals with those rare colorings would be Jacob's. Laban immediately separated the animals, put Jacob's into the hands of his sons, and had them move Jacob's few animals three days, journey away. Apparently Laban was making sure that Jacob would not neglect Laban's flocks in favor of his own.

What a bargain! With only a few animals going to Jacob, Laban foresaw riches for himself and poor Jacob strapped to him for life. But the bargain did not work out that way, the animals did not bear their young in the way he had expected—in fact, they did just the opposite. Jacob's flocks and herds kept on increasing until he *had much cattle, and maidservants, and menservants, and camels, and asses (30:43)* even as Laban's were decreasing. So Laban decided to change Jacob's wages, but it didn't help at all. For six years he kept changing them, but the changes always turned out to enrich Jacob (31:7–9). Laban was powerless to stop the blessings that kept pouring over his nephew.

Protection from Laban

As Jacob's wealth increased, he saw a change in his uncle's family. Laban's sons were wrongly saying, *Jacob hath taken away all that was our father's . . . (31:1).*

How would Jacob know when to leave this conniving uncle and return home? Though he had not heard from his mother, he didn't need to. One night a dream came and in the dream a message: *Now arise, get thee out from this land, and return unto the land of thy kindred* [family] *(31:11–13).* At last it was time!

Fearing what Laban might do and knowing he might strip him of all he had, even his family, Jacob waited until Laban was away. *Then Jacob rose and set his sons and his wives on camels. And he carried away all his cattle, and all his goods which he had gotten . . . for to go to Isaac his father in the land of Canaan. And Jacob stole away unawares to Laban . . . in that he told him not that he fled (31:17–18, 20).*

When Laban learned his nephew Jacob had secretly left, he rounded up his men and chased after him either hoping to bring him back, or at the least, to keep Jacob's possessions and send him away empty handed; but just as years earlier Jacob's father, Isaac, had not been able to outwit the plans of the LORD (27:1–40), neither could Laban. The night before he caught up with Jacob, the LORD spoke to Laban and frightened him into leaving Jacob alone. God forbade him to say one threatening word to his fleeing nephew (31:22–24, 29).

Would Laban, in that last meeting with Jacob and his daughters, humble himself and face the truth? No, it was too hard. He painted himself pure as an angel from heaven, innocent and deeply hurt by his son-in-law. They separated, never to see each other again, and Jacob, after twenty years, was at last free from Laban's power. The other fear, however, still lay ahead.

Facing Esau

Preparing to meet Esau

And Jacob sent messengers before him to Esau his brother unto the land of Seir, the country of Edom. And he commanded them, saying, Thus shall ye speak unto my lord Esau; Thy servant Jacob saith thus, I have sojourned with Laban, and stayed there until now: and I have oxen, and asses, flocks, and menservants, and womenservants: and I have sent to tell my lord, that I may find grace in thy sight (32:3–5).

And the messengers returned to Jacob, saying, We came to thy brother Esau, and also he cometh to meet thee, and four hundred men with him. Then Jacob was greatly afraid and distressed (32:6–7a), certain they were not coming to celebrate his return. *And Jacob* [prayed and] *said, O God . . . the* LORD, *which saidst unto me, Return unto thy country . . . and I will deal well with thee: I am not worthy of the least of all the mercies . . . . Deliver me, I pray thee, from the hand of my brother . . . for I fear him, lest he will come and smite me, and the mother with the children (32:9–11).*

Shortly, an idea came. How could Jacob expect restoration when he had expressed no repentance? Though Jacob knew he could restore neither the birthright nor the blessing, he realized there was something he *could* do. He could try to recompense his brother—to make amends for his cold-hearted, selfish injustices. He could pour blessings on his brother.

[So he sent] *a present for Esau; two hundred she goats, and twenty he goats, two hundred ewes* [female sheep], *and twenty rams, thirty milch* [milking] *camels with their colts, forty kine* [cows], *and ten bulls, twenty she asses, and ten foals. And he delivered them into the hand of his servants, every drove by themselves; and said unto his servants, Pass over before me, and put a space betwixt* [between] *drove and drove (32:13b–16).*

And he commanded the foremost [servant], *saying, When Esau my brother meeteth thee, and asketh thee, saying, Whose art thou? and whither goest thou? and whose are these before thee? Then thou shalt say, They be thy servant Jacob's; it is a present sent unto my lord Esau: and, behold, also he is behind us (32:17–18).*

Whoever had the birthright was lord and master, but Jacob was reversing it, calling Esau his lord and master and himself the servant. That change in Jacob, that unexpected humility and meekness, would astonish Esau.

Jacob a new man

After Jacob had done all that he could to prepare, a stranger suddenly appeared, and *Jacob was left alone; and there wrestled a man with him until the breaking of the day (32:24).* You would think Jacob had enough troubles without this! According to some verses in a later book in the Bible, Hosea 12:2–4, Jacob, as he was wrestling with the stranger, was sobbing and praying.

And when he [the mysterious man] *saw that he prevailed not against him* [Jacob], *he touched the hollow of his thigh; and the hollow of Jacob's thigh was* [put] *out of joint, as he wrestled with him. And* [the man] *said, Let me go, for the day breaketh. And he* [Jacob] *said, I will not let thee go, except thou bless me. So he* [the man] *said unto him, What is thy name? And he said, Jacob (32:25–27).*

By speaking his own name Jacob, meaning a person who shamelessly takes the rights of another, the stranger was forcing Jacob to admit, "I am a liar and a cheater; I am unworthy of blessing." But there was more to the picture of Jacob. The years of reaping—of seeing what it was like to be on the other side of another supplanter—had been making Jacob into a new man, and the new Jacob needed a new name.

[And the stranger] *said, Thy name shall be called no more Jacob, but Israel* [meaning *he struggles or strives*]: *for as a prince hast thou power with God and with men, and hast prevailed* [triumphed] *(32:28).* After the stranger blessed him and left, Jacob said of him, . . . *I have seen God face to face, and my life is preserved (32:30).*

A new relationship with Esau

And Jacob lifted up his eyes, and looked, and, behold, Esau came, and with him four hundred men (33:1b).

When Esau looked toward Jacob, what was he seeing? He was seeing his brother—weaponless, no protection, hair and clothing in shambles, face dirty and tear-streaked limping alone toward him, bowing again and again. And Jacob *bowed himself to the ground seven times, until he came near to his brother (33:3).*

And Esau ran to meet him, and embraced him, and fell on his neck, and kissed him: and they wept (33:4). The broken relationship was restored.

My reflections on Jacob's reaping

I was happy with that story. It's good to hear accounts where sufferings—
the kind a person deserves—can have good endings.

Checking for understanding

1. How did Laban reap for his own wrongdoings toward Jacob?

2. Jacob had nothing to make right with his uncle, but much to make right with Esau. Give at least two actions Jacob took to win Esau's forgiveness.

3. Figure out approximately how many animals Jacob gave to Esau.

4. Tell why Jacob's actions toward Esau were acts of justice.

5. What did Jacob's new name, Israel, reveal about him?

6. According to Genesis 32:30, with whom did Jacob say he had wrestled?

7. Since Esau possibly brought the four hundred men planning a battle of revenge, what was it that changed his mind so that he would embrace and kiss his brother who had so wronged him?

8. Even though there was no battle, why was it beneficial for Esau to have the four hundred men with him? In your answer consider Genesis 32:13–18.

9. What made the ending of this story a good one?

From Haran to Canaan: Told from the Viewpoint of Jacob's Young Son, Joseph.

Based on Genesis 31—35

My first thoughts

ONE OF THE PROJECTS offered to our class was to write a summary of the events from Genesis 31 to 35. Several students signed up for that. The girl who had the best summary wrote it as if it were the journal of Jacob's young son, Joseph. She made a copy for each of us. This is what she wrote:

Young Joseph's Journal from Haran to Canaan

Leaving Grandfather Laban

Grandfather Laban was away when we left. He knew nothing about our father's plans—nothing about God's command to return to Canaan. I remember the departure well—the rushing to prepare, the flight, my grandfather's catching up with us, and the long, resentful talking between our father and grandfather.

Both men were worried that the other would make trouble. To make sure neither would do that, they made a covenant, a promise that both would do what was right for the women and the children and neither would make any problems for the other. My father then offered a sacrifice to God and had a meal served that no one seemed to enjoy. Our goodbye kisses in the morning, mixed with warnings by our father and grandfather to stay away and leave each other alone, didn't do a lot for our feelings. I was sad to find out that this was a final goodbye (Genesis 31:1–55).

Facing Uncle Esau

As we continued the journey south, my father sent messengers to tell Uncle Esau that we were coming. When the messengers returned with news that Esau was coming to meet us with 400 men, my father was scared to death. How he prayed! He does a lot of praying now. After that he began barking out orders to the servants, sending drove after drove of animals as presents to Esau—dreading his arrival. I had never seen my father that worried (32:1–21).

The night before Uncle Esau's arrival I didn't see my father at all. I don't know where he was. When he appeared in the morning, he looked as if he had been in a terrible, painful fight for his life. He was walking with a bad limp, his hair and clothing were covered with dust, and you could tell he had been crying (Hosea 12:2–4).

Seeing my uncle and his four hundred men in the distance, my father divided our family into three groups: The maidservants, Bilhah and Zilpah, and their children were in the front; behind them were Leah and her children; and last, in the place of greatest protection, my mother Rachel holding me close (33:1–2).

Even though my father had been terribly frightened last night, he wasn't anymore. Something mysterious had happened; now he was humble, limping toward his advancing brother and bowing repeatedly. When Esau reached him, they hugged and kissed and wept. I wanted to cry too—cry from relief for my father (33:4–11).

Troubles at Shechem

Events since then have been troubling: my brothers are the reasons. From my earliest years, I could tell they were either really out of hand, or they were really in charge. Something is wrong in the family, but my father doesn't pay much attention.

We had camped for a while near the Canaanite town Shechem. I remember when my half-sister Dinah went into Shechem to visit the girls there; she didn't come back that night. A young man, the prince of the town, saw her, fell in love with her, and forced her to sleep with him. My father let my brothers, Simeon and Levi, decide what to do. How he would regret it! They lied to the men of Shechem and made them think the prince could marry Dinah just as long as the men of their town would all be circumcised. Then, when the circumcised males lay on their beds in great pain—unable to move—the two went from house to house with their swords and slaughtered all the males. The rest of my brothers then joined them, plundering the homes, taking property and flocks, and forcing the women and children to come as captives. My father was horrified and furious, but I don't think there were any consequences for what they did, at least not then (34:1–31).

Meeting with God

After that, though, my father did seem more concerned about the family. He said we were going to the place where he had long ago dreamed about a ladder to heaven, the place where God had made great promises to him (28:10–15). First, my father said that any person who had any foreign gods was to bring them to him. He buried them in the earth under a great tree. I know my mother had some that she secretly stole from her father (31:19), and the women taken from Shechem must have had some too. (I took note that not one of those gods made any resistance about being dumped in a hole and buried.) After that, we all bathed and changed our clothes, for we were going to Bethel to meet with our father's God (35:1–15)!

Sorrows in Canaan

I could tell my father was happy at Bethel, for bad as our family was, the LORD God blessed us all. That blessing, though, did not stop my father's entering some of the worst years of his life. We were nearing our grandfather Isaac's dwelling, when, with only a few miles to go, my mother Rachel, the dearest person in my father's life, and in mine too, went into labor. She gave birth to my brother Benjamin and then she died (35:16–20).

Without my mother, I have no one but my father who cares about me. I know my brothers don't. I'm not sure my brothers care about my father either. Reuben, our eldest brother, went to bed with Bilhah, one of my father's wives (35:22).

Since my mother died, I have spent a great deal of time alone with my father, hearing stories almost too good to be true, stories of promises and prophecies made to his grandfather Abraham for our family. One prophecy was both good and bad. The LORD told Abraham that one day our people will leave Canaan, go into a foreign land, and there become slaves. Four hundred years later, after the Canaanites have become hopelessly evil, our descendants will leave the land of slavery, return to Canaan, and purify the land of its wickedness (Genesis 15:13–16). What could ever take us to a foreign land? Could the people of Canaan really become that evil? I think my own brothers are as bad as any of them. I suppose that prophecy is for many more years in the future.

My father doesn't want me to make the mistakes he himself made—not trusting our God, lying to get what he wanted, and being coldhearted toward the family. Unfortunately for me, he is making another mistake, making it clear I am his favorite son, which is not making me popular.

My reflections on the report

In these passages I am seeing the inside of Jacob's sons, and I don't like what I see: they are even worse than Jacob was. If that family truly was blessed as the report said, I'd hate to see what a non-blessed family looked like.

Checking for understanding

1. Jacob's family obviously had problems. If you had lived back then as a counselor guiding families in personal relationships, what two pieces of advice would you give Jacob to help him be a better father?

2. The death of Rachel deeply hurt both Jacob and Joseph. In spite of that, what benefit might have come to Joseph because of her death?

Jacob Crushed by His Sons

Based on Genesis 37

My first thoughts

I FOUND THE TITLE on the board disturbing: "Jacob crushed by his sons." I thought by now he had come to terms with his past and would stop having so many troubles, but the teacher said the lesson on Genesis 37 would present an even more troubling picture. Again, it didn't seem at all like a blessed life.

My notes on the teacher's lesson

Review of Jacob's sons

A family with four different mothers and a father unable to bond with his sons is bound to be dysfunctional, and this family was. In spite of God's promises, Jacob's life back in Canaan was acutely painful. His beloved wife Rachel died giving birth to Benjamin. The ten oldest sons were living like the Canaanites, and the life of the eleventh was in danger.

The development of hatred toward Joseph

Jacob had no idea how the feelings of his other sons were building up against his favorite son Joseph and apparently no idea of his own responsibility for it.

Joseph's reports to his father

These are the generations of Jacob. Joseph, being seventeen years old, was feeding the flock with his brethren; and the lad was with the sons of Bilhah, and with the sons of Zilpah, his father's wives: and Joseph brought unto his father their evil report (37:2). The brothers were furious. Even today some resent Joseph and call him a proud tattletale. They say the words *bad report* in the Hebrew language indicate he was giving the report with a bad attitude. Perhaps he was; perhaps he was immature in how he handled it, but nevertheless, if to spare himself trouble he had said nothing to his father, would he not have shared some part in their guilt? According to the biblical prophet Ezekiel who lived over a thousand years later, Joseph truly would have brought guilt on himself (Ezekiel 3:17–19).

Could it be Joseph was trying to move his seemingly uninvolved father to action—action that perhaps would bring a change to the lives of his brothers? In some ways Joseph was like the many prophets throughout the Bible, people who brought messages calling evildoers to repent, and just like the prophets, Joseph was endangering himself by his words.

Jacob's favoritism

Now Israel [Jacob's new name] *loved Joseph more than all his children, because he was the son of his old age: and he made him a coat of many colors (37:3).* The coat loudly announced that Joseph was his father's favorite and that the others, evidently, did not mean much at all. *And when his brethren saw that their father loved him more than all his brethren, they hated him, and could not speak peaceably unto him (37:4).*

Joseph's dreams

And Joseph dreamed a dream [that he evidently believed was a message from the LORD for himself and his brothers], *and he told it* [to] *his brethren: and they hated him yet the more. And he said unto them, Hear, I pray you, this dream which I have dreamed: For, behold, we were binding sheaves in the field, and, lo, my sheaf arose, and also stood upright; and, behold, your sheaves stood round about, and made obeisance* [bowed] *to my sheaf (37:5–7).* (A sheaf is a bundle of grain stalks bound together.)

And his brethren said to him, Shalt thou indeed reign over us? or shalt thou indeed have dominion [rule] over us? And they hated him yet the more for his dreams, and for his words (37:8). And he dreamed yet another, and told it [to] his brethren, and said, Behold, I have dreamed a dream more [another dream]; and, behold, the sun and the moon and the eleven stars made obeisance to me (37:9).

And he told it to his father, and to his brethren: and his father rebuked him, and said unto him, What is this dream that thou hast dreamed? Shall I and thy mother and thy brethren indeed come to bow down ourselves to thee to the earth? And his brethren envied him; but his father observed the saying (37:10—11).

Jacob had said nothing to Joseph about the first dream. Perhaps he enjoyed picturing the insolent brothers bowing to Joseph, but when the second dream indicated that he too would bow, he didn't seem to like that idea, and he silenced his son with a scolding. Jacob's attitude is surprising because in the past he, too, had had dreams that he believed were telling him what would happen in the future.

In defense of Joseph

Some claim that Joseph, by telling his dreams, was bragging. However, back then dreams were considered to be direct messages from God, so would not a seventeen-year-old boy want to talk with his family about them? Would it be right to hide the dreams just because others might resent them? Perhaps this record of Joseph's faithfulness in telling his dreams gave courage to Israelite prophets centuries later, when they too were rejected for messages they reported to the people.

The plans to be rid of Joseph

Into the pit

And his brethren went to feed their father's flock in Shechem. And Israel [Jacob] said unto Joseph, Do not thy brethren feed the flock in Shechem? come, and I will send thee unto them. And he said to him, Here am I. And he said to him, Go, I pray thee, see whether it be well with thy brethren, and well with the flocks; and bring me word again (37:12—14a). Jacob had good reason to worry about the welfare of his sons. Shechem, the place where they were feeding their flocks, was the place where the brothers had recently lied to the men of the city and then put all of them to death (34:1–31).

And when they [the ten brothers] *saw him* [Joseph] *afar off, even before he came near unto them, they conspired against him to slay him. And they said one to another, Behold, this dreamer cometh. Come now therefore, and let us slay him, and cast him into some pit, and we will say, Some evil beast hath devoured him: and we shall see what will become of his dreams* (37:18–20).

And Reuben heard it, and he delivered him out of their hands; and said, Let us not kill him. And [lacking the strength of character to completely halt their plans as the firstborn should have done], *Reuben said unto them, Shed no blood, but cast him into this pit that is in the wilderness, and lay no hand upon him; that he might rid* [remove] *him out of their hands, to deliver him to his father again* (37:21–22). Reuben planned to return later to the pit and rescue his brother.

And it came to pass, when Joseph was come unto his brethren, that they stripped Joseph out of his coat, his coat of many colors that was on him; And they took him, and cast him into a pit: and the pit was empty, there was no water in it (37:23–24).

Into slavery

And they sat down to eat bread [planning to leave him in the pit to die of exposure and starvation]: *and they lifted up their eyes and looked, and, behold, a company of Ishmaelites came from Gilead with their camels bearing spicery and balm and myrrh, going to carry it down to Egypt.*

And Judah said unto his brethren, What profit is it if we slay our brother, and conceal his blood? Come, and let us sell him to the Ishmaelites, and let not our hand be upon him; for he is our brother and our flesh. And his brethren were content (37:25–27). Whether Judah was feeling a slight sympathy for Joseph or whether he was greedy for money, Judah's action saved their brother's life.

Then there passed by Midianites merchantmen; and they drew and lifted up Joseph out of the pit, and sold Joseph to the Ishmaelites for twenty pieces of silver [the price of a boy slave]: *and they brought Joseph into Egypt* (37:28). Later events reveal that Joseph had pled with his brothers *in the anguish of his soul* not to sell him, but the brothers *would not hear* (42:21). His tears and pleadings could not break through their hatred.

The cover-up

And Reuben [who had not been there when they sold him] *returned unto the pit; and, behold, Joseph was not in the pit; and he rent* [tore a seam in] *his clothes* [a sign of great grief]. *And he returned unto his brethren, and said, The child is not; and I, whither* [where] *shall I go? (37:29–30).*

And they took Joseph's coat, and killed a kid of the goats, and dipped the coat in the blood; and they sent the coat of many colors, and they brought it to their father; and said, This have we found: know now whether it be thy son's coat or no (37:31–32).

Jacob's grief

And he knew [recognized] *it, and said, It is my son's coat; an evil beast hath devoured him; Joseph is without doubt rent* [torn] *in pieces. And Jacob rent his clothes, and* [as an additional sign of his anguish] *put sackcloth upon his loins* [waist], *and mourned for his son many days. And all his sons and all his daughters rose up to comfort him; but he refused to be comforted; and he said, For I will go down into the grave unto my son mourning. Thus his father wept for him (37:33–35).*

No one knew, not even Joseph, that his slavery and suffering in Egypt would be for him far better than a college education—an education exceeding anything he could have received in Canaan.

My reflections on Jacob's rejection of Joseph's dreams

If only Jacob had believed the dreams of the good son, he would not have believed the lies of the evil sons. If he had said to them, "I know Joseph is alive, and I know we will all bow to the ground when we see him," Jacob would then have gained courage and comfort, and his sons would have gained well-deserved nightmares.

Checking for understanding

1. When four of Joseph's brothers were involved in evil doings, Joseph reported it to his father. If you had been Joseph, would you have told your father? Why or why not?

2. Considering the events of Genesis 34, why might Jacob have been worried about his sons shepherding their flocks near Shechem?

3. Except for Reuben, would you think Judah was the best of the brothers or the worst of the brothers? Explain your answer.

4. The brothers used a kid, a baby goat, to deceive their father. Explain the irony of that act (See Genesis 27 if you need help.)

5. Genesis 15 foretold for the family a future life in a foreign land. How might the sale of Joseph be the first step in bringing that prophecy to fulfillment?

Judah's Sowing and Reaping

Based on Genesis 38

My first thoughts

THERE IT WAS ON the board: another story of another son and more sowing and more reaping. It seemed to me that almost everyone in Jacob's family—as the expression goes—*made his bed and had to lie in it*. In other words, they made some choices and had to live with the results. Their beds were usually miserable. This chapter picks up with the life of Judah who recommended, rather than leaving Joseph to die in the pit, selling him into slavery.

My notes on the teacher's lesson

Review of the family crimes

Joseph had known all along that his brothers were evil. He knew about Reuben's adultery with a stepmother; he knew about the horrible massacre of the Shechemites by Simeon and Levi and of his father's anger with them; and he knew about the evils of the handmaids's four sons. He also knew he had heard nothing about any discipline from their father, and as far as the record went, there had been none.

It seemed the brothers had not only gotten away with those wrongdoings, but had also, united by hatred and jealousy, gotten rid of Joseph with no witness against them and no consequences. Apparently life was moving along pleasantly, at least for most of them. Judah seemed to be having a hard time. Perhaps they all were.

Judah's new life

As Jacob sat clothed in sackcloth, weeping, grief-stricken, refusing to be comforted, the happiness the brothers probably hoped for from the removal of their father's pet never came. Perhaps that was why Judah moved away from the family.

And it came to pass at that time, that Judah went down from his brethren, and turned in to a certain Adullamite [an inhabitant of the Canaanite city, Adullam] *whose name was Hirah. And Judah saw there a daughter of a certain Canaanite, whose name was Shuah; and* [indifferent to what he knew of Canaanite beliefs, he married her]. *And she conceived, and bare a son; and he called his name Er. And she conceived again, and bare a son; and she called his name Onan. And she yet again conceived, and bare a son; and called his name Shelah (38:1–5a).*

So even though Judah had left his father's family, he had a new one—his own. In his new life and new surroundings, he was with people who probably knew nothing of his deeds, little of his background, and little about his brothers. Even while his father's beloved son, Joseph, labored as a slave, Judah was raising his own beloved sons, apparently unaware that they were absorbing Canaanite values and behaviors so contrary to the values of his "fathers," Abraham, Isaac, and Jacob.

The lives of Judah's first two sons

Following the custom of those days, when Er was at the age to marry, *Judah took a wife for Er his firstborn, and her name was Tamar (38:6).* The joy of adding Tamar to the family and the happy hopes of an heir for Er did not last long though, for *Er, Judah's firstborn, was wicked in the sight of the LORD, and the LORD slew* [killed] *him (38:7).* It was now Judah's turn to experience the loss of a beloved son—the dreadful pain he and his brothers had put upon their father—and he was about to have that pain doubled.

And Judah said unto Onan, Go in unto thy brother's wife, and marry her, and raise up seed to thy brother (38:8). Er's widow, Tamar, had not yet borne children, so according to the custom, Er's unmarried brother Onan was to marry her.

The first son by that second marriage would be Er's, having all the rights that Er's own son would have had. *And Onan knew that the seed* [son] *should not be his; and it came to pass, when he went in unto his brother's wife, that he spilled it* [the semen] *on the ground, lest that he should give seed to his brother. And the thing which he did displeased the* LORD: *wherefore he slew him also (38:9–10).*

If Judah and nine of his brothers were evil and yet the LORD brought no punishment on them except the punishments of guilt, then how great must have been the evil of Judah's sons that at their young ages the LORD removed them from the land of the living!

Judah's defrauding of Tamar

Then said Judah to Tamar his daughter-in-law [perhaps believing Tamar was to blame for the deaths of his sons], *Remain a widow at thy father's house, till Shelah my son be grown: for he said, Lest peradventure he die also, as his brethren did. And Tamar went and dwelt in her father's house (38:11).*

Back at her father's home, Tamar would have counted the few years until she would marry again being no longer a widow, but a wife and mother with home and happiness. Distressingly, the waiting passed beyond a proper length, and *she saw that Shelah was grown, and she was not given unto him to wife* [marry] *(38:14b).* Though Tamar was legally engaged to Shelah—an engagement as binding as marriage—Judah was shamelessly ignoring his obligation to let her marry and have a family, a great necessity for a woman in their culture.

Tamar's solution

Even as Tamar began to consider what to do, a new grief came into Judah's life; his wife died. Perhaps that was when the idea came. Gathering the right clothes, Tamar waited for news from her friends who probably knew she was to marry Shelah and knew that Judah could not be trusted. Evidently they kept her posted on Judah's business and his travels, and at last the right news came.

And it was told Tamar, saying, Behold thy father-in-law goeth up to Timnath to shear his sheep. And she put her widow's garments off from her, and covered her with a veil [which a prostitute would do], *and wrapped herself, and sat in an open place, which is by the way to Timnath; for she saw that Shelah was grown, and she was not given unto him to wife (38:13–14).*

When Judah saw her, he thought her to be a harlot [prostitute]; *because she had covered her face. And he turned unto her by the way, and said, Go to, I pray thee, let me come in unto thee; (for he knew not that she was his daughter-in-law). And she said, What wilt thou give me, that thou mayest come in unto me? (38:15–16).*

And he said, I will send thee a kid from the flock. And she said, Wilt thou give me a pledge [a guarantee], *till thou send it? And he said, What pledge shall I give thee? And she said, Thy signet* [a cylinder which if rolled over clay left the imprint of his identification], *and thy bracelets* [from which his signet hung], *and thy* [shepherd] *staff that is in thine hand. And he gave it her, and came in unto her, and she conceived by him. And she arose, and went away, and laid by her veil from her, and put on the garments of her widowhood* [no one except herself knowing what she had done] *(38:17–19).*

And Judah sent the kid by the hand of his friend the Adullamite, to receive his pledge [his property] *from the woman's hand: but he found her not. Then he asked the men of that place, saying, Where is the harlot, that was openly by the way side? And they said, There was no harlot in this place. And he returned to Judah, and said, I cannot find her; and also the men of the place said, that there was no harlot in this place. And Judah* [preferring to lose his valuable signet rather than lose his name] *said, Let her take it to her* [for herself], *lest we be shamed: behold, I sent this kid, and thou hast not found her (38:20–23).*

(Someone today may argue that Judah's going to a harlot was not wrong, but clearly Judah believed it was wrong for he was afraid that public knowledge of it would bring shame upon him.)

Judah's response to Tamar's pregnancy

And it came to pass about three months after, that it was told Judah, saying, Tamar thy daughter-in-law hath played the harlot; and also, behold, she is with child by whoredom. And Judah [possibly greatly relieved at the thought of being rid of her] *said, Bring her forth, and let her be burnt. When she was brought forth, she sent to her father-in-law, saying, By the man, whose these are, am I with child: and she said, Discern, I pray thee, whose are these, the signet, and bracelets, and staff (38:24–25).*

Judah's next words were a confession such as, according to the records, had never before come from his mouth nor from the mouths of any of his brothers. *And Judah . . . said, She hath been more righteous* [upright] *than I; because that I gave her not to Shelah my son. And he knew her again no more* [had no further sexual relations with her] *(38:26).*

The fire preparations ceased. With three pieces of proof in his hand and his shame out in the open, Judah entered a new stage in his life, just as his father had—the stage of being humbled. The changes would continue in his life. Before Genesis is over, he, too, will be a new man.

The descendants of Tamar and Judah

And it came to pass in the time of her travail [labor], *that, behold, twins were in her womb. . . . And . . .* [the firstborn] *. . . was called Pharez* [also known as Perez]. *And . . . his brother . . . was called Zarah (38:27, 29–30.)* Later great significance and importance would come through Pharez. That child, son of unwanted Tamar and deeply shamed Judah, became the link from his father, Judah, to the most renowned family line in the Bible. That line led to the great King David, and one thousand years after King David, through that same line to Jesus of Nazareth called the Christ.

My reflections on Judah's failures

I sense that shame was teaching Judah that the joys of secret wrongdoings were far more short-lived than the humiliations that followed. I wonder how much more shame he must go through.

Checking for understanding

1. What was biblically wrong about Judah's decision to marry Shua's daughter? (38:1–5)

2. Name Judah's three sons and tell why the first-born died.

3. Why did Judah tell his second son to marry Tamar?

4. Explain Tamar's reason for sitting by the roadside disguised as a prostitute.

5. Judah admitted it was unrighteous (or wrong) of him not to let Tamar marry his youngest son, but we don't know if he felt guilty about anything else. List any other behavior of Judah in this chapter which you think was wrong.

6. What made Pharez (Perez)—about whom we know almost nothing—significant in the Bible?

Joseph's Further Humiliation

Based on Genesis 39—40

My first thoughts

BEFORE GOING ON WITH the life of Joseph, the teacher reminded us that the Bible is filled with stories and stories *within* stories. She reminded us also of the elements of stories—the setting, the characters, a problem, and finally the resolution or settlement of the problem. It's like a mystery that must be solved or a conflict that must be turned to peace. In the story of Joseph's father, Jacob, we have seen plenty of problems, but only small resolutions—as his making peace with his brother Esau, but at the same time, not making peace with his family. It was the same, our teacher told us, for Joseph's story. There are small settlements all leading, hopefully, to a state of peace, but the title written on the board indicates a new problem—a story about to get worse.

My notes on the teacher's lesson

The new setting in Joseph's life

In Genesis 37 we saw Joseph taken southwest from his father's shepherd-household in southern Canaan to Egypt, where Potiphar, captain of the guard under Pharaoh, bought him as a slave.

A new slave, especially when he didn't know the language, likely began with the lowest tasks, disgusting work which anyone could do, but which only a slave with a particular view of life could do with enthusiasm.

Potiphar must have been receiving unusual reports about Joseph, the slave who seemed more concerned for the slave owner and his affairs than for himself. Genesis 39 gives a reason why Joseph was different.

And the LORD was with Joseph, and he was a prosperous man; and he was in the house of his master the Egyptian (39:2). Working for a high Egyptian official, he would be in a position to learn Egypt's inner workings—not merely its language, but also its economy, its finances, its laws, and its management of people—everything the overseer of a prosperous estate had to know. Evidently, Joseph was a fast learner, and as his understanding grew, so did the success of Potiphar's personal estate.

And his master saw that the LORD was with him, and that the LORD made all that he did to prosper in his hand. And Joseph found grace [or favor] *in his sight, and he served him: and he* [Potiphar] *made him* [Joseph] *overseer over his house, and all that he had he put into his hand (39:3–4).* In that work Joseph would come to understand great matters of which Hebrew shepherds in Canaan would know almost nothing and would have almost no way of learning about them. For Joseph, being in Potiphar's house was truly better than the best college education he could have ever had.

And it came to pass from the time that he had made him overseer in his house, and over all that he had, that the LORD blessed the Egyptian's house for Joseph's sake; and the blessing of the LORD was upon all that he had in the house, and in the field. And he left all that he had in Joseph's hand; and he knew not ought [anything] *he had, save* [except] *the bread which he did eat (39:5–6a).*

Joseph ran Potiphar's whole estate—the slaves, the fields, the finances, and new business dealings—everything about the operations except the food his master ate. The master trusted him fully in all he did. That was the setting of Joseph's slave work.

The malicious disturbance

Once Joseph learned how to run his master's business, it was time for the next step. That step required that Potiphar turn against Joseph. However, since Potiphar could see that the LORD was with him and that Joseph was making him extremely prosperous, what could turn him against that loyal young man? A third character could—Potiphar's wife. She could turn her husband against this faithful, prosperous young man.

And Joseph was a goodly [handsome] *person, and well favored. And it came to pass after these things, that his master's wife cast her eyes upon Joseph* [with lust]; *and she said, Lie with me (39:6b–7).* What an opportunity for Joseph! He could have an affair with his master's love-struck wife and get away with it. Did she not have a right to order Joseph, a slave, to do her bidding? Evidently she thought she did.

But he refused, and said unto his master's wife, Behold, my master wotteth [knows] *not what is with me in the house, and he hath committed all that he hath to my hand; There is none greater in this house than I; neither hath he kept back any thing from me but thee, because thou art his wife: how then can I do this great wickedness, and sin against God? (39:8–9).*

Some have questioned how Joseph could say that adultery was a sin since the Ten Commandments were not given to his family until centuries later. The world of Joseph's day, however, took adultery seriously. In the Code of Hammurabi, written about the time of Abraham but only discovered in the last century, adultery could be punished by drowning.

And it came to pass, as she spake to Joseph day by day, that he hearkened [listened] *not unto her, to lie by her, or to be with her. And it came to pass about this time, that Joseph went into the house to do his business; and there was none of the men of the house there within. And she caught him by his garment, saying, Lie with me: and he left his garment in her hand, and fled, and got him out (39:10–12).*

False charges against Joseph

There she stood. She had used all the powers of her raging lusts, her position, her manipulations, her claims of love, and all she had was the garment of his rejection in her hand. In an instant her lusts turned to the most intense fury.

And it came to pass, when she saw that he had left his garment in her hand, and was fled forth, that she called unto the men of her house, and spake unto them, saying, See, he hath brought in an Hebrew unto us to mock us; he came in unto me to lie with me, and I cried with a loud voice: And it came to pass, when he heard that I lifted up my voice and cried, that he left his garment with me, and fled, and got him out (39:13–15).

You can almost hear her tears, her sobbing, her pretended shock and anguish, her claims of purity and innocence even as she was plotting a cruel revenge. *And she laid up his garment by her, until his lord* [master] *came home. And she spake unto him according to these words, saying, The Hebrew servant, which thou hast brought unto us, came in unto me to mock me: and it came to pass, as I lifted up my voice and cried, that he left his garment with me, and fled out (39:16–18).*

Joseph in prison

And it came to pass, when his master heard the words of his wife, which she spake unto him, saying, After this manner did thy servant to me; that his wrath [fury] was kindled. And Joseph's master took him, and put him into the prison, a place where the king's prisoners were bound: and he was there in the prison (39:19–20).

Why would Potiphar imprison Joseph rather than execute him? Moses does not say. Also, why would Potiphar put Joseph into that particular prison, the prison in his own house? (40:3) Potiphar, as executioner, kept the king's prisoners until the king pronounced a verdict of innocence or guilt, but Joseph was not the king's prisoner, and he was not awaiting a verdict of innocence or guilt. Again, why? Moses leaves it to the readers to decide.

The most important question was, "Why did the God that Moses wrote of not save Joseph from the lies, shame, and imprisonment?" Moses *does* answer that question, but only later.

But the LORD *was with Joseph, and showed him mercy, and gave him favor in the sight of the keeper of the prison. And the keeper of the prison committed to Joseph's hand all the prisoners that were in the prison; and whatsoever they did there, he was the doer of it. The keeper of the prison looked not to any thing that was under his hand; because the* LORD *was with him, and that which he did, the* LORD *made it to prosper (39:21–23).*

What must Joseph have been like that the keeper of the prison knew he could trust him? He must have been like a prince, happy with the joy of work and free from bitterness and self-pity.

The new prisoners and their dreams

And it came to pass after these things, that [for some unknown reason] *the butler of the king of Egypt and his baker had offended their lord the king of Egypt. And Pharaoh was wroth [angry] against two of his officers, against the chief of the butlers, and against the chief of the bakers. And he put them in ward* [prison] *in the house of the captain of the guard, into the prison, the place where Joseph was bound* [confined] *(40:1–3).*

The chief butler was in charge of safeguarding the king's wine. If the wine were poisoned, the butler took death for him, drinking the poisoned wine before the king could. In the same way, the chief baker was in charge of safeguarding the king's food, possibly testing it before the king ate, dying for him if the food was not safe.

And the captain of the guard charged Joseph with them, and he served them: and they continued a season in ward (40:4).

The butler's dream and its meaning

And they dreamed a dream both of them, each man his dream in one night, . . . the butler and the baker of the king of Egypt, which were bound in the prison. And Joseph came in unto them in the morning, and looked upon them, and, behold, they were sad. And he asked Pharaoh's officers that were with him, saying . . . , Wherefore [why] *look ye so sadly to day? (40:5–7).*

And they said unto him, We have dreamed a dream, and there is no interpreter of it. And Joseph said unto them, Do not interpretations belong to God? tell me them, I pray you (40:8). Joseph was certain that if the dreams were messages from God, the LORD could reveal the meanings to him.

And the chief butler told his dream to Joseph, and said to him, In my dream, behold, a vine was before me; and in the vine were three branches: and it was as though it budded, and her blossoms shot forth; and the clusters thereof brought forth ripe grapes: and Pharaoh's cup was in my hand: and I took the grapes, and pressed them into Pharaoh's cup, and I gave the cup into Pharaoh's hand (40:9–11).

And Joseph said unto him, This is the interpretation of it: The three branches are three days: yet within three days shall Pharaoh lift up thine head, and restore thee unto thy place: and thou shalt deliver Pharaoh's cup into his hand, after the former manner when thou wast his butler (40:12–13).

What a marvelous interpretation—if it was true! If Joseph was correct, then Pharaoh was about to declare the butler innocent of all charges and suspicions. Joseph followed his interpretation with a request.

But think on me when it shall be well with thee, and show kindness, I pray thee, unto me, and make mention of me unto Pharaoh, and bring me out of this house: for indeed I was stolen away out of the land of the Hebrews:

and here also have I done nothing that they should put me into the dungeon (40:14–15).

Since Joseph was sure the interpretation was right, he must have seen freedom around the corner. What rejoicing!

The baker's dream and its meaning

When the chief baker saw that the interpretation was good, he said unto Joseph, I also was in my dream, and, behold, I had three white baskets on my head: and in the uppermost basket there was of all manner of bakemeats [baked goods] for Pharaoh; and the birds did eat them out of the basket upon my head (40:16–17).

Joseph at once understood the dream and its dreadful meaning. A new temptation probably arose—the temptation to disguise the meaning of the baker's dream and relieve his anxiety—let him live his last three days in peace—but Joseph evidently believed painful truth is better than false comfort. Here he is again, a picture of the Bible's prophets who did not let fear keep them from delivering unpleasant messages. As the class would soon see, it would have made a tragic difference in Joseph's future if, to make the baker happy, he had given a pleasing interpretation to the dream.

And Joseph answered and said, This is the interpretation thereof: The three baskets are three days: yet within three days shall Pharaoh lift up thy head from off thee, and shall hang thee on a tree; and the birds shall eat thy flesh from off thee (40:18–19). Though the butler would again serve the king his wine, the baker would swing from a tree—the food of vultures.

Fulfillment of the dreams

And it came to pass the third day, which was Pharaoh's birthday, that he made a feast unto all his servants: and he lifted up the head of the chief butler and of the chief baker among his servants. And he restored the chief butler unto his butlership again; and he gave the cup into Pharaoh's hand: but he hanged the chief baker: as Joseph had interpreted to them (40:20–22).

Continued unsettling for Joseph

As the butler departed from the prison, no doubt he left Joseph with warm goodbyes and with assurances that he would speak to Pharaoh for him.

What a joyous time for Joseph! At last he could return home. He would see his father and join the family once again. The injustices would end—at least he would hope so. But the injustices in Egypt did not end, for the days, the weeks, and the months passed, and finally it was clear that no one was coming because *the chief butler did not remember Joseph, but forgot him* (40:23).

Resolution had not come, and sorrowful disappointment continued. It must have been like a kind of death.

My reflections on Joseph's humiliations

How humiliating to be hated! How humiliating to be a slave, and a slave accused of attempted rape! How humiliating to feel you have so little significance that when you are out of sight, those you helped forget you. At the same time though, I wondered if being forgotten by others could sometimes be for good. I am almost certain that Joseph's return home at that time would have had dreadful complications tearing the family even further apart. Why go back into a setting of hatred, jealousy, and dangers?

Checking for understanding

1. Compare Joseph's life as a slave to Potiphar with his life back home with his family and explain why he was better off in Egypt.

2. According to Genesis what made Joseph so successful in his work?

3. Explain the two reasons Joseph refused to sleep with Potiphar's wife.

4. If Joseph had given in to Potiphar's wife, would it have given Joseph *more* freedom and power or *less*. Explain your answer.

5. What might have been the reasons that Potiphar did not execute Joseph?

6. How was Joseph's work and life in the prison the same as his work and life when he was a slave for Potiphar?

7. Do you think there could have been any reason that the butler might have chosen to forget Joseph? Explain your answer.

Joseph and Timing

Based on Genesis 41

My first thoughts

BEFORE THE TEACHER EXPLAINED the title of this lesson, she had us turn to a chapter over half way through the Bible, Ecclesiastes 3. The book, she explained, was written by a descendant of Jacob long after he and his sons had died. The assignment was to review Joseph's life from the perspective of Ecclesiastes 3:1—*To every thing there is a season, and a time to every purpose under the heaven.*

We were to see the importance of particular "times" in the life of Joseph.

My notes on the teacher's lesson

Review of significant timing in Joseph's life

- Slave traders came by at the same time Joseph was down in the pit.

- Reuben, who had planned to save Joseph, was not with the brothers at the critical time of the sale.

- Potiphar was at the slave market in Egypt right at the time Joseph was put up for sale.

- Joseph walked into Potiphar's house on business at a time when no one was there except Potiphar's lust-crazed wife.

The events of this new lesson have the same sense of perfect timing.

The timing of Pharaoh's dreams

And it came to pass at the end of two full years, that Pharaoh dreamed (41:1a). And it came to pass in the morning that his spirit was troubled; and he sent and called for all the magicians of Egypt, and all the wise men thereof (41:8a). The Egyptians believed that their many gods gave supernatural power to special people, turning them into magicians and wise men who then became the king's advisors. *And Pharaoh told them his dream; but there was none that could interpret them unto Pharaoh (41:8b).*

Then spake the chief butler unto Pharaoh, saying, I do remember my faults this day: Pharaoh was wroth [angry] with his servants, and put me in ward in the captain of the guard's house, both me and the chief baker. And we dreamed a dream in one night, I and he; we dreamed each man according to the interpretation of his dream (41:9–11).

And there was there with us a young man, a Hebrew, servant to the captain of the guard; and we told him, and he interpreted to us our dreams; to each man according to his dream he did interpret. And it came to pass, as he interpreted to us, so it was; me he restored unto mine office, and him he hanged (41:12–13). Notice that if Joseph had lied about the baker's dream just to give the baker three days of false hope, the butler would not have told the king that Joseph could interpret correctly.

Then Pharaoh sent and called Joseph, and they brought him hastily out of the dungeon: and he shaved himself, and changed his raiment, and came in unto Pharaoh. And Pharaoh said unto Joseph, I have dreamed a dream, and there is none that can interpret it: and I have heard say of thee, that thou canst understand a dream to interpret it. And Joseph answered Pharaoh, saying, It is not in me: God shall give Pharaoh an answer of peace (41:14–16).

The dreams and their meanings

And Pharaoh said unto Joseph, In my dream, behold, I stood upon the bank of the river: and, behold, there came up out of the river seven kine [cows], fat-fleshed and well-favored; and they fed in a meadow: and, behold, seven other kine came up after them, poor and very ill-favored and lean-fleshed, such as I never saw in all the land of Egypt for badness: and the lean and the ill-favored kine did eat up the first seven fat kine: and when they had eaten them up, it could not be known that they had eaten them; but they were still ill-favored, as at the beginning. So I awoke (41:17–21).

And I saw in my dream, and, behold, seven ears came up in one stalk, full and good: and, behold, seven ears, withered, thin, and blasted with the east wind, sprung up after them: and the thin ears devoured the seven good ears: and I told this unto the magicians; but there was none that could declare it to me (41:22–24).

And Joseph said unto Pharaoh, The dream of Pharaoh is one: God hath showed Pharaoh what he is about to do. The seven good kine are seven years; and the seven good ears are seven years: the dream is one. And the seven thin and ill-favored kine that came up after them are seven years; and the seven empty ears blasted with the east wind shall be seven years of famine. This is the thing which I have spoken unto Pharaoh: What God is about to do he showeth unto Pharaoh (41:25–28).

Behold, there come seven years of great plenty throughout all the land of Egypt: and there shall arise after them seven years of famine; and all the plenty shall be forgotten in the land of Egypt; and the famine shall consume the land; and the plenty shall not be known in the land by reason of that famine following; for it shall be very grievous. And for that the dream was doubled unto Pharaoh twice; it is because the thing is established by God, and God will shortly bring it to pass (41:29–32).

Shocking! For seven years they would have incredibly abundant harvests; the next seven years they would have nothing but barren fields and starvation. Joseph went on speaking.

Joseph's advice

Now therefore let Pharaoh look out a man discreet and wise, and set him over the land of Egypt. Let Pharaoh do this, and let him appoint officers over the land, and take up the fifth part of the land of Egypt in the seven plenteous years [a tax of twenty percent—low compared to many countries today]. *And let them gather all the food of those good years that come, and lay up corn under the hand of Pharaoh, and let them keep food in the cities. And that food shall be for store to the land against the seven years of famine, which shall be in the land of Egypt; that the land perish not through the famine (41:33–36).*

The time, at last, for justice

And the thing was good in the eyes of Pharaoh, and in the eyes of all his servants. And Pharaoh said unto his servants, Can we find such a one as this is, a man in whom the Spirit of God is? And Pharaoh said unto Joseph, Forasmuch as God hath showed thee all this, there is none so discreet and wise as thou art: Thou shalt be over my house, and according unto thy word shall all my people be ruled: only in the throne will I be greater than thou (41:37–40).

And Pharaoh said unto Joseph, See, I have set thee over all the land of Egypt. And Pharaoh took off his ring from his hand, and put it upon Joseph's hand, and arrayed him in vestures of fine linen [the clothing of royalty and high officials], *and put a gold chain about his neck,* [a prized reward for great service] *(41:41–42).*

With the king's signet ring, Joseph had power to make any law he wished, make any changes in the land he desired, go anywhere he wanted, and rule exactly as he saw fit.

And [Pharaoh] *made him to ride in the second chariot* [which rode beside the king]; *which he had; and they cried* [or called out] *before him, Bow the knee: and he made him ruler over all the land of Egypt. And Pharaoh said unto Joseph, I am Pharaoh, and without thee* [without your permission] *shall no man lift up his hand or foot in all the land of Egypt. And Pharaoh called Joseph's name Zaphnath-paaneah* [zahf-nath–pay-a-NEE-a]; *and he gave him to wife Asenath the daughter of Potipherah priest of On. And Joseph went out over all the land of Egypt (41:43–45).*

Joseph arose that morning an imprisoned, disgraced, forgotten slave. He went to bed that evening second highest ruler of Egypt, the greatest nation in the world.

The time of fulfillment begins

And Joseph was thirty years old when he stood before Pharaoh king of Egypt. And Joseph went out from the presence of Pharaoh, and went throughout all the land of Egypt. And in the seven plenteous years the earth brought forth by handfuls. And he gathered up all the food of the seven years, which were in the land of Egypt, and laid up the food in the cities: the food of the field, which was round about every city, laid he up in the same. And Joseph gathered corn as the sand of the sea, very much, until he left numbering; for it was without number (41:46–49).

Silos, storehouses, and wagonloads of food covered the landscape, keeping carpenters busy building more. The wagons continually went out to the fields and returned, overflowing with food. Egypt was ready to save the world!

Even though Joseph had freedom to do whatever he chose, including freedom to contact his father, he chose not to use that privilege. From his own dreams, he knew that one day he would see both his father and all his brothers again, but he also knew it was not yet time. He would wait patiently.

My reflections of Joseph's life

At last Joseph's life began to made sense. The times of rejection, slavery, lies, prison, and neglect—they all came together for him. The hatred of the brothers had thrust him into the perfect place. Slavery in Potiphar's house had taught him language, agriculture, finances, politics, and leadership. The false accusations of attempted rape had placed him in the prison where he became acquainted with the king's butler and interpreted his dream. The butler's forgetfulness had kept Joseph in prison until the time to interpret the Pharaoh's dreams—the time for Joseph to become ruler of Egypt. Those thirteen years in the greatest nation of that time had prepared him with the education and the wisdom needed to bless his world.

Checking for understanding

1. Joseph was a straightforward man from his youth. He told the family his dreams. He told Potiphar's wife why he rejected her, and he told the baker the true meaning of his dreadful dream. None of them wanted to hear what he said. Explain how in each of these three cases his honesty benefitted him.

2. Joseph was twenty-eight when he interpreted the butler's dream. How old was he when the butler told Pharaoh about him?

3. When Pharaoh first spoke to Joseph, he said he had heard that Joseph could interpret dreams. How did Joseph's response in verses 14–16 show his humility?

4. Briefly explain the meaning of Pharaoh's two dreams.

5. List at least four ways Pharaoh honored Joseph. (Genesis 41:37–45)

6. Suppose you decided to write a novel about Joseph's life. Describe, in at least two sentences, what you imagine Potiphar's wife did or said when her husband told her Joseph was out of prison and ruling Egypt.

The Brothers Face Joseph

Based on Genesis 41:53—42:38

My first thoughts

WE'RE ALL LOOKING FORWARD to today's study. I'm figuring that with all of Egypt bowing to Joseph, he must have been remembering those dreams back when he was with his family, dreams of his brothers bowing to him. Since he would know that when famine came, men from all countries would be coming to Egypt for food, it seemed to me Joseph would know that would have to include his brothers. I'm wondering what he will do. I'm especially wondering what the brothers will do. Joseph will have them right where he wants them.

My notes on the teacher's lesson

The coming of the famine

And the seven years of plenteousness, that was in the land of Egypt, were ended. And the seven years of dearth [food shortage] *began to come, according as Joseph had said: and the dearth was in all lands; but in all the land of Egypt there was bread. And when all the land of Egypt was famished, the people cried to Pharaoh for bread: and Pharaoh said unto all the Egyptians, Go unto Joseph: what he saith to you, do* (41:53–55).

One of our business-minded classmates (always thinking about logistics) brought up the question of how a man without our technology could coordinate every town—its leaders, its work crews building storage houses, the storage of the grain, and then coordinate its food distribution. Once Pharaoh said, *Go unto Joseph: what he saith to you, do (41:55b)*, Joseph had to be ready, and when that order came, he was. Truly, Joseph was a genius of organization.

And Joseph opened all the storehouses, and sold unto the Egyptians; and the famine waxed sore [increased greatly] *in the land of Egypt. And all countries came into Egypt to Joseph for to buy corn; because that the famine was so sore in all lands (41:56b–57).*

Joseph's brothers go down to Egypt

Since only the Egyptians were prepared for the seven years of famine, by the second year Joseph's family back in Canaan was running out of food. As we would see later, Joseph longed to help them, but he had to know first if his ten brothers had changed. Whether or not they had changed would determine how he would be able to relate to them.

Now when Jacob saw that there was corn in Egypt, Jacob said unto his sons, Why do ye look one upon another? And he said, Behold, I have heard that there is corn in Egypt: get you down thither, and buy for us from thence; that we may live, and not die. And Joseph's ten brethren went down to buy corn in Egypt. But Benjamin, Joseph's brother, Jacob sent not with his brethren; for he said, Lest peradventure mischief befall him (42:1–4).

When they entered Egypt, did the ten brothers scan slave faces, wondering if they might see the brother they had sold over twenty years earlier? If they did think about Joseph, they quickly forgot him when they entered his presence and *bowed down themselves before him with their faces to the earth (42:6b).* They had no idea that the man standing before them was the one whom they had despised and abused and sold into slavery—no hint that they were looking on the face of one who knew them and who had the power to bring total justice upon each of them.

Joseph's first step: Awaken their consciences

And Joseph saw his brethren, and he knew them, but made himself strange unto them, and spake roughly unto them; and he said unto them, Whence [from where] *come ye? And they said, From the land of Canaan to buy food (42:7).*

And Joseph knew his brethren, but they knew not him. And Joseph . . . said unto them, Ye are spies; to see the nakedness of the land ye are come. [We all loved how he was talking to them—we wanted revenge.] *And they said unto him, Nay, my lord, but to buy food are thy servants come. We are all one man's sons; we are true men, thy servants are no spies (42:8–11).*

And he said unto them, Nay, but to see the nakedness of the land ye are come. And they said, Thy servants are twelve brethren, the sons of one man in the land of Canaan; and, behold, the youngest is this day with our father, and one is not [in other words, he is dead] *(42:12–13).*

After learning that his father and Benjamin were both still living, the "dead" brother continued his accusations. *And Joseph said unto them, That is it that I spake unto you, saying, Ye are spies: hereby ye shall be proved: By the life of Pharaoh ye shall not go forth hence* [from here], *except* [unless] *your youngest brother come hither* [here]. *Send one of you, and let him fetch your brother, and ye shall be kept in prison, that your words may be proved, whether there be any truth in you: or else by the life of Pharaoh surely ye are spies. And he put them all together into ward three days* [perhaps the same prison where he had spent many years] *(42:14–17).*

Joseph had no intention of making the family back in Canaan wait for food. On the third day of their imprisonment, he said to the brothers, *This do, and live; for I fear God: If ye be true men, let one of your brethren be bound in the house of your prison: go ye, carry corn for the famine of your houses: but bring your youngest brother unto me; so shall your words be verified, and ye shall not die (42:18b–20a).* In order to return to Egypt for food, they must bring Benjamin back with them.

The brothers confess to one another their guilt

As they stood before Joseph, pangs of conscience gripped their hearts. *And they said one to another* [perhaps for the first time since they sold Joseph], *We are verily* [truly] *guilty concerning our brother, in that we saw the anguish of his soul, when he besought us* [pleaded with us], *and we would not hear; therefore is this distress come upon us. And Reuben answered them, saying, Spake I not unto you, saying, Do not sin against the child; and ye would not hear? therefore, behold, also his blood is required*—God is at last punishing us for what we did to Joseph *(42:21–22).*

And they knew not that Joseph understood them; for he spake unto them by an interpreter. And [Joseph, deeply moved] *turned himself about from them, and wept; and returned to them again, and communed* [talked] *with them, and took from them Simeon,* [the next to oldest who should have protected Joseph when firstborn Reuben was not there] *and bound him before their eyes (42:23–24).* Simeon would stay there in prison until they returned with Benjamin.

Then Joseph gave them grain in their sacks plus food for the journey home. They did not know that Joseph had put something else into their sacks—something that would frighten and further test them. Joseph had commanded his servants, not only to fill their sacks with corn, but also to put every man's money back into his sack.

Joseph's second step: Test their honesty

And they laded their asses with the corn, and departed thence. And [when they stopped for the night] *as one of them opened his sack to give his ass provender in the inn, he espied* [saw] *his money; for, behold, it was in his sack's mouth. And he said unto his brethren, My money is restored; and, lo, it is even in my sack: and their heart failed them, and they were afraid, saying one to another, What is this that God hath done unto us? (42:26–28).* The rest of them did not know yet that money was in each of their sacks too.

Jacob's fears

And they came unto Jacob their father unto the land of Canaan, and told him all that befell unto them; saying, The man, who is the lord of the land, spake roughly to us, and took us for spies of the country. And we said unto him, We are true men; we are no spies: We be twelve brethren, sons of our father; one is not [is dead], *and the youngest is this day with our father in the land of Canaan (42:29–32).*

And the man, the lord of the country, said unto us, Hereby shall I know that ye are true men; leave one of your brethren here with me, and take food for the famine of your households, and be gone: And bring your youngest brother unto me: then shall I know that ye are no spies, but that ye are true men: so will I deliver you your brother, and ye shall traffic in the land (42:33–34).

Fear and suspicion about the money

And it came to pass as they emptied their sacks, that, behold, every man's bundle of money was in his sack: and when both they and their father saw the bundles of money, they were afraid (42:35). Since Jacob's ten sons had never proven themselves to be especially honest, when all that money came out of their sacks, perhaps Jacob wondered if they had sold Simeon and that was the real reason for the money in their sacks. When Jacob learned that the ruler of Egypt demanded that Benjamin be brought to him in Egypt, Jacob's distrust poured out of him.

Fear to trust his sons with Benjamin

And Jacob their father said unto them, Me have ye bereaved of my children: Joseph is not, and Simeon is not, and ye will take Benjamin away: all these things are against me (42:36). In some way he seemed to be blaming his sons for Joseph's disappearance. Had he always suspected them? If he let the brothers take Benjamin to Egypt, he feared they would never bring him back.

Then Reuben spoke up, perhaps trying to reinstate himself in the eyes of his father and in the eyes of his brothers who knew too well his cowardly firstborn failures and his immorality (35:22). To convince their father to let Benjamin go with them to Egypt, he made a dramatic, senseless promise, *saying, Slay my two sons, if I bring him not* [back] *to thee,* as if two dead grandsons would somehow make up for the loss of Benjamin *(42:37).*

And he [Jacob] *said, My son shall not go down with you; for his brother is dead, and he is left alone: if mischief befall him by the way in the which ye go, then shall ye bring down my gray hairs with sorrow to the grave (42:38).* Clearly, Jacob had not changed—he had a favorite. No son was loved as much as Benjamin.

Time passed and everyone waited: the family in Canaan carefully measuring out their food, surely praying for the famine to end; Simeon, in the Egyptian prison, uncertain if he would ever be rescued; and Joseph, not far away from him, preparing for the return of his brothers. If the family's hopes for the end of the famine had been answered, poor Simeon might have waited forever, but Joseph, of course, knew that would not happen; he knew the famine would go on much longer. In the meantime, he would wait too.

My reflections on the deserved sufferings of Joseph's brothers

Gradually, I am feeling some sympathy for the ten brothers because I, too, know what it is to have regrets; I guess everyone does. I know they don't deserve mercy, but even so, I know I would want it.

Checking for understanding

1. How were Joseph's brothers to prove they were not spies?

2. Why did Joseph pick Simeon as the brother to remain in the prison?

3. How did Reuben's offer to take responsibility for Benjamin show his lack of wisdom?

4. Our conscience is that inner sense or knowledge of what is right and what is wrong. When we violate our conscience, doing what we know is wrong, the memory often brings those violations back to haunt us with guilt and shame. Joseph's brothers knew they had done great wrong. Prove that the brothers carried haunting regrets for their past.

Final Tests of Joseph's Brothers

Based on Genesis 43 and 44

My first thoughts

SINCE JOSEPH'S BROTHERS REGRETTED selling him into slavery, I'm wondering if Joseph should forgive them and forget about the past; that seems a noble thing to do. Most of the class says, *No.* They don't feel you should deal that way with abusers. The brothers might have been sorry for what they did to Joseph, but that didn't mean they cared a speck for the new favorite, Benjamin. They might happily treat him the same way they treated Joseph. The class thought that even though Joseph cared about his brothers, he was trying to find out whether or not they had changed. I'm not sure; he's been pretty rough on them so far.

My notes on the teacher's lesson

Persuading Jacob to let Benjamin go to Egypt

Jacob probably thought the weather, or whatever caused the famine, would surely begin to improve—it always had in the past. Yet no matter how much he might have prayed and tried to convince himself that the famine would soon end, nothing was growing, and the family was again running out of food.

Proof of Jacob's continued favoritism

Perhaps Joseph was puzzled that his father did not send Benjamin down to Egypt at once and that he let Simeon stay so long in the Egyptian prison, but if he had heard his father's words, he would have understood. *My son shall not go down with you; for his brother is dead, and he is left alone* [as if their father had no other sons]. *If mischief befall him by the way in the which ye go, then shall ye bring down my gray hairs with sorrow to the grave (42:38).* If Joseph had heard those words, he would have known his father still had a favorite and could still be creating jealousy and resentment among the sons.

Jacob's grudging permission

And it came to pass, when they had eaten up the corn which they had brought out of Egypt, their father [ignoring the orders to send Benjamin to Egypt,] *said to his sons, Go again, buy us a little food. And Judah spake unto him, saying, The man did solemnly protest unto us, saying, Ye shall not see my face, except your brother be with you. If thou wilt send our brother with us, we will go down and buy thee food: But if thou wilt not send him, we will not go down: for the man said unto us, Ye shall not see my face, except your brother be with you (43:2–5).*

When Judah could get nowhere with his father, he gave him a promise. *I will be surety* [a guarantee] *for him . . . . If I bring him not unto thee, and set him before thee, then let me bear the blame forever (43:9).*

Judah was promising to take full responsibility for Benjamin and to take upon himself any blame that might arise for this youngest favorite son.

And their father Israel said unto them, If it must be . . . , do this; take of the best fruits in the land in your vessels, and carry down the man a present, a little balm, and a little honey, spices, and myrrh, nuts, and almonds: and take double money in your hand; and the money that was brought again in the mouth of your sacks, carry it again in your hand; peradventure [perhaps] *it was an oversight (43:11–12).*

Take also your brother, and arise, go again unto the man: and God Almighty give you mercy before the man, that he may send away your other brother, and Benjamin. If I be bereaved of my children, I am bereaved. And the men took that present, and they took double money in their hand and Benjamin; and rose up, and went down to Egypt, and stood before Joseph (43:13–15).

More tests for the brothers

Passing the honesty test

And when Joseph saw Benjamin with them, he said to the ruler of his house, Bring these men home . . . and make ready; for these men shall dine with me at noon. . . . And the men were afraid, because they were brought into Joseph's house; and they said, Because of the money that was returned in our sacks at the first time are we brought in; that he may seek occasion against us, and fall upon us, and take us for bondmen [slaves], *and our asses (43:16, 18).*

And they came near to the steward of Joseph's house [the man who managed Joseph's household], *and they communed* [talked] *with him at the door of the house, and said, O sir, we came indeed down at the first time to buy food: and it came to pass, when we came to the inn, that we opened our sacks, and, behold, every man's money was in the mouth of his sack, . . . and we have brought it again in our hand (43:19–21).*

And he [the steward] *said, Peace be to you, fear not: your God, and the God of your father, hath given you treasure in your sacks: I had your money. And he brought Simeon out unto them. And the man brought the men into Joseph's house, and gave them water, and they washed their feet; and he gave their asses provender* [food] *(43:23–24).* How bewildering that would have been for the brothers!

The jealousy tests

And when Joseph came home, they brought him the present which was in their hand into the house, and bowed themselves to him to the earth. [How we all loved picturing them with their faces to the ground.] *And he asked them of their welfare, and said, Is your father well, the old man of whom ye spake? Is he yet alive? And they answered, Thy servant our father is in good health, he is yet alive. And they bowed down their heads, and made obeisance (43:26–28).*

And he lifted up his eyes, and saw his brother Benjamin, his mother's son, and said, Is this your younger brother, of whom ye spake unto me? And he said, God be gracious unto thee, my son. And Joseph made haste . . . and he sought where to weep; and he entered into his chamber, and wept there. And he washed his face, and went out, and refrained himself, and said, Set on bread (43:29–31).

The servants had set a table for the brothers, assigning to each a particular seat. They had another table for the Egyptians, who would have abhorred the thought of eating with those shepherds. A third table was just for Joseph, a place from which he could observe his brothers.

As the brothers looked around their table, they would have been struck with awe, an awe surely mixed with anxiety—the ruler of Egypt had seated them by age, from the eldest to the youngest. Seeing that this great man knew the specific birth order of eleven brothers, most born in the space of seven years, what else might he know? Did he know the evils of their past?

And he took and sent messes [servings of food] *unto them from before him: but Benjamin's mess was five times so much as any of theirs. And they drank, and were merry with him (43:34).* Joseph observed the reactions of the brothers toward Benjamin. Would they resent Joseph's favoritism toward him? Evidently they did not.

The love test

The brothers had passed the first tests, but had they truly changed, or were they being merry simply out of relief? The last test would tell him.

And he commanded the steward of his house, saying, Fill the men's sacks with food, as much as they can carry, and put every man's money in his sack's mouth. And put my cup, the silver cup, in the sack's mouth of the youngest, and his corn money. And he did according to the word that Joseph had spoken (44:1–2).

As soon as the morning was light, the men were sent away, they and their asses (44:3). Little did they know the story was about to take a terrifying turn. Right after they left the city, *Joseph said unto his steward, Up, follow after the men; and when thou dost overtake them, say unto them, Wherefore* [why] *have ye rewarded evil for good? (44:4b).* The steward was to accuse the brothers of stealing the ruler's silver cup. The steward followed the directions. *And he overtook them, and he spake unto them these same words (44:6).*

And they [the brothers] *said unto him, Wherefore saith my lord these words? God forbid that thy servants should do according to this thing: behold, the money, which we found in our sacks's mouths, we brought again unto thee out of the land of Canaan: how then should we steal out of thy lord's house silver or gold? With whomsoever of thy servants it be found, both let him die, and we also will be my lord's bondmen* [slaves] *(44:7–9).* Since the cup will be found in Benjamin's sack, the brothers were unknowingly telling the steward to put him to death and to make the rest of them slaves! If that would happen, no one would ever return to Canaan, and Jacob would die of the most intense grief and sorrow knowing nothing.

"Proof" of Benjamin's guilt

Then they speedily took down every man his sack to the ground, and opened every man his sack. And he searched, and began at the eldest, and left at the youngest: and the cup was found in Benjamin's sack (44:11–12).

The appearance of the cup was worse than anything that had ever happened in their lives—events far beyond their control were tearing their world apart. To make it even worse, in their hearts they were sure the troubles were coming from their past, and they knew they deserved them. *Then they rent* [ripped] *their clothes, and laded* [loaded] *every man his ass, and returned to the city (44:13).*

Twenty-one years earlier, the brothers eagerly got rid of their father's pet, Joseph. They are now faced with the same opportunity to get rid of their father's pet, Benjamin. Joseph wouldn't need to ask whether they had genuine love for their father and for their youngest brother. He would see for himself.

The answer to the final test

And Judah and his brethren came to Joseph's house; for he was yet there: and they fell before him on the ground. And Joseph said unto them, What deed is this that ye have done? (44:14–15a).

And Judah said, What shall we say unto my lord? what shall we speak? or how shall we clear ourselves? God hath found out the iniquity [the great sin] *of thy servant.* It appears that Judah was at last confessing that great evil lay in their past, evil that God was finally bringing to justice. *Behold, we are my lord's servants, both we, and he also with whom the cup is found (44:16).*

And he [Joseph] *said, God forbid that I should do so: but the man in whose hand the cup is found, he shall be my servant; and as for you, get you up in peace unto your father (44:17).* In other words, Joseph would not make the brothers slaves; they could go home. Neither would he kill Benjamin; rather, Benjamin would stay and be Joseph's own personal slave.

At last Joseph would have his answer. Did they care about their brother, and did they care about their father? If they were jealous, they would gladly get rid of Benjamin.

Judah's plea

Then Judah came near unto him, and said, Oh my lord, let thy servant, I pray thee, speak a word in my lord's ears, and let not thine anger burn against thy servant: for thou art even as Pharaoh. My lord asked his servants, saying, Have ye a father, or a brother? And we said unto my lord, We have a father, an old man, and a child of his old age, a little one; and his brother is dead, and he alone is left of his mother, and his father loveth him (44:18–20).

And thou saidst unto thy servants, Bring him down unto me, that I may set mine eyes upon him. And we said unto my lord, The lad cannot leave his father: for if he should leave his father, his father would die. And thou saidst unto thy servants, Except your youngest brother come down with you, ye shall see my face no more (44:21–23).

And it came to pass when we came up unto thy servant my father, we told him the words of my lord. And our father said, Go again, and buy us a little food. And we said, We cannot go down: if our youngest brother be with us, then will we go down: for we may not see the man's face, except our youngest brother be with us (44:24–26).

And thy servant my father said unto us, Ye know that my wife bare me two sons: and the one went out from me, and I said, Surely he is torn in pieces; and I saw him not since: and if ye take this also from me, and mischief befall him, ye shall bring down my gray hairs with sorrow to the grave (44:27–29).

Those words told Joseph that the cause of their old resentments remained. Their father still spoke as if Rachel, Joseph, and Benjamin were all that mattered. The question remained: were the brothers still resentful? Did they forgive their father his faults?

Proof of Judah's great love

Judah continued: *Now therefore when I come to thy servant my father, and the lad be not with us; seeing that his life is bound up in the lad's life; it shall come to pass, when he seeth that the lad is not with us, that he will die: and thy servants shall bring down the gray hairs of thy servant our father with sorrow to the grave (44:30–31).*

For thy servant [I myself] *became surety* [a guarantee] *for the lad unto my father, saying, If I bring him not unto thee, then I shall bear the blame to my father forever. Now therefore, I pray thee, let* [me stay] *instead of the lad a bondman to my lord;* [let all the blame be laid on me] *and let the lad go up with his brethren. For how shall I go up to my father, and the lad be not with me? lest peradventure I see the evil that shall come on my father (44:32–34).*

Judah's heart was breaking for both his father and Benjamin as he, in essence, said, "I will stay here the rest of my life and be your slave. I will never return home. I will give up my whole life that I may save my brother and send him back to our father."

Joseph had his answer and was about to give his response.

My reflections on Judah

When Judah first appeared in Joseph's story, I thought he was the worst of all the brothers, but now, seeing his heart for his father and for his brother Benjamin, I realize he had changed. He was the best of brothers. Over the years, and perhaps through losing two of his own sons, (Genesis 38) Judah had truly become a new man. But just the same, Judah had a bad record. It was he who advised that they should send Joseph into slavery. Should Joseph make him pay for it?

Checking for understanding

1. What words of their father Jacob showed that the ten older brothers meant very little to him in comparison to Benjamin?

2. Explain how Judah persuaded his father to let Benjamin go down to Egypt.

3. When the brothers returned to Egypt, what was the first clue that they might have become trustworthy?

4. What do you think might have been the reason Joseph seated his brothers by their birth order?

5. From what you have seen, how was Joseph's treatment of Benjamin at the dinner a test?

6. Explain the wisdom of dealing with people who once had been abusers as Joseph dealt with his brothers.

Forgiveness and Comfort

Based on Genesis 45

My first thoughts

THERE WAS A LOT to forgive in Jacob's family. The only consequences so far that anyone seemed to have had were guilt and sadness—and no one ever said he was sorry for anything. How can a person repay and repair years of dishonesty and indifference? I used to think—before I took this class—that the people in the Bible were all good. I sure had that one wrong!

My notes on the teacher's lesson

As the teacher began this lesson, she reminded us of the last part of our previous study: Judah had just poured out his heart to the ruler Joseph, not having the faintest idea that the ruler was his brother. He had begged to be kept as a slave in Benjamin's place, heartsick for the welfare of their father who would die if the boy did not return home. That was where our study had ended.

Joseph's response to Judah's plea

Overwhelmed at Judah's love that would beg, not for his own life, but for the life of his "convicted" brother, *Joseph could not refrain himself . . . and he cried* [out], *Cause every man to go out from me (45:1a).* Every person went out—the officials, the guards, even the interpreter—everyone except his brothers. *And there stood no man with him (45:1b).*

And he wept aloud [so loud that he could be heard throughout the house]: *and the Egyptians and the house of Pharaoh heard (45:2),* but Joseph's brothers heard something even more shocking than the sounds of loud weeping. They heard words in their own Hebrew language coming from the mouth of the ruler—*I am Joseph.* They were terrified! They had not escaped their past deeds.

Joseph went on speaking to them. *I am Joseph your brother, whom ye sold into Egypt (45:4b).* The unthinkable secret was out! Benjamin was hearing what the ten older brothers had hidden for twenty-two years. Benjamin was hearing what would have happened to him, too, if his brothers had not changed! The rest of Joseph's words were not what they expected and not at all what they deserved.

Joseph's view of his brothers's crimes

Now therefore be not grieved, nor angry with yourselves, that ye sold me hither: for God did send me before you to preserve life (45:5). He was removing the responsibility from them. *And God sent me before you . . . to save your lives by a great deliverance. So now it was not you that sent me hither, but God: and he hath made me a father to Pharaoh, and lord of all his house, and a ruler throughout all the land of Egypt (45:7–8).*

He then told his brothers what he wanted them to do. *Haste ye, and go up to my father, and say unto him, Thus saith thy son Joseph, God hath made me lord of all Egypt: come down unto me, tarry* [delay] *not: and thou shalt dwell in the land . . . and thou shalt be near unto me, thou, and thy children, and thy children's children, and thy flocks, and thy herds, and all that thou hast: and there will I nourish thee; for yet there are five years of famine; lest thou, and thy household, and all that thou hast, come to poverty (45:9–11).*

And ye shall tell my father of all my glory in Egypt, and of all that ye have seen; and ye shall haste and bring down my father hither. And he fell upon his brother Benjamin's neck, and wept; and Benjamin wept upon his neck. Moreover he kissed all his brethren, and wept upon them: and after that his brethren talked with him (45:13–15).

What wonderful love that required no restitution—love that made plans for their future almost too good to be true! What love that saw their evildoings—the suffering their jealousy and hatred had brought on their father and Joseph, and the shame those wrongdoings had brought on themselves used as tools that had preserved their world from death!

Pharaoh's pleasure

And the fame thereof was heard in Pharaoh's house, saying, Joseph's brethren are come: and it pleased Pharaoh well, and his servants. And Pharaoh said unto Joseph, Say unto thy brethren, This do ye; lade [load] *your beasts, and go, get you unto the land of Canaan; And take your father and your households, and come unto me: and I will give you the good of the land of Egypt, and ye shall eat the fat of the land (45:16–18).*

Now thou art commanded, [continued Pharaoh], *this do ye; take you wagons out of the land of Egypt for your little ones, and for your wives, and bring your father, and come. Also regard not your stuff* [don't worry about bringing your own possessions]; *for the good of all the land of Egypt is yours (45:19–20).*

Apparently Joseph never told anyone who his kidnappers were, at least he told no one who did not need to know—and never talked about their cruel treatment of him. So knowing nothing about the past lives of Joseph's brothers, Pharaoh and all Egypt could happily open their hearts and their land to every one of Joseph's family.

Continued mercy on the brothers

And Joseph gave them wagons, according to the commandment of Pharaoh, and gave them provision for the way. To all of them he gave each man changes of raiment [clothing]; *but to Benjamin he gave three hundred pieces of silver, and five changes of raiment (45:21b–22).*

Clothing carries considerable significance throughout the book of Genesis. Joseph's brothers had long ago stripped him of his coat of many colors and had sent him unclothed, ashamed, and humiliated into slavery. Now they themselves have just stood before Joseph and Benjamin, stripped of their twenty-two year cover-up, a humiliating exposure worse than the loss of clothing. The truth was out. Benjamin knew, and their father would soon know too or at least, it would seem that he would know. The brothers were fully aware that it was in Joseph's power to strip them in every way and make them slaves themselves, but instead, he clothed them. They didn't even deserve to leave Egypt as freemen, yet they left dressed in the finest clothing of that land. For them, those clothes meant Joseph was forgiving them and covering them with respect, dignity, and value.

When Joseph sent his brothers back to their father, he gave them a command. *He said unto them, See that ye fall not out by the way (45:24b).* What would make them "fall out by the way"? Why would the ten brothers with the greatest possible news have a falling out—an argument or fight—in their travels home? Consider what faces them when they return. What will they say to their father? Each might wish to place the blame on someone else, but Joseph forbade such talk because all that they had done was forgiven. Perhaps he didn't even want them telling their father *anything* of what they had done.

The new beginning for Jacob's family

Old Jacob, trembling and fearful, waited in Canaan for his sons to return, dreading what news they might bring. I wondered what his thoughts would be in that long wait. When he was young, Jacob had bright prospects—his father's blessings and God's blessings. Maybe as he waited he thought of that night over fifty years earlier when he dreamed of the ladder reaching to heaven and heard the words of the one at the top promising to bless him and bring him back to Canaan—and that had happened, just as promised. But then, it seemed the blessings ended.

Did Jacob wonder if God was repaying him for his sins? Did he wish he could go back to his youth and start over again? Little could he have imagined that a new start was right on his horizon!

The return of the sons

If Jacob had been scanning the southern horizon hoping for eleven riders, he would have seen a large group of Egyptian wagons and travelers moving northward. "Not my sons," he might have thought, yet they were coming directly toward him, and then he saw—Benjamin was there, Simeon was there, and all the other nine! The eleven riders *were* his sons, but what were all those wagons with them? When the sons reached their father and told him, *Joseph is yet alive, and he is governor over all the land of Egypt . . . Jacob's heart fainted, for he believed them not (45:26).*

It seems that right after they told their father the good news, they would have had to admit the truth: their sale of Joseph into slavery, their cruelties, lies, and pretended innocence, but this chapter does not say that. Genesis only tells us that *they told him all the words of Joseph, which he had said unto them (45:27a)*. Had Joseph commanded them to say nothing of their crimes? It was almost as if their evil past had disappeared, as if there were no record of it.

Though their father had not at first believed that Joseph was alive, *when he saw the wagons which Joseph had sent to carry him, the spirit of Jacob their father revived: And Israel said, It is enough; Joseph my son is yet alive: I will go and see him before I die (45:27–28)*.

My reflections on Jacob's family

Wow! This chapter is brimming with forgiveness. I couldn't see how comfort could possibly come to such a family. All it had taken, though, was one person—the one wronged to see the sorrow of the wrongdoers, to forgive them and in spite of what they had done to care about them anyway.

I love these chapters—chapters where a messed up family could start all over again and have a new beginning. This is another story I plan to bookmark.

Checking for understanding

1. Joseph tested his brothers by casting blame on innocent Benjamin and telling the ten they could go home, leaving Benjamin to be his personal slave. Explain why leaving Benjamin was a perfect test of whether they had changed.

2. What was Joseph's belief about all the evils that had happened in his life?

3. Tell how Joseph's gift of clothing for his brothers is a picture of what forgiveness does to wrongdoers.

4. Joseph commanded his brothers not to argue on the way back to Canaan. What were the arguments he probably feared might arise?

5. According to what Moses wrote, how did great good come through Jacob's family even though he failed as a father?

Jacob's Years in Egypt

Based on Genesis 46–48

My first thoughts

THE WORDS ON THE board read, "Jacob begins to take charge of his family." We all agreed that it was about time.

My notes on the teacher's lesson

Jacob united with Joseph

Jacob has just learned that Joseph, the son whose death he has mourned for twenty-two years, is alive, well, and living only about 200 miles away. Why had Joseph not made contact with his father earlier? In his thirteen years as a slave and then as a prison inmate, he would not have had that freedom. Once he was released from prison, however, he could easily have sent a message, but knowing what lay ahead and knowing that famine would soon force his brothers into Egypt, waited.

He waited until he knew whether his brothers had changed, and at last he did know. At last he could send his father the message he had long wanted to send: *Thus saith thy son Joseph, God hath made me lord of all Egypt: come down unto me, tarry not: And thou shalt dwell in the land of Goshen, and thou shalt be near unto me, thou . . . and all that thou hast: And there will I nourish thee (45:9b–11a).* That shocking news had almost given Jacob a heart attack! (45:26).

Confidence to move to Egypt

Jacob's caravan moved slowly from Canaan, stopping in the south at Beer-sheba where his father and grandfather had once worshiped. There he *offered sacrifices unto the God of his father Isaac* (46:1b). Perhaps he wanted to know if God would be pleased with the move to Egypt. He had made enough mistakes and wanted no more.

The words to Jacob were, *Fear not to go down into Egypt; for I will there make of thee a great nation (46:3b).* That answer was much more than simply, "Yes, you must go." Jacob's family numbered only about seventy people; to be the size of a nation, surely they would have to increase to at least half a million. That would mean staying in Egypt for hundreds of years. (Sounds to me like the words of Genesis 15:13–16.)

And Jacob rose up from Beersheba: and the sons of Israel [Jacob] *carried Jacob their father, and their little ones, and their wives, in the wagons which Pharaoh had sent to carry him (46:5).*

And they took their cattle, and their goods, which they had gotten in the land of Canaan, and came into Egypt, Jacob, and all his seed with him (46:6).

Shortly before arriving in Egypt, Jacob sent Judah ahead to tell Joseph they would soon be there. *And Joseph made ready his chariot, and went to meet Israel his father . . . and he fell on his neck, and wept on his neck a good while (46:29).*

Jacob blesses Pharaoh

In the years before his journey to Egypt, Jacob had lived in a cloud of depression, but when *Joseph brought him in and set him before Pharaoh (47:7a),* Jacob's words showed a new spirit. Perhaps remembering the promises that he and his family would bring blessing to the world, *Jacob blessed Pharaoh (47:7b),* evidently believing he could bring more good to the king than the king could ever bring to him.

Pharaoh wanted to learn more about Jacob. *And Pharaoh said unto Jacob, How old art thou? And Jacob said unto Pharaoh, The days of the years of my pilgrimage are 130 years (47:8–9a).* That was quite short in comparison to the lives of his father and grandfather. According to the records, grandfather Abraham had lived *175 years* (25:7) and father Isaac *180 years* (35:28).

Then Jacob gave Pharaoh a brief summary of his life—no details, no mournful dwelling on his own sins and the sins of his family, just one sentence: *Few and evil have the days of the years of my life been, and* [my days] *have not attained unto the days of the years of the life of my fathers in the days of their pilgrimage (47:9b)*. That was all that Moses recorded of his words. After that, Jacob again *blessed Pharaoh and went out . . . (47:10)*.

Life in Egypt

Pharaoh, so deeply grateful for Joseph, had Jacob's family settle *in the best of the land . . . in the land of Goshen* on the eastern side of Egypt—the ideal place for shepherding *(47:6b)* and the ideal place for the family. Why was Goshen so ideal for shepherds as well as for their flocks? The Egyptians looked on shepherds not only as low class, but also as abominable. The occupation of Joseph's family and their location in Egypt would keep the family separated from the praises and pleasures of Egypt. That separation, though, would not keep them from prospering and multiplying exceedingly (47:27b). They prospered there and *had possessions therein, and grew, and multiplied exceedingly (47:27b)*; many, many children were born to Jacob's family there in Egypt.

Moses briefly described Joseph's policies during the famine—policies for which all of Egypt praised and thanked him—and then quickly moved the story seventeen years ahead to shortly before Jacob's death.

The importance of understanding chapters 48 and 49

For any who choose to read beyond the book of Genesis, our teacher said they would need to know what happened in the next two chapters, 48 and 49. Evidently some people skim over them and feel the two chapters are anticlimactic leftovers. The good stuff, they think, is all settled; forgiveness has swept in and repaired the family, the blessings are returning, and as soon as the funerals are over, we'll jump ahead hundreds of years to the first chapter of Exodus. They don't realize that if they skip what is said and done in chapters 48 and 49, they will have a continual problem understanding certain parts of the biblical story. The rest of this lesson deals with the significant events of Genesis 48.

The structure of the family changed

Jacob, sick in bed, knew it was time—he must tell his sons who would have the birthright and after that give to each of them his blessings. When Joseph heard that his father was sick, perhaps having no idea of his father's unusual plans, he took his two sons, Ephraim and Manasseh, to visit him. Once they arrived, Jacob had two great surprises for Joseph.

The first surprise: Joseph, who was the next to last son in birth order, would have the birthright, the rights usually given to the firstborn. He would have the double portion of the inheritance from his father.

The second surprise: Jacob, without asking any permission from Joseph, had an adoption ceremony planned. He announced to Joseph, *And now thy two sons, Ephraim and Manasseh, . . . are mine . . . (48:5).* He was adopting Joseph's two sons, Ephraim and Manasseh, as his own—putting them on an equal level with their uncles!

How the birthright and adoption affected the whole family

Since Joseph probably had more wealth than all his brothers put together, why would the double-portion inheritance make any difference to him? That double-portion would be extremely important in the future of his own descendants. This particular inheritance would not have been about wealth, but rather about an inheritance in Canaan—a possession in the land that would not be theirs for hundreds of years!

Long after the deaths of Jacob's sons, the descendants or tribes coming from the twelve sons would enter into Canaan and divide the land into portions or territories.

Since the adoption gave Joseph's two sons equal standing with Joseph's brothers, the two boys would each have his own tribal territory just as Joseph's eleven brothers each had his own. In that way, Joseph was the father of two tribes (think double-portion): one tribe named for his son Ephraim and the other named for his son Manasseh. Readers who are not aware of this may sometimes find the future history difficult to unravel, and it may cause them to think the writers were making errors.

Jacob's grateful words

Jacob had so many sad and shameful memories, so many failures he could not change, and yet in spite of all that, he would die a happy man. What would give him this happiness? His words during the adoption give us the clues.

In that ceremony he spoke words that showed a grateful heart. He said nothing about the difficult past—much of which he had brought upon himself. Instead, he praised the God of his fathers Abraham and Isaac. He said he had been *redeemed from all evil (48:15–16a)*. One definition of *redeemed* is *delivered*, or *saved from evil*. As a young man Jacob had dug a pit of deceit and had fallen into it himself. He had wronged so many and had reaped their hatred. Those evils, however, were not the end of his story. He had been redeemed—rescued from the pit of his own making, lifted up to become a new and humbled man. Jacob showed no fear in his death, no heavy, guilty conscience. Rather, it seemed that he had died contented and at peace.

My reflections on Jacob and his family

I'm wondering if Jacob's sons felt that they, like their father, had been redeemed. I thought to myself, "What if the brothers had been like Adam and Eve, blaming someone else for what they had done, perhaps their father or even Joseph? What if they had been like Cain, who felt no regrets for his hatred and cruelty—only regrets for his shame and humiliation?" That kind of pride seemed to infect almost everyone in Genesis, but I didn't see it redeeming anyone. It didn't make anything right. I couldn't tell what the brothers were thinking.

All of us in the class, though, could tell that the promises to Abraham were being fulfilled (12:2–3). Abraham's grandson Jacob blessed the ruler of the greatest nation of their day, and Abraham's great grandson Joseph blessed the families of all the starving nations of their world.

Checking for understanding

1. What happened at Beersheba that gave Jacob the courage to go to Egypt?

2. Contrast the size of Jacob's family when they left Canaan with the size God told Jacob it would become in Egypt.

3. Give the ages at which Abraham and Isaac died.

4. Explain what Jacob gave to Joseph for his birthright portion.

5. One of the promises to Abraham in Genesis 12 was that through him all families of the earth would be blessed. In what way was Joseph,

Abraham's great grandson, a fulfillment of that promise for the world of his time?

6. In your opinion, what warnings and what encouragements would Moses expect the Israelites to get from his record of Jacob's life?

Jacob Blesses His Sons

Based on Genesis 49:1–28

My first thoughts

THE TEACHER ASKED US to write several short sentences on what we think an old dying father would say to his children before he dies. Some of the students read theirs to the class. They wrote words of love, praise, and encouragement. Then she asked us to write what we thought dying Jacob would say to his sons. Most of the class wrote almost the same words, certain it would be a comforting and memorable final time with their father. I was surprised when she said that if we had been there as guests, we might have felt extremely uncomfortable and might have wished we hadn't gone.

My notes on the teacher's lesson

The blessings

Jacob is about to be *gathered to his people*—about to die. First though, he must prepare his twelve sons for their futures. *And Jacob called unto his sons, and said, Gather yourselves together, that I may tell you that which shall befall you in the last days (49:1).* In that gathering he gave to each of them and to their descendants his blessings, even telling the futures of their tribes.

The blessing to Reuben

Reuben, thou art my firstborn, my might, and the beginning of my strength, the excellency of dignity, and the excellency of power (49:3). Reuben's heart must have swollen with happiness at those praises, having quick flashbacks of himself as that untroubled little boy, delightedly following his proud father in the fields and pastures. The next words, however, would have made his face burn, humiliated to hear about the evil he had hidden in the back of his memory. Perhaps he hoped his father had forgotten, if he had even known.

Unstable as water, thou shalt not excel; because thou wentest up to thy father's bed; then defiledst thou it: he went up to my couch (49:4). Was Reuben such an outstanding son, so splendid that he thought he could do anything—even sleep with one of his father's wives? (35:22). Did he think of himself as a worthy leader over his brothers even though years earlier he had failed in his firstborn duty to protect young Joseph? (37:21–30). And had he expected to gain his father's respect by offering the deaths of two of his own sons if he failed to bring Benjamin back from Egypt? (42:37). His behavior and words had proved to Jacob the inability of firstborn Reuben to rule himself. How much less would Reuben have the ability to rule the family!

Jacob's blessing was a warning to Reuben's descendants, as if to say, "It is not too late for you," but the Bible's later record of Reuben's tribe shows the same weaknesses in his descendants, the same indecision and the same failures to aid those in great need (Judges 5:15–16). The tribe never did excel.

The blessing to Simeon and Levi

The blessing to the fiery second and third sons, Simeon and Levi, was both a warning to their descendents and a protection. *O my soul, come not thou into their secret* [council]; *unto their assembly . . . be not thou united: . . . Cursed be their anger, for it was fierce; and their wrath, for it was cruel: I will divide them . . . and scatter them in Israel (49:6–7).*

Woe to the one who would join in with the plans of Simeon and Levi! Years earlier the two had violently murdered the trusting men of Shechem, and, when rebuked by their father, had sullenly excused and defended their injustice (34:1–31). Up until that day, the rebuke had been their only consequence, but they needed more for the sake of themselves and for the sake of the nation. Those hot-tempered brothers must be separated from each other and scattered among their fellow tribe members, not having their own sovereign territories. Simeon's descendants, once they moved into Canaan, were assigned to live in cities within Judah's tribe. Levi's tribe was assigned to live in cities scattered, not within one tribe, but within all the tribes.

The descendants of the two brothers needed to take the words as a warning. Levi's tribe took the warning. Simeon's did not. Simeon's tribe strove for little, accomplished little, shrank in size, and was eventually absorbed into Judah's tribe, making his family incapable of any widespread, organized trouble.

Several centuries later a descendant of Levi with Levi's same fiery nature murdered an Egyptian. His violence forced him into a fugitive's life, a desert-life where he could cause no harm and where his fiery nature could be brought under control. His name was *Moses*, the nation's future leader who would lead them back to Canaan. Moses should have been a great encouragement to the Israelites that the mistakes and disgraces of a person's foolish, impulsive youth did not necessarily doom that one to a disgraced future.

Others in Levi's tribe had the same characteristics. Great numbers of them rose up in mighty indignation to wipe out the worshiping of a golden calf (Exodus 32:25–29). For their zeal they were rewarded; they became the spiritual leaders, the priests of the nation, representing the people to the LORD their God and teaching them how to have forgiveness of their sins. Who would have dreamed that Levi, a stubborn, vengeful man with a record of cruelty, could have such descendants? And what an encouragement to all the family that their futures were neither doomed because of their own follies nor were their futures doomed because of any failures of their parents!

The blessing to Judah

The blessing to Judah might have surprised the first three sons. Everyone knew his terrible record. Judah was the brother who had advised selling Joseph into slavery, had then gone to live among the Canaanites where he married a Canaanite woman, and had raised two sons who were so evil that God took their lives. In addition, he would not take responsibility for his son's widow; he slept with a woman he thought was a prostitute, and when he learned she was pregnant, ordered her to be burned to death (Genesis

38). Jacob, though, never mentioned the evildoings of Judah; rather, he pronounced huge blessings on him!

Judah, thou art he whom thy brethren shall praise: thy hand shall be in the neck of thine enemies; thy father's children shall bow down before thee. . . . The sceptre shall not depart from Judah, nor a lawgiver from between his feet . . . (49:8, 10). Though Joseph received the birthright, with two tribes descending from him, Judah received the leadership part of the birthright (I Chronicles 5:1–2).

Why would Jacob tell Judah that his brothers would praise him, that they would bow to him, that he would conquer his enemies, and that rulers would come from his line of descendants? Something had changed in Judah—they all must have seen it. When years earlier he took back his unjust condemnation of his daughter-in-law, he confessed, *she hath been more righteous than I (38:26b),* and from then on had taken her into his family and provided for her. In addition, he, more than all his brothers, showed deep sorrow for their united lies and cruelty and begged to give up his own life and become a slave forever for the sake of his father and Benjamin. The change made in his character would bring honor and rewards to his descendants. His greatest descendant in the Old Testament was the hugely successful King David, the same who as a youth had killed the giant Goliath. His greatest descendant in the New Testament was Jesus, called the Christ.

The blessings to seven more of the sons

Jacob's sons Zebulun, Issachar, Dan, Gad, Asher, Naphtali, and Benjamin each received a brief blessing for their descendants. Some would receive blessings related to their character, some to their individual talents, and some to the location of their Canaan land inheritance.

The blessing to Joseph—a model for weak, helpless family members

Why would blessings to the most successful of Jacob's sons be an encouragement to any weaker or less talented family member? Though Jacob referred to Joseph's strength and stability throughout the cruelties forced upon him, he did not credit Joseph with that strength. No one should be jealous of him. From Jacob's blessings to Joseph, the other tribes would see that Joseph's strength was not the focus of their father's words—the strength of their God was his focus.

Jacob used four different names for God—*the mighty God of Jacob, the shepherd, the stone of Israel, the Almighty* (49:24–25). He believed that their God had been a powerful shepherd to Joseph along every part of his abused, danger-filled, often lonely path, a path of learning and training, preparing him for his extraordinary future work.

He wanted the seemingly weaker descendants to look, not *within* themselves for significance and success, but instead, to look *outside* of themselves; he wanted them to look for significance and success as coming from the God of Abraham, Isaac, and Jacob alone. That would be a theme and a foundational law commanded to all their people throughout all the rest of the Bible.

My reflections on Jacob's blessings for his sons

Jacob's words must have humiliated some of his sons, but how good for their descendants. They did not have to make the mistakes of their fathers. Better, I thought, to have a humiliating warning than to live in self-deceived, self-satisfied pride. We've seen that over and over again in Genesis.

Checking for understanding

1. Tell one way the blessings given to Jacob's sons were different from the blessings on most birthday cards.

2. Explain the warning wrapped up in Reuben's blessing, warnings which, hopefully, some would take seriously.

3. For what reason did Jacob warn against taking advice from either Simeon or Levi?

4. Simeon's tribe paid no attention to their warnings. Levi's did. How was the future of Levi's tribe better than Simeon's?

5. Name two honors that would come to Judah's tribe.

6. How might Jacob's words to his son Judah encourage future *prodigals*—descendants who had disgraced themselves in shameful living?

7. As a review, make a stick-figure family tree of Abraham, Isaac, Jacob, and Jacob's children, including the wives of Abraham, Isaac, and Jacob.

Two Deaths

Based on Genesis 49:29—50:26

My first thoughts

I FOUND GENESIS 50, the last chapter in the book, jolting—totally unexpected. I was shocked reading the description of Jacob's funeral. I was shocked reading the message Joseph received from his ten older brothers, and I was shocked at the unexpected ending of the book.

My notes on the teacher's lesson

Jacob's burial plans and funeral

One hundred forty-seven year old Jacob, having blessed his sons and knowing he was about to die, gave his sons this command: *Bury me with my fathers (49:29)*. The family owned a burial site in Canaan where he wanted to be buried. He firmly believed the prophecy that his descendants would return one day to Canaan, purify it of evil, and bring blessing to the world; and he wanted his body to be there, too.

Would his descendants believe the prophecy or even remember it? And if they did, would they be faithful to return? Hopefully, Jacob's command before he died would keep those thoughts nailed into their memories.

Jacob's impressive funeral might also have helped keep those thoughts in their minds. Jacob had no idea before he died how memorable his funeral would be. The directions were exact. *I am to be gathered unto my people: bury me with my fathers in the cave that is in the field of Ephron the*

Hittite . . . in the land of Canaan, which Abraham bought . . . for a possession of a burying place. There they buried Abraham and Sarah his wife: there they buried Isaac and Rebekah his wife; and there I buried Leah (49:29b–31).

With a clear mind, satisfied that he had made his wishes understood, *he gathered up his feet into the bed, and yielded up the ghost* [the old word for spirit] *and was gathered unto his people* [who had died before him]. *And Joseph fell upon his father's face, and wept upon him, and kissed him (49:33–50:1).*

And Joseph commanded his servants the physicians to embalm his father: and the physicians embalmed Israel. And forty days were fulfilled for him; for so are fulfilled the days of those which are embalmed: and the Egyptians mourned for him threescore and ten days (50:2–3). In the ways in which the Egyptians mourned the death of a great man, they mourned for Jacob.

The funeral

About two months after Jacob's death, word must have been spreading among the southern settlements of Canaan. A large procession was coming from the direction of Egypt! Was it an army? No, they were carrying a regal coffin. Who was the esteemed, honored person in that royal coffin? Who was this who chose burial in the backwaters of Canaan rather than in a splendid pyramid in Egypt?

It was Jacob, brought by his sons for burial. What an unforgettable funeral procession traveling those many miles from Egypt to Canaan! With them were *all the servants of Pharaoh, the elders of his house, and all the elders of the land of Egypt, and all the house of Joseph, and his brethren, and his father's house* [except for their little ones]. *And there went up with him both chariots and horsemen: and it was a very great company. And they . . . mourned with a great and very sore lamentation: and he made a mourning for his father seven days. And when the inhabitants of the land, the Canaanites, saw the mourning . . . they said, This is a grievous mourning to the Egyptians. . . (50:7b–11).*

Nowhere else in Scripture is such a great funeral recorded. Who would have dreamed! Who would have dreamed that the greatest nation in the world would mourn Jacob's death and give him the greatest funeral recorded in the Bible. Jacob himself would have been shocked too.

No doubt for many generations Jacob's family would repeat the story of how all the great men of Egypt—a huge procession of all Egypt's leaders—traveled to Canaan to bury their father. That memory would help keep alive in their minds that Egypt was only a temporary home and that one day all of their father's descendents would return to Canaan.

The brothers's shocking message to Joseph

After the funeral was over and all were back in Egypt, Jacob received a shocking message from his older brothers. With their father gone, an old fear had risen up. In the seventeen years in Egypt, even with Joseph's mercy and kindness to them, they had never experienced peace. A terrible cloud of guilt and fear still hung over them—true guilt for all the evils they had brought into Joseph's life and great fear of all the justice he might be planning.

Their one hope was Joseph's love for their father. Knowing Joseph would do whatever their father asked, the brothers sent a messenger to him claiming that they had had a meeting with their father before he died (though who knows if they really did).

The message was, *Thy father did command before he died, saying, So shall ye say unto Joseph, Forgive, I pray thee now, the trespass of thy brethren, and their sin; for they did unto thee evil: and now* [the message continued], *we pray thee, forgive the trespass of the servants of the God of thy father (50:16b–17a).*

There is no record in Genesis that the brothers had ever before asked for forgiveness. They had admitted they were wrong, but had they ever asked for forgiveness—that pride-crushing request? Had they been more concerned about the shame they had earned than the pain they had brought on Joseph and their father? When Joseph received their message, he wept, realizing they had never felt assured of his forgiveness.

After the messenger had gone to Joseph, the brothers went themselves *and fell down before his face; and they said, behold, we be thy servants (50:18b).* They offered no excuses, made no attempts to explain their evildoing, did not try to place the blame on their father's favoritism, just pled Joseph's forgiveness of their death-deserving crimes—ready to be his slaves.

Joseph's forgiving view of his brother's evil

And Joseph said unto them, Fear not: for am I in the place of God? But as for you, ye thought evil against me; but God meant it unto good . . . to save much people alive (50:19-20). He knew they had meant evil—he was not denying that. At the same time, though, he was certain that their God had worked good through their crimes to save them and to save their world from starvation.

Joseph went on with words of comfort: *Now therefore fear ye not: I will nourish you, and your little ones. And he comforted them, and spake kindly unto them (50:21).* He knew they were deeply sorry for their evildoings. There would be no punishment, no payment for their evils, no grudges, no cool distancing himself from them. Rather, Joseph would nourish them: he would make sure all their needs were kindly and fully met. At last they would have the peace and the certainty that like their father they had been redeemed from their evil past.

Did Joseph owe apologies to his brothers?

Many commentators believe that when Joseph was young, he was a boaster and braggart. If they are correct that Joseph had brought the brothers's hatred on himself by proud, immature behavior, should he not have asked forgiveness from them too? Instead of asking forgiveness, though, as they were asking of him, he agreed that they truly had done evil, but then immediately comforted them by the reminder that God had taken their evil actions and had used them to bring about great good.

If Joseph truly was an honorable, honest man, would he not admit that he too had done wrong—if he had? To accuse Joseph of bragging and boasting does not seem to fit into this picture of him.

Joseph's burial plans and death

Joseph, like his father, was so certain they would return to Canaan that fifty years later when he himself was dying, he made the family take an oath: *And Joseph said unto his brethren, I die: and God will surely visit you, and bring you out of this land unto the land which he sware to Abraham, to Isaac, and to Jacob. And Joseph took an oath of the children of Israel, saying, God will surely visit you, and ye shall carry up my bones from hence (50:24-25).* When the time came for the Israelites to return to Canaan, he wanted his body to go with them.

Genesis ends with this verse: *So Joseph died, being a hundred and ten years old: and they embalmed him, and he was put in a coffin in Egypt (50:26).*

That unburied coffin would wait many, many years, continually reminding the family that Egypt was not their final home. Who, though, would ever want to leave Egypt? Life was so good in the land of the Pharaohs.

My reflection on the end of Genesis

The end of Genesis surprised me. I thought the words, *Joseph . . . in a coffin in Egypt*, was a terrible ending, leaving us hanging like a soap opera! I wondered how long that casket awaited burial. Our teacher said that we would have to read further in the Bible to know, that we had not yet come to the end of the story. So I did read further—about ten chapters into Exodus. After I read them I was sure that if Jacob's descendants could have looked over my shoulder and seen what lay ahead, they would have made an immediate "exit" out of Egypt, not waiting for the Exodus departure hundreds of years into the future.

Checking for understanding

1. Moses, in describing the moment of Jacob's death, did not use the words *death* or *dying*. Give his two indirect expressions (Genesis 49:33) for telling us that Jacob died.

2. Explain the reason that Joseph, even though he knew his brothers had meant evil against him, had no desire to pay them back (Genesis 50:20).

3. How would the sight of Joseph's unburied coffin encourage the Israelites?

4. Contrast the way Genesis 1 begins this book, with the way Genesis 50 ends the book.

Epilogue

Our teacher's words in her wrap-up of Genesis

"In our study of Genesis," our teacher began, "we joined Moses' first audience listening to the events he wanted his people to know—the events he wanted them to pass on to future generations. The goal of this study has been to open the door, at least a crack, to that ancient record and its wisdom.

"We studied the stories—the first parts of the great storyline that begins in the first chapter of Genesis and continues to the last chapter of the Bible. Hopefully, sometime you will be able to study the Bible in greater depth—a depth that includes not only the enlarging storyline, but also the Bible's literary styles. You will want to know the difference between prose, poetry, prophecy, figures of speech, and more.

"Two common and fascinating styles are *chiasmus* [kai-AZZ-mus] and *parallelism*. Both have mirror-type repetitions—good for memory, and good for finding the main point of the writing. An Internet search of "chiasmus in the Bible" can give you many examples of this literary device. Another good Bible search would be "parallelism." An understanding of parallelism guides you when you read the Bible's poetry—particulary in Job, Psalms, Proverbs, Ecclesiastes, and Song of Solomon, as well as scattered throughout the whole Bible.

"You are aware by now that you cannot stop your reading at the end of Genesis; Joseph's coffin is not the end. Genesis is only the beginning. If the Bible had nothing more after Genesis—if Moses had forever laid down his pen—you would have only the foundation of what could have become a great house. You would have a foundation, but a foundation lacking sitting rooms, kitchens, dining rooms, stairs to climb, and windows from which to see afar. If Genesis were all that you had, you would be left with unanswered questions, a book without an ending, and a book, no doubt, long forgotten.

"By this time you know Abraham's family well enough to read further. Yes, you will come to chapters that go on and on with lists of names for each man had to know his personal family tree—his ancestors. You will read chapters in Leviticus, Numbers, and Deuteronomy where strange ceremonies and detailed laws also seem to go on and on for Moses wrote that they had to know how to be in a right relationship with the LORD their God. By the time you reach the book of *Joshua,* however, those people will at last be in the land promised to Abraham, still having the promise of bringing blessing to the whole broken world. That is the story of the rest of the Bible.

"You are now well prepared to take up the Bible and read on. May the wisdom in it enrich all your future studies and future years."

Bibliography

Abington v. Schempp, 374 U.S. 203 10 L. Ed. 2d 844, 83 S. Ct. 1560 (1963).

Lynch v. Donnelly, 465 U.S. 668, 104 S. Ct. 1355 (1984).

Maps

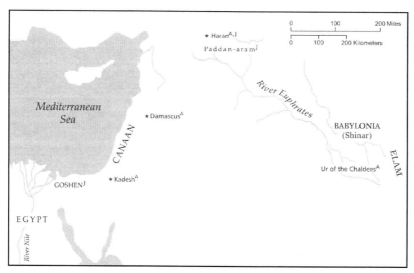

The geography of the ancestral narratives.
Places associated with a particular ancestor are
highlighted with a star, and the initial of the ancestor follows
the place name: A(braham), I(saac), or J(acob).

The geography of the ancestral narratives.

Places associated with a particular ancestor are
highlighted with a star, and the initial of the ancestor follows
the place name: A(braham), I(saac), or J(acob).